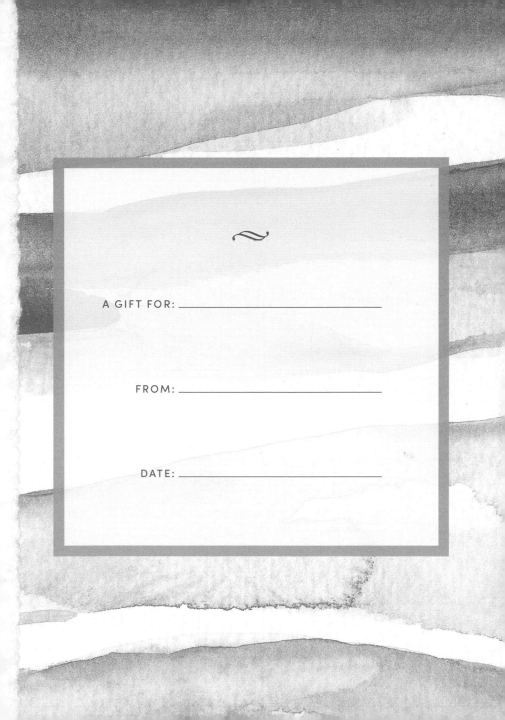

A GIFT FOR: _____

FROM: _____

DATE: _____

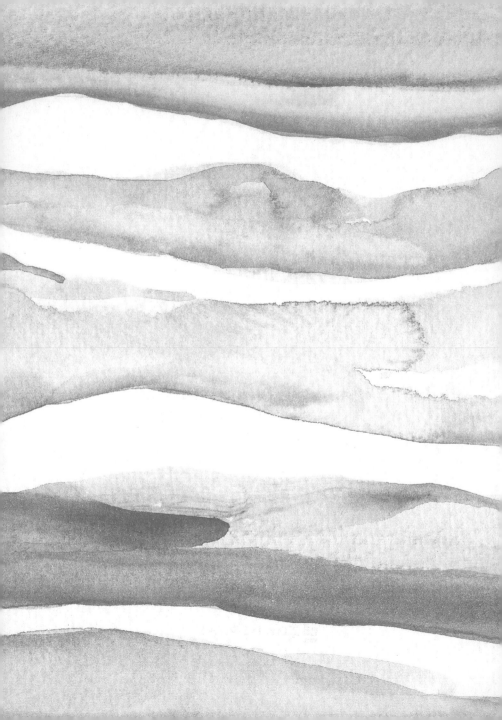

Calm

YOUR

Anxious
Mind

DAILY DEVOTIONS TO MANAGE
STRESS AND BUILD RESILIENCE

Carrie Marrs

ZONDERVAN

Calm Your Anxious Mind

© 2021 by Zondervan

Requests for information should be addressed to:

Zondervan, 3900 Sparks Dr. SE, Grand Rapids, Michigan 49546

ISBN 978-0-310-45574-5 (Hardcover)
ISBN 978-0-310-46122-7 (Audio)
ISBN 978-0-310-45573-8 (eBook)

Introduction

How's today been for you?

Maybe it was smooth sailing until a life-curveball totally rattled you. Or you've been trying to tune out a string of concerns running like a newsfeed at the back of your mind. A swirl of tasks, questions, and worries might have you knotted up inside, or a growing pile of problems might be feeling heavier by the hour.

You could even be in a darker place. Maybe you're reeling from a series of life-punches. Maybe hope feels out of reach.

When was the last time you breathed deeply? Or felt a grounding sense of peace, a surge of confidence, or a joyful lightness? It's not just you. Everybody's got their stuff. Even if today's been a good day, the waters may get rough again. We all face challenging times and the mash-up of feelings that come with them.

We were made with complex emotions, big hearts that care, and powerful brains that want to figure things out. Put us in a broken world and things are bound to get complicated.

But guess what? God knows how we're built, He knows what we're in the middle of, and He can handle it all. He says to us, "Come here. *Closer.* Lay it all out. We'll look at it together. Yes, I see it all. Will you let Me carry that for you? Will you let Me provide what you need for this journey? Now, keep close as we go on together."

"Cast all your anxieties on Me," He says. "Be anxious for nothing and pray instead," He says. "I'll be your strength, be all the help you need, and make a way toward your bright future with Me."

And so this is a book about moving through our struggles with the Mighty One. The One who knows us best and loves us most, who has abundance and beauty and dreamy goodness in mind for us. The One who calls us into His power and fullness of life.

Listen, I've dealt with fear and anxiety for as long as I can remember. I still deal with it! For me, part of being alive and worshiping God means continually staring down my monsters and returning to truths I can hang on to. It means forming habits that keep me healthy, connected, and productive. I've learned I have to cultivate a mindset and lifestyle that help me be joyful, grateful, and alive with purpose. It requires brutal honesty and a teachable spirit. But much of it has to do with staying in tune with the Voice of Love.

So let's dive into this together.

We're going to talk about winning the battle of the mind and managing feelings and being still so we can receive peace. We'll look at the crazy force called hope and dependence on the One with all the resources. We'll explore some of His amazing gifts: healing relationships, wisdom for wellness, a spirit of power, and heaps of agency. We'll think about how we can live in the light every day and become sunshine for our part of the world.

Our God is an awesome and compassionate God. He didn't leave us to our sin; He's not leaving us to our anxiety either. He will create a way forward for us, just like He has before.

He's full of comfort and love and power. He's offering you peace and wisdom and freedom.

Come see.

~

You Are Known and Held

Anxiety is like a fog that keeps you from seeing what's right in front of you. It fools you into thinking you're alone. It gets you constantly anticipating danger, expecting the worst.

In reality, though, you're never alone. The One who is with you understands you perfectly. He knows your whole story and holds your future. He'll hold all your hopes, fears, and feelings too, if you'll let Him. He'll help you sense more than just potential danger.

The fog *will* lift eventually. In the meantime, He'll be your safe place.

Keep breathing. He's got you. He's right here.

Not a Solo Mission

The LORD your God will be with you wherever you go.
Joshua 1:9

I don't know about you, but when my anxiety spikes, I feel like I'm completely alone in a rocket ship getting propelled toward a scary, uninhabitable planet. I'm headed for an atmosphere that doesn't allow normal breathing.

I can see other humans, but they don't get my rocket ship problems. I feel like even if I called out to them, they couldn't understand or are just too busy with their normal life stuff.

I wind up feeling pretty trapped.

But then it's like I suddenly notice a surprise passenger on the rocket ship, and He knows how to ground me. He's well aware of how I ended up hurtling this direction and can bring me back to safety.

When anxiety rises up in you, you might feel alone. But that is not the reality, dear one. What *is* true is this: the Spirit of God is with you wherever you go.

He can ground you. He can bring powerful truths to mind, calm your breathing, send helpers. He'll point you to people who are indeed within reach and willing to meet you where you are. It's not as bad as you think, and it's going to get better. You're teamed up with the One who sets you on steady ground and makes your footing sure.

God, help me sense Your presence—right now.

His Heart's Wrapped Up with Yours

He will quiet you with His love.
Zephaniah 3:17 NKJV

Have you ever seen a mother with her newborn baby? The little creature might have started in a worked-up state, wriggling and whining, huffing and puffing. Then he's put into the arms of the one he belongs to.

And something shifts. Something powerful arrives. The baby starts to quiet down as all his senses begin to pick up on what the mother is communicating with her loving gaze and strong embrace.

You haven't seen my face before, but I've been thinking of you non-stop. I've been pumping life into your veins. I've been dreaming up sweet moments for us. I've been getting so much ready for you that you're gonna love. My heart's been wrapped up with yours from the very beginning.

And that baby transforms into the calmest, most content little bundle of cuteness you've ever seen.

Right now, wherever you are in the big story of your life, you might be kinda worked up. You've got a lot on your shoulders and on your mind. At times, you find your heart uneasy, even racing.

Have you forgotten that Someone has a loving gaze for you? He has all kinds of powerful messages for you. He's longing to give you so much—enormous love, perfect provision, intimate connection.

God, help me know more of Your heart of love for me.

Deeper Still

There is no pit so deep that He is not deeper still.
Corrie ten Boom, *The Hiding Place*

There are days when your problems and concerns feel so large and so looming, you just can't escape them.

Questions about the future fill your mind. *What if things don't get better? What if the worst happens?* Their weight is enough to sink you.

There's yet another question to add to the others: *Am I too deep in this stuck place for anyone to reach in and pull me out?*

David talked about being in a pit of despair in Psalm 40. Everything seemed to be going wrong in his life, and he was freaking out about a bleak future. He wa s stuck in the mud and mire—stuck in fear and hopelessness.

Guess who got him out of there?

Listen, you're looking at legitimately hard things. Life can be grueling and heartbreaking. But it's not too much for your Rescuer. The pit you're in *is* deep—but not deeper than His love. No matter how you feel right now, believe me when I tell you: this is not too hard for Him.

Your problems will never outmatch His power. That goes for your current anxiety and every problem you'll face in the future. He will meet you where you are and lift you up. Just look up.

Find me in this pit of anxious thoughts, God.
Reach in and pull me into Your light.

Breathe

If your heart is broken, you'll find GOD right there; if you're
kicked in the gut, he'll help you catch your breath.
Psalm 34:18 MSG

"C an you take a deep breath for me?" the doctor asks, stethoscope poised. "And another?" Pause. "And another?"

I wonder if you've taken deep breaths like that since your last visit with the doctor. Some people think it's hokey, but it's actually scientifically legit. Slow abdominal breathing stimulates your vagus nerve, which prompts relaxation in your nervous system. It can actually bring down your stress and anxiety level.[1] So why not give it a shot?

Some people recommend inhaling for five seconds, then exhaling for five seconds.[2] Others say breathe in for four, hold for four; breathe out for four, hold for four.[3] Still others recommend inhaling for four seconds, holding for seven, and exhaling for eight.[4]

However many seconds you do, the most important thing is that you take deep, slow breaths using your diaphragm, the muscle in your lower ribs. You can choose to breathe only through your mouth, or only through your nose, or use a combination.[5]

Do this when your internal pressure is rising, for sure. But really, do it anytime. Stimulating your vagus nerve regularly will make you feel calmer and more relaxed.[6]

Lord, help me slow down my breaths. Calm
my body, my heart, and my mind.

Not Too Much

"My love won't walk away from you."
Isaiah 54:10 MSG

Have you ever felt like you were too much for someone to handle? It's that moment when your feelings are on display, your struggles in full view, and the other person is nervously eyeing the door. Before long he just might blurt out, "Whoa," as he steps back and shows you his palms.

And now you feel like a freak show.

Get close and listen. You are a beautiful creation of God, unique and wondrous and lovely. He made you amazing. Now, struggling—that's just part of the human package. You're being honest and real about what you're feeling, which takes courage. If any shame over struggling starts to sneak into your heart, kick it right out.

While other people may choose to bolt, Jesus never does.

He's not eyeing the door. He's not backing away saying, "Whoa, this is too much for Me." He actually leans in. He shows you His nail-pierced palms. He reminds you of His bigger-than-you-can-fathom, relentless love.

He didn't run away from your sin problem; He ran after it and conquered it. Your anxiety? Not even close to being "too much" for Him.

God, thank You for sticking with me no matter what.

He *Really* Knows You

*You formed me in my mother's womb. . . . You know
me inside and out. . . . Like an open book, you
watched me grow from conception to birth.*
Psalm 139:13, 16 MSG

W ho in your life knows you best? Probably your best friend who
finishes your sentences. Or is it your sibling who can tell all
your embarrassing stories? Maybe it's actually your mentor who knows
your strengths and weaknesses.

Yep, these people have seen you up close—they are super familiar
with you. But, compared to the way God knows you, they simply know
things *about* you.

God dreamed you up. You are His awesome idea. He knows you
inside and out. Every wound, fear, and mistake. Every triumph, hope,
and highlight. He sees all the crazy, hard things you've endured, what
has formed you, and how you've grown. He sees all your fabulous
abilities, potential for greatness, and love in your heart. He totally gets
your personality quirks and sense of humor.

With Him, you don't have to explain yourself or your circumstances or your issues. He gets it. Don't bother trying to put on some
kind of performance. Just exhale. Be real. He knows everything there
is to know about you, and He adores you.

God, I'm amazed that You know me better than I know myself.

He Holds You Close

Even if my father and mother abandon
me, the LORD will hold me close.
Psalm 27:10 NLT

"Ow! Ow, ow, *owwwwww!*" After my seven-year-old daughter takes a big fall and the pain is intense, she lets out a visceral yell. I'll hug her and she'll cry. She'll say, "It hurts." I'll say, "It hurts." Sometimes we end up saying that over and over, and eventually we get quiet as we keep hugging. I just sit in that feeling with her.

Sometimes you and I need to do exactly that in God's arms. Sometimes there isn't a lot more to say than "It hurts." He enters into that pain with us. He sees every tear and knows every ache.

While we sleep with tearstained faces, He stays by our side. In the morning, He remains as close as ever. We can say of the God of all comfort, "When I awake, I am still with you" (Psalm 139:18).

Let yourself be held like a child by your loving Father. Tell Him how it feels.

"It's heavy."

"It's scary."

"It's confusing."

"It's exhausting."

Be with Him through it all.

Father, I'm letting myself fall into Your arms. Hold me tight.

Take a Look

"What comes out of the mouth comes from the heart."
Matthew 15:18 HCSB

Sometimes you're in a dark or stuck place in life, but you can't put your finger on why. You can start to trace it by having more self-awareness. So often we're just trying to get through the day, and we're not exactly in tune with the nuances of what we're doing. But our behavior is information; whatever is going on *in* us eventually comes *out* of us. Once we acknowledge our behavior, we can begin to identify what feelings or needs are part of it.

So take an inventory. What have you been doing lately? What have your tendencies, reactions, and coping mechanisms been? Don't automatically scan over the "bad" behaviors. This is information-gathering time, not judging-and-shaming time. Did you snap at someone you love? Did you put off that important task yet again? Did you numb yourself with a Netflix binge? *Sure did.* Okay. Noted.

Now, what feelings might be behind these behaviors? If this kind of introspection makes you want to run, I get it. But just remember: you can't work through an issue you refuse to look at, and it's going to keep hanging around until you do. There's so much power in simply acknowledging where you are. Find your courage and take a good look. You'll be so glad you did later on.

Open my eyes to see what I'm doing, God. Help
me see my starting point for growth.

Vocab Refresher

Good words are worth much, and cost little.
George Herbert

R emember when you learned lists of vocabulary words in school? Suddenly, you no longer got cold or hungry or excited. You were frigid. Ravenous. Delirious!

Sometimes, when we're acknowledging our feelings, it helps to dig a little deeper than *sad* or *mad*. Sure, that's in there. But you've got a plethora of distinctions and complexities going on too. You're wonderfully made. You're no two-dimensional creature with black-and-white simplicity and cookie-cutter qualities. If you can describe more of what's going on, it can help you come to terms with where you are and how to move forward.

Look up a list of terms for feelings and see what fits. Here are a few: embarrassed, misunderstood, apprehensive, aggravated, disturbed, on edge, skeptical, remorseful, betrayed, isolated, distracted, frazzled, resigned, exasperated, overwhelmed. Do any of these describe how you feel today?

You may not be proud of some of the words that describe your current state, but don't beat yourself up, okay? Nobody's perfect, so don't bother pretending to be anything you're not. Just be honest.

God, give me the courage to be honest with myself and with You.

All the Feelings

You, Lord, are a compassionate and gracious God,
slow to anger, abounding in love and faithfulness.
Psalm 86:15

As you become deliberately self-aware, there's something super important to remember: you need to acknowledge your feelings and experiences *with compassion*.

Make observations about your behavior and past without immediately shaming yourself. Why? Because God has so much compassion for you—an ocean's worth of compassion for you. Open your heart to that and receive it from Him. Practice it in your own thoughts.

Sometimes it helps to think of it like this: How would you respond to a child sharing his feelings? Or a friend opening her heart to you? Treat yourself with the same gentleness and kindness. Think of the words you would say to them. Then say them to yourself.

Do not be hard on yourself. You are not a robot; you are a living being with frailties and wounds and limitations—and so is everyone else you know! All your feelings, even the ones you're not a fan of, are part of being human. God completely understands them, and He accepts you.

Thank You, God, for the ocean of compassion You have for me.

Curiosity

It is a narrow mind which cannot look at a
subject from various points of view.
George Eliot, *Middlemarch*

D o you like putting jigsaw puzzles together? Picture when you see a distinctive marking on a puzzle piece and think, *I bet I can figure out where this goes.* You try to fit it into one spot and it doesn't work, so what do you do? You look closer. If you approach the piece with curiosity and patience, you'll eventually find where it connects.

We need to have a spirit of curiosity as we're practicing more self-awareness. It's a little weird to think of being curious about yourself, but the truth is, we don't automatically understand ourselves really well. God designed us with some pretty complicated wiring. We're not fully cognizant of how past experiences have affected us or why we react to people the way we do, which is why therapists have jobs.

Instead of dismissing a feeling, acknowledge it—and then ask questions. *How is this related to past experiences and other times I've felt this way? How is this related to what I believe about myself, about God, about the world?* It's like looking at that puzzle piece. You examine, then wonder. *What's it like? What might it be connected to?*

As you do, God just might guide your thoughts to some important insights.

Lord, help me be curious and patient enough to
see what You want me to see in myself.

Deep-Down Realities

Search me, God, and know my heart; . . .
know my anxious thoughts.
Psalm 139:23

When David invited God to know his heart in Psalm 139, it wasn't because God didn't already know it. David was saying, "Show me what's going on in here, God. Help me know myself more like You know me."

Like I've said before, we don't always know ourselves really well. Invite the Spirit of God to reveal some important realities to you: *Am I looking for approval in my relationships? Am I trying to find purpose only through my achievements? Am I seeking significance on social media? Am I trying to gain self-worth through my possessions or lifestyle? Am I avoiding wounds that need healing or questions that need addressing?*

Maybe He'll gently unveil some really big questions at the deepest part of you: *Am I doing enough? Am I failing too much? Am I seen and loved? Do I matter? Am I safe? Do I fit in? Can unconditional love and grace actually be real? Will I ever be able to forgive, adjust, recover, heal? Is there hope for me to grow in the ways I long to?*

Dear one, you *are* loved—more than you know. Find these secret places in yourself. Meet with God in them. Let Him speak to every anxious thought and big question.

God, I know You can see what I can't. Show me what I need to see.

A Big Blinking Arrow

*"I will bring health and healing to it; I will heal my people
and will let them enjoy abundant peace and security."*
Jeremiah 33:6

My instinct is to resent anxiety. You too?
For years it just seemed like a sign of general weakness, another way I wasn't measuring up. Even if my anxiety stayed private and only I knew about it, I was mad at myself for not being Wonder Woman. Maybe it was even a faulty part of my faith in God.

Later, though, I realized that anxiety can be like a big neon arrow, pointing to wounds that need healing or to fears and unmet needs that ought to be addressed. It's connected to deep parts of me, areas where God wants to bring His power and goodness and peace.

Most of us are walking around with unresolved pain and unidentified needs. There may be tender areas or major traumas from our younger years. There may be too much on our plate, a lie that's limiting us, or just an ongoing need to not feel so alone.

Don't resent or quickly dismiss your anxiety. Look at it long enough to learn what it's connected to. Invite God to meet those needy and broken areas with His help and healing.

*God, help me be patient with my anxiety. Bring Your
strength and goodness to everything it's connected to.*

Express Yourself

I cry to you for help when my heart is overwhelmed. Lead me
to the towering rock of safety, for you are my safe refuge.
Psalm 61:2–3 NLT

When's the last time you wrote out how you were feeling? It turns out that experts can list oodles of benefits of journaling.[7] Among other things, it can really help you understand yourself, process what you're experiencing, and pray.

Don't know where to start? What's been on your mind? Whatever you write doesn't have to meet any standards. You're creating a safe place to express yourself. It may seem basic, but it might prevent you from feeling like you need to combust later.

Journaling isn't only a form of release; it often brings clarity too. Sometimes I start out in a wad, a big mess of worries and frustrations. Once I find some words and put them out there, in dialogue with God, His Spirit leads my thoughts. Scriptures come to mind. Hope and peace and wisdom show up. By the time I'm wrapping up, I often have new praises in my heart and direction for what's next.

At the very least, I'm calmer. I have assurance that I'm not alone, I'm known, and I'm on a path with God. I've opened up about where I am and what I'm experiencing. I've put a spotlight on my struggle, and He has met me in it.

He will meet with you too. He's ready anytime.

Father, hold my feelings and wounds. Hold my fears and hopes.

Pour Out Your Soul

I am a woman who is deeply troubled. . . . I was
pouring out my soul to the LORD. . . . I have been
praying here out of my great anguish and grief.
1 Samuel 1:15–16

S ometimes you don't have time to journal—and the anxiety is
cranking up. Wherever you are, get real with God. Maybe cry. For
Hannah, it was at an altar, but for you it could be in a car or outdoors.

Hannah was desperate to become a mother. For years, her infer-
tility had been breaking her heart. Eventually her anguish came
flooding out of her at a public altar. She silently prayed out her grief
and longing and crushed-up heart to God. She wasn't praying the
way people typically did, by speaking out loud, so the priest actually
thought she was drunk. But Hannah was earnestly confiding in God,
asking Him to help her in her agony, and telling Him she still hoped
for Him to act.

God absolutely answered Hannah's prayer. She became the
mother of Samuel and continued to honor God with the rest of her
life. And she left an example for generations of what to do when you
are deeply troubled.

Pour out your soul to God. Get real and let it all out in the presence of the One who knows you and holds you.

God, here are all my longings and hurts and tangled-
up feelings. I pour them all out to You.

You're Not Meant to Carry All That

Give your burdens to the LORD, and he will take care of you.
Psalm 55:22 NLT

H ave you ever gone backpacking? Those giant packs are no joke—some people walk around with sixty pounds on their back! Can you imagine going through your daily routine with one of those strapped to you? You wouldn't feel free to do all you were meant to do with that beast constantly aggravating you and wearing you down.

Aren't we sort of like that when we drudge through our days feeling miserably burdened?

God says, "I see you've got a heavy-duty burden going there. Will you let Me take some weight off?" If we say yes, He'll choose a way to do that in His wisdom. Sometimes He takes burdens away. Sometimes He sends helpers. Other times He makes the hard things feel lighter and doable. His powerful presence changes our experience of them.

It's a bit like when I call my sister and say, "Here's what's weighing on me." I can't explain why, but simply talking it out and having her listen makes me feel lighter. Or like when I'm carrying ten grocery bags and my husband says, "I can take some of those," with an outstretched hand.

Listen, you need to remove something you've been carrying alone on your shoulders. I'm betting all that is not meant for one human. Surrender it into God's able hands.

Help me feel lighter, God. Free me up to do what I'm meant to do.

In His Care

The Spirit of God has made me; the breath
of the Almighty gives me life.
Job 33:4

H ave you been pausing to take deep breaths? Remember how you can stimulate that vagus nerve and prompt your nervous system to relax?

The next time you do that long, deep breathing, think on this: even though your heart is uneasy as you're carrying uncertainties, and parts of life just feel wrong, *you are breathing.* God is making you alive right now. On purpose.

Even if it feels like your world's spinning out of control and you can't imagine how things will ever get better, you're breathing. You're meant for this moment and what God has for you in it.

God wants you alive for something beautiful and purposeful. You'll have to trust Him, and sometimes that feels hard. No matter what you do, though, He'll remain insistent about bringing you into His goodness. That's one thing in your life you *can* be certain of.

So breathe deep and ponder this mystery, that the Almighty put His breath in your lungs. Offer yourself up to Him. Think, *My soul is still in His care. It always will be.* He's giving you the gift of life in this moment. He can keep giving you what you need for each moment to come.

Almighty God, thank You for giving breath.

Holding Hands

"I will take hold of your hand."
Isaiah 42:6

There's nothing like holding the hand of someone you love. You've probably done it countless times throughout your life. Each experience has had its own distinctive sensation or meaning. Maybe the hand you held was soft or clammy or scratchy-dry. The hand felt electric on a date. It felt like home with a family member. It felt connected in a circle of believers. Most times, it made you feel safe and loved and special.

Now, go with me here. Imagine what it would be like to hold God's hand.

No, really, take a minute and try to picture it.

How would you describe how His hand feels? *Big. Strong. Warm.* How would it make you feel? *Secure. Loved. Special.*

How would it affect how you view where you are and what's next? *Not alone. Helped. Less afraid.*

Jesus walked this earth and used His hands to love and help people just like you. Only heaven knows how many hands He held and hearts He comforted.

Let His Spirit do that for you now. The next time an anxious thought springs up, imagine yourself reaching out to grab His big, strong hand. He will hold you fast.

God, help me to keep grabbing hold of You.

Right by Your Side

Where can I go from your Spirit? Where
can I flee from your presence?
Psalm 139:7

I have abandonment issues. Like anyone else, I've had friends profess forever bonds, then drop away, and boyfriends who just quit calling. But the deeper cuts were when my dad moved out when I was thirteen and when my mom died when I was seventeen. I learned really fast that God was the only One who stayed.

God's presence is truly relentless. He's with you in the hospital room, in the lawyer's office, and at the job interview. He's with you in the panic attack and the sleepless nights. He's there when you're stood up, lonely, or nervous.

Wherever you are, whenever it is, whatever is happening, you can count on this: the Spirit of God will not quit on you. If you think you're alone, you've put up blinders. You can't see what's right next to you.

God didn't make you so He could abandon you. He made you so you could be in a loving, intimate relationship with Him, and He's serious about it. So take off those blinders and look around. *He's right here.* He always has been. And He's not leaving. Ever.

Spirit of God, You're closer to me than my own breath.
Help me remember and sense that You're right here.

The God Who Sees

"You are the God who sees me."
Genesis 16:13

You know those moments when you feel overlooked or misunderstood? A woman named Hagar had a lot of those.

God had promised Sarah and Abraham that they'd have a baby, but after ten years, they were done waiting on God. They instead decided to try to grow their family through a maidservant named Hagar—a standard cultural practice back then.

So Abraham slept with Hagar, and she got pregnant. When she turned hostile toward Sarah, Sarah fired back the contempt, and the fighting culminated in Hagar running away.

Hagar was out in the desert by herself when an angel of God appeared. His message to her was, "Running away isn't the answer. Go back. Continue in your role there. But know this: you'll have a huge family. God heard you, Hagar. God answered you." She was stunned and overjoyed. "You are the God who sees me!" she said.

Can you see the generosity in God's heart here? He saw how this woman had been mistreated, along with her mistakes, and poured out loving gifts to her.

We're all eager to feel seen. But people will only ever see parts of us. God is the One who really sees it all. God has His loving attention on you, dear one.

God, You are the One who truly sees my heart and my story.

Who Forgot?

*"Can a mother forget the baby at her breast and have
no compassion on the child she has borne?"*
Isaiah 49:15

When my anxiety is high, it can be hard to sense the presence of God. It can feel like He's far away, like He's forgotten me.

The Israelites felt this way when they were exiled in Babylon. All signs pointed to God turning His back on them—they were captives in a foreign land, missing the home they loved, just miserable. But Isaiah basically said to them, "Are you kidding? God is like a devoted mother who is forever connected to her kid. There's no way God could forget you!" Isaiah went on to describe how God would do some legendary rescuing. He'd bring His people back home, make wrong things right, and give them all kinds of new joys.

So back up. God never forgets His people? But what about those moments I'm pretty sure He has? When my feelings take over?

Oh. *Right.* It's actually me who's forgetting Him.

My tasks and concerns and fears can essentially become my focus. Guess what? It's hard to do all that while not forgetting some things— including the fact that God knows exactly how I am and what I need.

Remember, His heart is all wrapped up with yours. You're His heart's treasure and are never out of His thoughts.

God, help me not forget Your never-ending love.

God's Tattoo

"I have engraved you on the palms of my hands."
Isaiah 49:16

D o you have a tattoo? What is it? If you got one today, what would it be? It'd be something that matters to you. Someone you love. A message that fills your heart. A memory that points to who you are. That tattoo would show your connection with this ultra-important person or idea.

The Israelites did something kind of like this. They marked their hands by puncturing them with an image that represented their temple or city. They wanted to express what their hearts were saying: *We're as devoted as we can be. We are all in.*

There's a good chance this was exactly what God was alluding to when He told His people, "I have engraved *you* on the palms of My hands."

How would you feel if someone put your name on his body for all the world to see? Just picture it for a minute. It'd be so crazy-bold and striking and certain. So permanent. What would that tattoo be saying to the world? *Yep, I love her. I'll forever want to be around her. I am hers and she is mine. I wouldn't want it any other way.*

God has that heart for you. It's undying affection times a million. He's as devoted as He can be. When it comes to loving you, He's all in.

God, nobody loves like You. Thank You for a
love that's so much bigger than me.

Confess and Be Light

I confessed all my sins to you. . . . And you
forgave me! All my guilt is gone.
Psalm 32:5 NLT

A little boy lay awake in his bed, unable to sleep. Why? He'd stolen money from his mom's wallet. Finally, he got up and told his mom, and then he could finally rest.

The weight of unconfessed sin causes anxiety no matter how old we are. But God is lightning-quick with forgiveness.

Sometimes we deceive ourselves and think we're fine. When we do that, we're not accepting what He says is good and right. We're pushing away His Spirit, hindering the beautiful work He can do in us. All of this opens us up to anxiety.

So we need to ask the Spirit to lead us into truth and get honest with ourselves. As the Spirit points out sin, we agree with Him. We say, *God, I love what You love and hate what You hate. I did that wrong thing. Forgive me. Help me turn away from what's wrong and grow in virtue.*

From that moment on, we make room for His Spirit to work His wonders in our lives.

God lifts up the one who is honest and contrite. He gives grace to the one who raises her hand, saying, "It was me. Forgive me." Humble yourself before Him today. See how He lightens your heart.

Forgive me for the ways I've not embodied Your truth and
beauty, God. I don't want anything to come between us.

Ask All the Questions

Faith does not eliminate questions. But
faith knows where to take them.
Elisabeth Elliot, *A Chance to Die*

The sharp turns and long detours in our lives can leave us feeling fatigued: the cancer that came back, the baby you lost, the job you can't find. You can end up gasping, crying, and questioning.

Those questions don't have to consume you. God is all ears. He deserves reverence, but that doesn't mean you have to be guarded with Him. He already knows you perfectly; it's not like you'll shock Him. Have you heard the questions people in the Bible asked God?

Abraham asked, "What good are all your blessings when I have no son?" (Genesis 15:2 TLB). Job asked, "Why then did you bring me out of the womb?" (Job 10:18). Paul repeatedly asked, "Will you remove this thorn in my flesh, this thing that torments me?" (see 2 Corinthians 12:7–8).

They didn't bottle up their confusion or run away from God in despair. Philip Yancey observed, "As often as not, spiritual giants of the Bible are shown *contending* with God. They prefer to go away limping, like Jacob, rather than to shut God out."[8]

You can go to God with every single question, even ones you can only bring yourself to whisper. He is here for it all.

God, thank You for not turning away from my
confusion. Thank You for staying and listening.

Allow Yourself to Grieve

Give sorrow words; the grief that does not speak knits
up the o'er wrought heart and bids it break.
William Shakespeare, *Macbeth*

Sometimes our anxiety is wrapped up in loss and we haven't fully processed the grief of that loss. Let me give you a few examples.

A friend betrayed your trust and drifted away, so you've lost the meaningful bond you had with her. Establishing trust with new friends now will be tough.

Your position at work was eliminated, and you're totally disoriented. You've lost the career trajectory you worked hard for and the financial security you were counting on.

You've moved to a new place where you don't know anyone. You've lost a way of life that was familiar, and now it's time to create a new local support system from the ground up.

In each scenario, someone has something to grieve. If anything like this has happened to you, open the window of your heart so God's light can reach inside. There could be sad or hurt parts of you that you can tend to and invite God into.

We're constantly adapting to the changing parts of our lives. Sometimes that's good; other times it's a whole lot to process. Ask God to show you how He can help you heal.

You know me best, God. Reveal what I need
to process and grieve with me.

He's Been There

We do not have a high priest who is unable to empathize with our weaknesses, but we have one who has been tempted in every way.
Hebrews 4:15

I couldn't keep my eyes open during that presentation." "I had to read this four times before I understood it." "I get my roommate to hide all the chocolate so I don't eat it all."

I love when people open up about their struggles. *Me too,* they're saying. Relief washes over me. We're all in the same boat.

You know who else understands? Jesus. He's fully God and *fully human.* He got hungry, thirsty, and weary. He got upset and anxious. Sound familiar? He felt overwhelming emotions. He flipped over temple tables in anger. He prayed with "loud cries and tears" (Hebrews 5:7 NET). His soul became deeply troubled.

By what? Many things: the injustices all around Him, the sorrow of His loved ones, the self-righteousness of the Pharisees. Sometimes it was what He saw coming, like the betrayal of Judas or the physical suffering on the cross. Anticipating that crushed Him with grief even "to the point of death" (Matthew 26:38).

Don't think for a minute that He doesn't get it. Jesus took on our humanity so He could redeem it.

So turn to Him in your struggle. He'll help in the moment and heal completely in the future.

Jesus, thank You for entering into my human struggle so completely.

He Weeps Too

He was . . . a man of sorrows, acquainted with deepest grief.
Isaiah 53:3 NLT

H ow do you think God views your heartache? You might get a good idea from what happened with Mary. She was one of Jesus' best friends, and her brother died. Jesus went to Mary and saw her weeping in her grief. He could have been awkward, maybe tried to console her with a little side hug. He could have been silent and stoic, maybe given her some time and space to calm down.

But Jesus did nothing of the sort. He responded with great emotion. "A deep anger welled up within him, and he was deeply troubled. . . . Then Jesus wept" (John 11:33, 35 NLT). He was outraged, so very disturbed, by the brokenness and heartache in the world. The effects of sin were sitting in front of Him, and He hated it. This wasn't what He wanted for His creation.

Jesus raised Lazarus from the dead, giving a glimpse of how He'd later conquer death for us all. "I am the resurrection and the life," He'd said earlier (v. 25). Underneath this was a promise: one day He would bring wholeness and healing. He'd make things right.

Do you know that the God you belong to knows your sorrow? That when you cry, He just may cry too? His grief over your pain and anger at any wrongness in your world runs deep. He is there with you, and one day He'll make all things right.

God, I can't begin to grasp the depths of Your heart.

Curl Up like a Child

"Let the little children come to me."
Matthew 19:14

D o you remember as a kid having moments of unease, then feeling pulled like a magnet toward an adult? Mom was my go-to for lots of moments—hurt when I wiped out in the driveway, sad when someone called me a nerd, or nervous about the first day of school.

As adults, we don't get so upset or scared or nervous like that. Okay, fine, we do. But we definitely don't need to sit in somebody's lap. Okay, yes, that'd actually be nice. We're fully functioning adults, but we've never outgrown our need for care and comfort.

Do you know how Jesus treated children? They felt pulled like a magnet to Him, and He couldn't have been happier about it. He wouldn't let anyone interfere with that sweet together time. They must've been piled all over Him, giggling or playing or just resting. Can you imagine how much love, comfort, and peace they must have felt when they were with their Maker?

You are God's child, His more-special-than-you-could-know creation. And He's looking at you with warm eyes that say, *Come.*

So do it. Come running to Him and be yourself. Wrap up in a blanket and imagine His arms wrapped around you. Talk with Him. Read truth and think on it. Make Him your go-to for all kinds of moments.

Father God, I just want to curl up in Your big, strong lap.

He Holds Your Future

"If it is the Lord's will, we will live and do this or that."
James 4:15

Americans spend *two billion* dollars on the psychic industry every year.[9] People claim psychic readings make them feel better, evidently because they're desperate to have fewer unknowns.

It's only natural to want to know what's coming. Sometimes questions about the future won't stop darting to the front of my mind. *What's going to happen? I have to know!*

But God designed our lives to include unknowns. He's all about the surprises and big reveals. Plus, we aren't really built to handle or process more of life than a day's worth at a time—knowing about the future would be a massive overload for our systems. Do you really want to try to mentally deal with a lifetime's worth of experiences right now, today? I'm curious, but I don't really want that. I'm betting you don't either.

So it really comes down to not *What?* but *Who?*

The One who is good and gracious and powerful. The One who created you in love and invited you into heaven.

You don't have to wonder if God's going to let the chips fall where they may. God is holding your future just as surely as He's giving you breath in this moment.

God, You created a beautiful world. I trust You
will create a beautiful future too.

Accepted and Supported

His love endures forever.
Psalm 100:5

We've talked about how God has His arms wide open to you. He wraps them around you and holds you. What does this mean to you?

I'd say that His open arms mean you're always welcome. You could be a wild, hot mess and He'd still say, *Come,* with all the compassion in the world.

His arms wrapped around you means you're accepted. He says, "I have grace for all of that. It's like your issues make up one speck of sand, and My grace is all the sand in the world. It's far more than enough to cover it."

His arms that keep on holding you mean you're loved. "I made you and you are lovely. I love you as you are. I'll also help you grow in beautiful ways and become who you're meant to be."

Fred Rogers, who was known for treating every person he encountered with great respect and dignity, said, "Knowing that we can be loved exactly as we are gives us all the best opportunity for growing into the healthiest of people."

God accepts you exactly as you are. And He has more for you. He wants to position you for healing and growth—and that "position" is with Him, in His love and support and wisdom.

God, because of who You are, I am always loved and lovely.

Hope for Good Change

The LORD hears his people when they call to him for help.
Psalm 34:17 NLT

I have crippling anxiety. I just *cannot* stop worrying."
"I had my second panic attack last week."
"I can't sleep because I'm so stressed and unsettled."
How often do you hear people say things like that? If you do, you're with a transparent group of people, and that is awesome.

It's okay to struggle. God is not scowling at you for having problems. You are His precious work in progress! He accepts you even though you're not perfect, so don't get swallowed up in guilt.

Our anxiety requires our curious attention and God's tender care. Once we understand its roots, patterns, and accompanying beliefs, we can work with the Spirit to get out of its grip.

We should address anxiety from multiple angles, including mindfulness, meditation, prayer, self-care, support from others, life balance, and healthy habits that make us holistically stronger. These things can help change our perspective and mindset.

Wherever you are today, don't be afraid to be honest. God will make it possible for you to take steps forward, to go deeper into His abundant life. Because of who you're with, there's always hope for good change.

God, I'm ready to stay honest and take steps
with You toward peace and freedom.

~

The Overcomer Is Here

Y ou're definitely not alone. Who is with you? The One who can handle anything.

He's your partner in all you face. He's your advocate, defender, provider, comforter, helper, and guide. You can count on Him.

Let yourself just sit at His feet and take in His heart. Spend some time every day meditating on His character. Return to stories of His jaw-dropping power. Remind yourself who you get to do life with. You are united with the Overcomer.

The Mighty One is for you.

Warrior God

*"In this world you will have trouble. But take
heart! I have overcome the world."*
John 16:33

A re you mad that life isn't easy? I have those days too. It's like I
forget Jesus came out and said it: "It's gonna get rough." And that
was for the first disciples who were heading into violent, frightening,
dangerous situations. My life seems like a Disney movie compared to
theirs.

Even so, once I accept it's not going to be easy, I'm not so flustered
and put out when things go sideways. Once I have Jesus' perspective,
I have the right perspective. I can go into my days mentally armed for
rolling with the punches.

Thankfully, Jesus didn't stop talking after giving a grim forecast.
Why not? Well, look at who He is and what His mission on earth was.

Jesus did exactly what the prophet said He'd do: "The LORD
will march forth like a mighty hero; he will come out like a warrior,
full of fury. He will shout his battle cry and crush all his enemies"
(Isaiah 42:13 NLT).

Jesus is a fighter. He is an overcomer. And He's the One who's
with you. So that heavy hard stuff you're facing today? He is going to
help you through it all.

I'm ready to do this day with You, Jesus, the Fighter.

You're Family

"Because I live, you also will live."
John 14:19

Y ou belong to your family in a unique way. You share a name, a reputation, and resources. The fact that you're united with them affects your identity and horizons—it may open up a lot of possibilities in life for you.

If your faith is in Jesus, you are united with Him. And that opens up a whole new existence for you.

You used to be dead in sin. Spiritually speaking, you were motionless with no pulse, unable to help yourself. God showed up and brought you to life. He overcame the entire dead-in-sin problem. He overcame all that was separating you from Him. Grace rushed in to meet every failure and rut and wound. Newness took over. Resurrection became your future.

You've got the life of Jesus in you today, and you get to live more like He did, connected to the Father. You belong to God.

Can you hear what Jesus is saying to you?

Because I was raised, you will be raised.

Because I live, you will live.

Because I have overcome, you will overcome.

Because I had victory, you will have victory.

You're with Me now.

Jesus, I believe there's nothing in my life You can't overcome.

Kingdom of Light

There were loud voices in heaven, which said: "The kingdom
of the world has become the kingdom of our Lord and
of his Messiah, and he will reign for ever and ever."
Revelation 11:15

E ver slip into survival mode? When we're stressed, fear and negativity creep in. Things look bleak. We lose perspective that our lives are part of something bigger—that we're part of God's kingdom of light, which is ever expanding in this world.

It all started with Jesus. He announced that He was ushering in a new kingdom. What was the proof? He was transforming whatever He touched: "The blind receive sight, the lame walk, those who have leprosy are cleansed, the deaf hear, the dead are raised, and the good news is proclaimed to the poor" (Matthew 11:5).

If your faith is in King Jesus, then you belong to His kingdom, which is conquering the darkness. Eventually it'll completely take over, and it's going to last forever.

But you're not on earth only to wait around for heaven. Jesus wants to bring more of His powerful light into your life right now. He's building His kingdom, and He wants you to help build it. Does something in your life need to be restored, renewed, or redirected? Or revived, replaced, or re-created? He can do all of that and more.

Jesus my King, I invite more of Your light and reign
and transforming power into my life.

He Sets Prisoners Free

He leads out the prisoners with singing.
Psalm 68:6

Two men sat in a prison cell, reeling from the humiliation of being stripped in public and the agony of getting beaten to a pulp. Their feet were in stocks and their bodies were bloody and bruised.

They had no Houdini tricks up their sleeves. No nice, sneaky guards to help them. They simply had no way out.

Then, the earth started shaking. The prison started crumbling. Every door flew open and every chain broke apart. Paul and Silas—and every other prisoner in the building—were freed (Acts 16:22–26).

God overpowered that prison. It's like what He did for the Israelites when they were enslaved in Egypt or stuck in exile. He sets out to "free captives from prison and to release from the dungeon those who sit in darkness" (Isaiah 42:7).

God is on a mission to free people today too. Whatever is binding you up, whatever unhealthy thing is controlling your life, He wants to free you from it.

Are you feeling trapped and helpless? Does it seem like you have no way out? The freedom-loving God can always make a way. Cry out to the One who knows exactly where you're sitting and how to get you out of there.

I know You can create a way out for me, God.
I want to start living with freedom.

43

He Is the Healer

He relieved the inwardly tormented. He cured the bodily ill.
Matthew 8:16 MSG

A man suffering from leprosy felt sores all over his body. A little girl lay in her bed, her chest as still as stone. Another man sat discouraged by a pool. He'd been suffering from his crippling disease for thirty-eight years.

These were broken people. And then they came into contact with the Healer. The One who had brought them to life in the beginning changed their current existence (Matthew 8:2–3; 9:18–25; John 5:1–8).

After God provided water in the desert for the Israelites, He said, "I am the LORD, who heals you" (Exodus 15:26). This is who our God is. In His great, transformative power, He brings newness, health, and wholeness.

So, because of who He is, we bring Him our suffering bodies, broken hearts, and chaotic minds. We ask for His transforming touch. We know He can renew or revive what seems hopelessly ruined, wrong, or dead.

We're not just damaged goods or broken beyond repair. He can bring us healing that offers a glimpse of heaven, where we'll be truly whole and fully alive forever.

Let yourself hope today.

My hope is in You, the Great Life-Giver and Healer.

The Eyes of the Blind

[You will] open eyes that are blind.
Isaiah 42:7

A man woke up in the morning and blinked his eyes in darkness, just like every other morning before. Born blind, he'd spent years without any light to guide him.

Then one day he met Someone who threw open the shutters in his world, and he stepped into a whole new way of living.

Jesus curiously combined His own saliva with the dust on the ground to make a mud paste, then rubbed it on the blind man's eyelids. It was like when He'd formed the first human, from the dust of the ground, just before He breathed life into him. When the blind man rinsed off the paste, he saw for the first time the vivid color, sharp detail, and striking design all around him (John 9:1–7).

Has God ever opened your eyes to something in your life, maybe something you'd been missing right in front of you? He may have something new to reveal to you today.

Do you feel stuck in a dark place? He could throw open the shutters for you and change your whole view.

God sees all, and He can open your eyes to see more of what He does. Maybe a habit that's holding you back. A sin that's hurting your soul. A behavior that's pushing away a friend. Ask Him to open your eyes to whatever He wants you to see.

God, I want to know what You have for me in the light.

He Provides for the Hungry

He satisfies the thirsty and fills the hungry with good things.
Psalm 107:9

T housands of people were hanging out with Jesus in the middle of nowhere, and before long they were famished.

A poor widow ran out of bread ingredients, the last bit of food she had. It looked like she and her son would go hungry.

An entire people group wandered in the desert with nothing to eat. They were positively desperate.

Everyone in these situations went from being needy to satisfied, all because God is a provider. Bread and fish mysteriously multiplied (Mark 6:35–44). Flour and oil kept showing up in empty containers (1 Kings 17:7–16). Quail and manna appeared in the desert (Exodus 16:3–14).

Jesus said He was the Bread of Life, bread that came down from heaven, the ultimate provision from God (John 6:35). He nourishes and takes care of our souls.

Do you have all that you need today? Whatever part of your life feels empty or unmanageable, whatever way your soul is hungry, let God be your provider. Trust the One who created the world to create a way to meet your needs.

Good Father, I open my hands and wait, ready
to receive the good things You'll give.

He Seeks the Needy

You, LORD, hear the desire of the afflicted; you
encourage them, and you listen to their cry,
defending the fatherless and the oppressed.
Psalm 10:17–18

A foreigner constantly feels confused, rejected, and unstable in a place that is strange to him. A widow sits alone panicking over the question of how she'll buy food and keep her home. An orphan sobs at night, gutted by loneliness.

God sees every one of these people, and He weeps. And then He runs to them. He calls for the reinforcements. His Spirit activates helpers to reach each dearly loved person and lift them out of dark places.

Jesus came to earth to seek and save the lost—the messed-up and broken ones, like me. Like you. He seeks out the oppressed, scoops them up, and sets them upright: Here's a meal. Here's a bed. Here's a job. A friend or caretaker or parent. A place to belong and feel secure.

His passion for people and for meeting them in their neediness is crying out for page after page of the Bible. It's calling out to your heart right now. *I see what you need. Yes, I know your need is so huge it's almost crushing you. My heart breaks for My child. Let Me step in now and meet it.*

God, I open my heart to Your vast compassion.
Help everyone else who is suffering too.

He Brings Justice

God is a just judge, and God is angry with the wicked every day.
Psalm 7:11 NKJV

W e live in a world that, indeed, tragically includes unfairness. Incarcerated innocents, mass shootings, sex trafficking, child abuse—incomprehensible atrocities that break us. We're horrified and shaken and angry. But we're not as angry as God is.

The psalmist David knew that, so that's why, whenever he encountered violence and wickedness, he ran to God. At one point he prayed, "Break off their fangs, O God! Smash the jaws of these lions, O LORD! . . . The godly will rejoice when they see injustice avenged. . . . 'There is a God who judges justly here on earth'" (Psalm 58:6, 10–11 NLT).

We see no way to make sense of suffering or make wrong things right. But we know a God who can. We'll see Him do some of it now and eventually sweep away all injustice forever.

Run to God about any unfairness and ask Him to shut it down. Don't think for a minute He isn't watchful and outraged and moving the universe toward righteousness. Hang on to the promise that He will end the suffering of His people and place them in His wholly just heaven.

Only You are truly just. Come call the shots, set things straight, and heal us. Show the world what You say is right and good.

He Gives Beauty for Ashes

[God will] care for the needs of all who mourn in Zion, give them
bouquets of roses instead of ashes. . . . Rename them "Oaks
of Righteousness" planted by GOD to display his glory. They'll
rebuild the old ruins, raise a new city out of the wreckage.
Isaiah 61:2–4 MSG

Stella weeps after giving birth to a baby with no heartbeat. Years later, her four children are piling on top of her, each one's giggles louder than the next.

Sam panics when he's diagnosed with cancer. Years later, a routine scan comes back clear as he's training for running a marathon.

Mae is heartbroken as she watches her husband move out. Years later, their bond is the strongest it's ever been. They write love notes to each other every day.

These are snapshots of lives that have been touched by the God of beauty, the One who gifts us with renewal and sweet surprises.

Even when things feel hopeless, He says, "This can change. You can have joy instead of mourning and praise instead of despair. You can even become like a strong oak tree, one I planted to show the world My beauty."

It may take time, but you can count on Him to free you. Ask Him to shine a brilliant light in any dark shadows and fill you up with deep goodness and new joy.

I believe You always have more beauty to give, God.

He Is the Light of the World

The light shines in the darkness, and the
darkness has not overcome it.
John 1:5

A curious child wanders away from a campsite at dusk to pick flowers, but she quickly loses her way. Before long it's pitch black and she's lost in the woods. There are threatening noises that scare her, sharp rocks that cut her, and fallen branches that trip her. Unable to understand her surroundings or to protect and help herself, she is seized by terror.

If you could run into the woods with a flashlight to help her, you'd do it in a heartbeat, wouldn't you? If it were your own child, you wouldn't let anything stop you.

You and I are like that lost child in the dark. Sometimes we're caught up in confusion—living with painful wounds and looming threats that leave us seized by fear. We're in a darkness we don't understand, a sin-broken world that ultimately leads to death. It's terrifying.

Like the sun that shines on the earth to bring life, Jesus is the true Light that brings us life. He promises that if you look to Him and say yes to Him, you won't have to stumble in darkness. You'll have His light to guide you.

Jesus, I'm so relieved You're more powerful than the
darkness. Fill my world with Your light.

He Is Peace

He himself is our peace.
Ephesians 2:14

When was the last time you longed for more peace in the world, or in your heart? Like two seconds ago? Me too.

Our sin generates a chaotic existence that God never wanted for us. He grieved the lack of peace in this world so deeply that He sent His own Son to make things right.

Jesus absorbed all our sin and its wreckage on the cross so that we could reconnect with the Father. He removed the barrier that kept us from God's incredible peace—which is about so much more than just stopping fights or quieting noise. It's about wholeness, safety, justice, "multidimensional, complete well-being."[1]

We now belong to the Prince of Peace's kingdom. Heaven's peace is our destiny, and until then, He can miraculously create peace in our hearts and relationships, no matter what we're in the middle of.

Jesus wants to amaze you on the frantic or fearful or dark days. He wants to inject His peace into your life and usher in even more gifts: steadiness, strength, and resilience. Patience, compassion, and gentleness.

Open your heart to the Source of all true peace and wholeness. He's right here.

Prince of Peace, overpower the chaos in my heart.
Replace it with Your gift of peace.

He Is Love

God is love. . . . This is how God showed his love for us: God
sent his only Son into the world so we might live through him.
1 John 4:8–9 MSG

We tell each other, "I love you!" and we mean it. But we can't claim to mean what God does when He says it.

God's love says, "I created you in love, and you always have My attention. I'll save you from your enemy. I'll send My Son into the world to complete My rescue mission. I'll adopt you and make you part of My family forever." Jesus' love says, "I'll meet you where you are and be a servant and a sacrifice. I'll teach you and heal you. I'll suffer and give up My life for you." The Spirit's love says, "I'll stay closer than your breath. I'll live inside you. I'll guide you, comfort you, and empower you."

The Father, Son, and Holy Spirit have always shared a joyful, perfect love. Out of their joy and abundance, they created people.

Take a minute and process it: this aspect of God's character is fundamental to *the whole reason we're even here.*

His love is perfect, pure, and life-giving. His love delights and pursues. It cheers and lifts. It's "better than life," the psalmist said (Psalm 63:3). It's the most beautiful thing in the universe. This is a love that can carry you through every day on earth and carry you home to heaven.

God, I want to spend every minute in Your perfect love.

He Is Committed to You

*I'll marry you for good—forever! I'll marry you true
and proper, in love and tenderness. Yes, I'll marry
you and neither leave you nor let you go.*
Hosea 2:19–20 MSG

One day a wife tells her husband, "I've fallen out of love with you. I've moved on with someone new." What would a natural response of the betrayed spouse be? Shock, anger, jealousy? That person is done—no consideration of second chances.

God says, "You and I are like this. I have a heart of a spouse for you. I'm thoroughly committed. When you forget Me and run away and break promises, I'm jealous. I'm hurt. But I'm still all in."

Okay, back up. God wants to be like a spouse to us? Well, *He is love*. He made people for a loving relationship with Him. He came up with marriage, and it's a construct we can grasp.

God wants us to know that His promises have the ultimate staying power. That when the one He loves turns away from Him, He runs after her. No matter what she has done, she's His love!

Deep intimacy, tender affection, undying commitment, neverending forgiveness—God's heart for you is like a superhero spouse. His love is unfailing, always and forever, period.

*God, I've never known a love like Yours.
It's stronger than anything I've ever felt.*

He Gives Wisdom

Only the LORD gives wisdom; he gives
knowledge and understanding.
Proverbs 2:6 NCV

I just don't know what to do. What a mind-boggling mess."

"What does it look like to be a good parent now?"

"How can we possibly rebuild the trust we've lost?"

There are countless moments when we're at a loss, baffled by the complexity of our problems.

God, however, is never puzzled. He created the whole world and all of life in His wisdom. Plants, animals, oceans, mountains, people, galaxies—they all function based on His orderly design. We can't even fathom all He's accomplished through His wisdom.

Nothing is hidden from Him either. Nothing surprises or stumps Him. There's just no end to what He understands.

For every problem, He sees an answer. For every impossible situation or ethical question, He knows what is good and right. For every twisty maze, He can whisper to you which turn to make.

So, when you get confused, don't throw your hands up in despair. Don't stay parked in a freak-out zone or a place of hopelessness. He's got treasures of wisdom available to you. Just ask, then wait to see how He'll help you.

Thank You that I don't have to live in over my head,
God. Show me what's good and right today.

He Is Goodness and Beauty

The LORD is good.
Psalm 100:5

I s God *really* good? Many of us live with this question as we feel the weight of suffering. We may not be saying the words, but it's deep inside us, and we experience the effects. Our hearts aren't at rest. We're constantly worried about what's coming. We sometimes feel defeated and helpless. We project our negative emotions and difficulties onto God, then we're not so sure He's attentive or trustworthy.

The truth is, nothing and no one can change the character of an infinite God. He has no skewed motives, no corrupt desires, no darkness at all. He is perfect and pure and lovely.

Now, those hard things in your life? He'll find a way to use them to carry out His purposes, to shape you in beauty and bring blessings. It'll take time, and you won't be able to understand it along the way, but the Almighty will accomplish His "good, pleasing and perfect will" (Romans 12:2).

Listen close, dear one. Your good God created you to share His goodness with you, not to keep it from you. Don't let anything—not the pain or questions or difficulties of this life—convince you otherwise.

All the good things in my life are from You, God.
You are good, and You want goodness for me.

He Knows About Suffering

He was looked down on and passed over, a man
who suffered, who knew pain firsthand.
Isaiah 53:3 MSG

I magine listening to someone complain about their "hardships"—
the horrors of going too long without a facial or missing their annual
European vacation—just after you lost your job and took your mom
to chemo. You can't help but wonder, *Is this person out of touch with*
actual suffering?

Jesus isn't that kind of person. The King of heaven could have
come to earth and lived like a king with every privilege. But He didn't.
He was born in a barn, had humble parents, and had no standout
qualities in His appearance. He experienced hunger and homelessness,
bullying and rejection, loneliness and abandonment, betrayal and false
accusation. He endured incomprehensible suffering leading up to and
on the cross.

Does Jesus understand what you're in the middle of? Does He
grasp how hurting people throughout the world are feeling? Absolutely.
He's been through it Himself. His suffering was living in a world subject to the brokenness of sin, and so is yours.

Jesus really gets it. His heart is full of compassion for you and He
stays with you through every hard thing.

Jesus, thank You for suffering for me and with me.

He Is the Comforter

"As a mother comforts her child, so will I comfort you."
Isaiah 66:13

When has someone brought you comfort? Maybe a friend delivered warm soup when you were sick. Or she listened to your heartache, hugged you when you cried, or stood with you when you were criticized.

Every experience of comfort throughout your life came from the heart of your Father. He is the God of *all* comfort (2 Corinthians 1:3).

"Comfort my people and speak tenderly to them," God told Isaiah, when the Israelites were living as foreigners in exile (see Isaiah 40:1–2). Relief and blessings were headed their way. "The Holy Spirit, the Comforter, will come," Jesus told His disciples as He prepared them for His departure. "He'll be with you forever" (see John 14:16).

We can see glimpses of God's tender heart in other scriptures too. The Samaritan binding up wounds of the man left on the road. The prodigal son's father hugging and kissing his beloved boy. David, moved by the intimacy of his God, saying, "Even in the darkest of places, You comfort me" (see Psalm 23:4).

This is the One calling you to come closer. Let Him encourage and strengthen your heart. Let Him surround you with His bigger-than-everything love and fill you with His mightier-than-everything peace. Open up your heart to what the God of all comfort wants to give you.

God, help me feel the comfort of Your closeness now.

He Is Not Fickle

God is not a man, so he does not lie. He is not human, so he
does not change his mind. Has he ever spoken and failed to
act? Has he ever promised and not carried it through?
Numbers 23:19 NLT

R aise your hand if you often receive texts like this: *Totally slept*
in—rain check? Oops, I forgot! Sorry, I can't make it after all.

We've also experienced more severe disappointments. People broke
big promises to us and left us hanging, shocked, and raw and reeling.
And that's exactly why it's so hard for us to grasp that God is constant
in who He is. He doesn't change His mind or have mood swings. He
is perfectly steadfast in His love and attention.

We don't ever have to wake up and wonder, *Does He really still love*
me and want to be close to me? Is He actually going to show up for me
when I need Him? Will He walk out on me?

No. He is always caring for you. He follows through on what He
says. Throughout the ages God has never changed and He never will.
He's the same yesterday, today, and tomorrow.

So that settles it. Your God—your comforter, strengthener,
and guide—is absolutely the most reliable thing in your world. The
unmovable mountain you can count on.

Now the question is, are you living like it? What if you did?

God, forgive me for projecting my changeableness
onto You. You are always better than I think.

He Is a Caregiver and Guide

The LORD is my shepherd; I have everything I need. He lets me
rest in green pastures. He leads me to calm water. He gives
me new strength. He leads me on paths that are right.
Psalm 23:1–3 NCV

Have you ever done any babysitting? Maybe you chased after straying kids, passed out juice boxes, and dried tears. You gave those kids what they needed and made all the difference in their world.

God is a caregiver, the best one you've ever seen. He's a shepherd who watches over all His sheep. Sometimes they're stubborn or senseless or distracted. He patiently stays with them, guiding them away from dangers and into nourishing spaces. He leads them to life-giving water and gives them new strength.

God is attentive and consistent in your life, saying, "Here, let Me show you how to be well. You need care! I'll help you." And "I know the right path to take. Follow Me."

He'll take care of you and guide you in this world, then lead you into a new heavenly life, where you will never again get lost, hunger or thirst, or face any danger.

Here is your loving pursuer, your nurturing caregiver, your wise guide. Ask Him to provide the nourishment and help you need today.

You know what I need and what steps I should take, God.
Help me stay close to You so I can receive Your care.

He Is a Protector

The Lord is faithful, and he will strengthen
you and protect you from the evil one.
2 Thessalonians 3:3

I t's a classic moment in movies when someone's at home in the dark and gets spooked by a noise. They pick up some makeshift weapon, whatever they can grab, and creep around, feeling a bit bolder.

But anything we could grab in those kinds of moments wouldn't help us in our biggest fights in this world, because those fights are not against flesh and blood. They're against God's enemy. God says He protects His people like a mother eagle "teaching its young to fly, catching them safely on its spreading wings" (Deuteronomy 32:11 GNT).

Jesus prayed for the protection of His people like this: "Holy Father, protect them by the power of your name. . . . My prayer is not that you take them out of the world but that you protect them from the evil one" (John 17:11, 15). The Evil One who wants to keep you from the abundant life of God. That snake who says to your heart, *Did God really say that?*

Meanwhile, your Good Shepherd holds His rod of protection. Any thoughts that tempt you away from truth—Jesus can take His rod to each one.

Protect my heart and mind right now, God. Fill me with Your
love and truth, and fight off anything that goes against them.

He Never Fails or Gives Up

There has never been the slightest doubt in my mind that the
God who started this great work in you would keep at it and bring
it to a flourishing finish on the very day Christ Jesus appears.
Philippians 1:6 MSG

God is never one to shy away from an epic, long-term project. Creation was His first endeavor. He didn't wimp out after day four. When He formed His own people, He didn't let their slavery in Egypt stand in His way. He charged in there and magnificently delivered them. Then He initiated covenants with them that would forever bind them to Him.

"He is the faithful God who keeps his covenant for a thousand generations" (Deuteronomy 7:9 NLT). He always accomplishes His purposes. And you are now wrapped up with those purposes.

You're the clay, and He's the Potter. He made you a new creation through Jesus, and now He's going to keep working in your heart and life. Got a lot of mistakes and problems? Tragedies? You're still in His hands. He can work with all of that.

Instead He says, "Just you wait . . . There's so much brilliance ahead! I'm making all things new!" Even though you'll fail, He won't. He says He's going to make you like Jesus? Build His kingdom through you? Bring justice and peace? You better believe it. These are all His epic long-term projects, which are totally His thing.

I am in awe that You never fail, God!

He Calms Storms

He got up and rebuked the winds and the
waves, and it was completely calm.
Matthew 8:26

H ave you ever been in a boat during a wild storm? Try to imagine it for a minute. It must be terrifying. It must make you think, *This is it for me. I don't think I'll survive this.*

That's pretty much where the disciples' heads were as a storm raged on the sea. Their boat was gaining increasingly more water, and they were losing their minds. Meanwhile, Jesus was asleep. The disciples woke Jesus, shouting. Mark records their words as, "Don't you care if we drown?" (Mark 4:38).

Jesus' response was, "Why are you so afraid?" (Matthew 8:26). "Where is your faith?" (Luke 8:25). His tone sounds like, *Don't you know Me at all? I've got this. You should be trusting Me with everything by now.* He stood up and immediately silenced the storm with a word.

The disciples were stunned at Jesus' jaw-dropping power, His complete and utter authority over the elements.

The power of Jesus is still real in *this moment.* Can He calm the storm in your heart? Does He care when you feel like you're drowning? Are there things in your life He could bring His jaw-dropping power to? The real question is, will you invite Him into your storm?

Jesus, bring Your storm-stopping power into my
heart and into my life. My trust is in You.

He Blasts Away Shame

There is now no condemnation for those who are in Christ Jesus.
Romans 8:1

D o you ever feel so frustrated with yourself that you think surely God is too? I totally go there. The shame is so real.

But then, finally, it hits me*: You must think a lot of yourself and your sin if you're acting like He couldn't knock it out. Do you really think that your sin could overpower His grace?*

Sure, I'll mess up, but I can't change who He is or what He's already done. "As high as heaven is over the earth, so strong is his love to those who fear him. And as far as sunrise is from sunset, he has separated us from our sins" (Psalm 103:11–12 MSG).

Maybe you can't shake a sense of guilt. Maybe you're anxious about how you could screw up in the future. *Potential shame.* We're really borrowing trouble now! But it can happen—if we're carrying around a weight from our past, we may automatically use it to fill in the blanks of our future.

But God already cast all your sins into the depths of the sea. He looked at them all, even the ones you don't know about yet, and declared you "not guilty." Whenever you hear shame's taunts, let God's message blast louder: "I don't condemn you; I accept you and love you."

God, I believe You over my feelings. I'll let
Your love scare off any shame.

He's the Best Lawyer Ever

We have an advocate with the Father—
Jesus Christ, the Righteous One.
1 John 2:1

That woman is worrying and whining today," says the accuser. "She's not trusting You again. Punish her and pronounce her a failure."

"Absolutely not," a strong voice cuts in. "That's all covered by grace—she's forgiven. Remember how I stepped in to take the punishment *for her*? I made sure that sin wouldn't get between her and the Father. Back off from My sister. She's forever loved."

Silence follows. Nobody can top that.

Who gave that irrefutable defense? Our advocate, Jesus.

He's the lawyer in the courtroom giving compelling arguments, saying, "Not true. Here's the proof."

Jesus is at the throne of God, standing by all He did to get and keep you in the family. He never shrinks back in embarrassment. He claims you as His sister or brother. He points to His undeniable accomplishment on your behalf. "Sure, she did that, but don't forget: she's with Me. Look what I did to make all of that go away."

He's your biggest supporter and will keep at it until the accuser's voice is permanently silenced.

Jesus, I'm stunned by Your sacrifice, Your defense,
and Your tireless commitment to me.

He Is Your Personal Prayer Warrior

He is able to save completely those who come to God through him, because he always lives to intercede for them.
Hebrews 7:25

How do you feel when someone is praying for you? Supported. Seen. Cared for. Honestly, maybe a little awkward or embarrassed with all the attention. But you certainly feel not alone. And hopeful—the hope of others helps build up yours.

God doesn't only lead other people to pray for you; He actually prays for you too. Again, your biggest supporter is stepping in for you. Jesus does for you what you can't do for yourself, just like when He defends you at the throne. With loving eyes, He's perceiving everything that's going on in you and around you: when you need courage, hope, and a reminder of what's true; when you're about to make a big decision and you need wisdom; when you need protection in a dangerous place.

Jesus doesn't miss a thing. He brings your needs to your God— much like the way He Himself prayed while on earth. He constantly reached up to His Father, deeply aware of His need. He's deeply aware of yours too.

It's just one of the many ways He's got your back and proves His love for you. Let your heart rest in that truth.

God, You prove Your compassion and love for me time and time again. This is who You are.

He Is Mighty

Wise in heart and mighty in strength, who
has defied Him without harm?
Job 9:4 NASB

I magine finding yourself in a battlefield. You make your way to a shelter and find your captain, a warrior through and through. Looking you in the eye, he lays out the battle plan. You feel your heart grow courageous in his presence. You'll fight every enemy together.

There are days we look at all the suffering and devastation in this world and want to cry in a closet. Disease and death, poverty and abuse, trauma and fear—this is all too much for us. We have to connect all these points of need, all these gaping holes of inability and overwhelming tragedies, to the Mighty One.

We're alive in this gap between God's kingdom beginning and being fully established. It's a window of freedom, giving time for people to follow His love into the light, and it involves the continued presence of darkness.

We might wonder, *Why is this still happening? Shouldn't our warrior have wrapped this up by now?* But there's far more to the epic story of the world than we can see. So we hang on to the One who comprehends it all and who will keep fighting until He defeats all evil.

Take heart, dear one. The battle is fierce. But He's fiercer.

I can't see the end yet, God, but I know You're the winner.
Make us strong. Keep fighting for our peace.

He Is Generous

We all live off his generous abundance, gift after gift after gift.
John 1:16 MSG

H ave you ever had an extraordinarily generous friend? Someone who looks for excuses to share something special with you and has a knack for picking out the perfect gift for you?

The generous heart of God is like that, but on a monumental scale. He's not stingy; He loves sharing His abundance.

All of creation is an expression of His generosity. So is the way He sustains it, bringing rain and harvests, making it lush and plentiful and rich with resources. When God told the Israelites how to harvest, He said, "Leave some behind for the poor and foreigner to grab" (see Deuteronomy 24:19). Yep, that's what He's like.

As His Spirit lives in us, He brings us more goodness: comfort, peace, guidance, protection, wisdom, power, love, patience, gentleness, and joy. He says, "I want to give all of this to you!"

Our anxiety is often rooted in feeling like we won't be able to get what we need. We can't shake the feeling that deprivation, whether spiritual or physical, is just around the corner. But Jesus spoke to this issue, saying that we can trust our Father to provide for us (Matthew 6:25–34). He already knows what we need—better than we do!

So draw near to Him. Ask Him to make your heart and your life overflow with His abundance.

God, help me remember that You're eager to give beautiful gifts.

He Is the Source

*Jesus answered, "If you knew the generosity of God
and who I am, you would be asking me for a drink,
and I would give you fresh, living water."*
John 4:10 MSG

The woman at the well was living with a restless soul. She had a seemingly unquenchable thirst for something *more*. Then Jesus told her something that would change her life forever.

"Those who drink the water that I will give them will never be thirsty again. The water that I will give them will become in them a spring which will provide them with life-giving water and give them eternal life" (John 4:14 GNT).

When we receive God's eternal life, we know our ultimate future will be endlessly brilliant. But we also receive resources for here and now.

Jesus understands this world better than you do and is more powerful than anything in it. He knows how you can live fully and freely. And He's endlessly generous in enabling you to do that.

So the next time you're anxious, stay close to His heart and let Him reach every part of your life. Keep saying, "I believe You can help me in this moment." And as you look out to days ahead of you, tell Him, "I want to live into the goodness You made me for."

*Almighty God, I believe that You are able to provide for
me, take care of me, and help me in every way.*

MARCH

~

Mind Management

Y ou know who your partner is. You know what He can do and that He's thrilled about you. Moving forward with Him is going to change how you think and live.

It's time to start working with Him to steer your thoughts toward His goodness, to fight hang-ups and pessimism, and to win the battle of the mind.

He will equip you with all you need: life-changing truth, practical tools to make things doable, and the Spirit's bigger-than-everything power. He's the One who fights for you and fights with you. He'll help you every step of the way.

Reframe That Weakness

"My power is made perfect in weakness."
2 Corinthians 12:9

I am all about using alarms on my phone to do life. Have you ever thought of anxiety as a sort of alarm? What if anxiety is something that signals it's time for God's strength to move into our weakness? What if the thing that causes anxiety for you—or the anxiety itself—is like Paul's thorn in the flesh?

Paul described having an infuriating difficulty in his life, a thing that relentlessly plagued him. (I'm willing to bet he experienced anxiety over it.) Whatever it was, he wanted it out of his life.

Then he reached a turning point in how he understood it. God was allowing this thing to be in Paul's life because it made him aware of his need for God. And so Paul reframed how he saw the whole thing: "I quit focusing on the handicap and began appreciating the gift. It was a case of Christ's strength moving in on my weakness. Now I take limitations in stride. . . . I just let Christ take over! And so the weaker I get, the stronger I become" (2 Corinthians 12:9–10 MSG).

Let your struggling lead you to the Source. Allow it to push you into further dependence. His power will fit just right with your neediness.

My heart is racing—so now, I'm praying. Bring
Your power to my weakness, God.

Is That a Lie?

"[The Enemy] is a liar and the father of lies."
John 8:44

Anxiety can be an arrow, pointing out wounds and needs to bring to God. It also can be based on real threats such as a tsunami headed our way.

On the flip side, anxiety can be based on lies. They can trip us up and shove us into some truly frightening territory.

There is no way forward. I have no options. God has left me alone.

God's power isn't big enough to handle this hard thing. It is all up to me, and I've come to the end of myself.

I'm worthless and unforgivable. No one will do anything to help me.

Scripture tells us those things aren't true. Yes, our feelings are intense, but we can know that something truer, deeper, and stronger than our feelings can start running the show. The Spirit of truth can lead us into new experiences.

Jesus said, "Do not be anxious about your life" (Matthew 6:25 ESV). He was talking about worrying about tomorrow and not trusting God— your incredible Father who is wild about you—to meet your needs. Jesus wants truth to rule in our minds: God is all-powerful and present, our helper and provider—always.

Ask Him to help you spot the lies and keep coming back to what's true.

Spirit of truth, lead me into new thoughts, feelings, and experiences.

You're Captain of Your Ship

Be careful what you think, because your thoughts run your life.
Proverbs 4:23 NCV

I am blown away by how much a shift in thinking can change how I feel. Our thoughts create our perspective on reality, and a shift in thought can dramatically change our experience.

My thoughts are my domain. It's my job to steer them in the right direction and make sure truth is out in front, leading the others. I can have a wild range of thoughts in the space of an hour. Some of them can perpetuate anxiety and multiply bad feelings. But I'm at the captain's wheel, and even a little nudge in one direction changes my trajectory.

I am broken; it's hopeless; I'm sad. Nothing and no one can change this. Or, after a nudge toward truth, I'm navigating in a new direction: *I am broken, but God is with me. There's always hope no matter how I feel.*

You are the captain of your ship too. It's your job to decide what to focus on, not to get tossed around by every thought and feeling. Jesus' words, "Do not be anxious about your life," imply some choice, some agency (Matthew 6:25 ESV). Life is not simply happening to you. You're standing at the captain's wheel, and there are a lot of directions you can take this boat. You can choose to work with the Spirit, who's standing there with you, to steer with confidence.

Spirit of God, awaken me to my agency and guide me into truth.

Special Tools

May the God of peace . . . equip you with everything good for doing his will, and may he work in us what is pleasing to him.
Hebrews 13:20–21

This month we're jumping into the battle of the mind. We'll need to be strategic, and we'll need supplies:

Self-awareness—I notice my anxious thoughts and address them before I spiral.

Reframing—If I can change the way I view something, I can see more possibilities. I can learn to live with it or identify actions to effect change.

Meditating on truth—I stamp God's Word onto my brain. I return to it when my feelings explode. It helps me create new thought patterns.

Prayer—I continually invite the Spirit to guide my thoughts, renew my mind, and transform me. I turn my concerns into prayers.

Will anxiety magically go away for good? No. Our freedom will be complete in heaven. But we can be a whole lot freer here and now if we get intentional and partner with the Miracle Worker.

God, I'm ready to start using every tool You want to give me.

Eyes Open, Captain

The wisdom of the prudent is to give thought to their ways.
Proverbs 14:8

S ometimes the highs and lows in life come so fast it feels as though we're living on a roller coaster, a hectic ride with random jerks and turns. Even though we can't avoid unexpected experiences, we can feel more stable if we learn to manage our internal lives.

We can use self-awareness to work toward self-mastery. We want to observe our thoughts, feelings, and actions and see ways they're connected. For example, *This is way harder than I thought it'd be. I feel overwhelmed and nervous. I'm making mistakes because I'm so anxious.*

Observe without judgment. Notice that all the thoughts and feelings come and go. Recognize that you are not your thoughts and feelings; you are experiencing them. You are the captain of the ship, and those thoughts and feelings are what you are navigating.

This is the beginning of owning your position as captain. You're not just a helpless passenger on a roller coaster of your emotions. You're at the wheel of the ship, looking straight at your surroundings, acknowledging the current situation so you can stay alert to your options.

As you become more self-aware, hang on to this reality: no thought or feeling has to control you. You get to decide what to do with them.

God, help me become more aware of my internal
life so I can manage it with Your wisdom.

Track It and Trace It

An intelligent heart acquires knowledge, and
the ear of the wise seeks knowledge.
Proverbs 18:15 ESV

I f you want to manage your weight or your budget better, you might track what you eat or spend. It helps to understand what you're already doing and what you could change.

Experts recommend tracking your experiences of anxiety for the same reason. Write about every experience of anxiety you can remember having recently: what thoughts you had, what prompted them, and what you felt and did after you had them.

Once you have some info in front of you, answer some questions: Do you see any patterns or regular triggers? Is there a belief, fear, or past experience that might be leading to your anxious thoughts?

Ask God to reveal the thought patterns and behaviors He wants you to notice. Whatever you find, just be honest, and remember we've all got something to work through.

John Locke said, "What worries you masters you."[1] I don't want any worry to master me. I'm sure you don't either. Let's be brave enough to get a thorough understanding of our worries so we can break free of them.

Lord, help me do the work of self-awareness
so I can move into Your freedom.

What's Yours, What's His?

Let the wise listen. . . . Let the discerning get guidance.
Proverbs 1:5

W hen we bought a new pink bedframe for my daughter, she couldn't wait to build it with her dad. She grabbed the instructions, looked at it with confusion, and then held it up to him. "Huh? Daddy?" she said.

Once you've got some info on your anxiety patterns, you need to ask your Father about what you're looking at. You need His wisdom, guidance, and help. *What's my part to do, and what's Yours?*

If there's a big question about His character, yourself, or the world that has surfaced, ask Him to speak His truth to it. Open your Bible and open your heart.

If there's something within your control, some action you can take to address a concern, jump on it. Afterward, if you keep feeling anxious about it, you can remind yourself you've done what you can.

If there's nothing you can do about the issue, resolve not to carry it anymore.

Maybe you're worrying about an upcoming decision and living with uncertainty. Then you can say, *I'm watching and waiting, God. I trust You'll make it clear in time. Prepare the right thing for me, and prepare me for the right thing.*

I'm ready to act and ready to wait. Whatever You say, God.

Think What He's Capable Of

Celebrate God all day, every day. I mean, revel *in him!*
Philippians 4:4 MSG

Sometimes I get really bummed out that I can't control everything. Because I've got *great* ideas.

It's like my unspoken words to God are, *Hello, don't You see what I'm capable of? Just hand that whole issue over to me, thanks.*

It's hilarious and a little sad, because never in my life have I done anything perfectly. Meanwhile, God is the essence of perfection. He sees my brain overestimating my ability and overlooking His. Then He graciously pulls me back to reality.

When Paul was telling believers that they ought to pray about everything—and not worry about anything—he started out by talking about celebrating God. He said rejoice in His awesomeness. Do it as often as you breathe. Have a mindset that keeps coming back to God's acts of power, His beauty in nature, His grace filling our lives. Nothing is beyond the Almighty.

Because of who He is, because of what He's capable of, trust Him with your life. Keep putting all your concerns in His hands.

And see if you can enjoy the fact that it's not all up to you. It's up to the One who is perfect.

You're so amazing, God! Run my life with Your wisdom.

Obsess or Pray?

Do not be anxious about anything.
Philippians 4:6

W hen you've got problems, stew over them. When you've got questions, obsess over them."

Is that what God said to do? No? Oops, that's what I've been doing.

Paul said, "Do not be anxious about anything," right after he said, "Remember how good and wonderful and brilliant God is." When you've got a God like *this*, you don't have to live like *that*. Whenever I live like *that*, I give my good God reason to think, *She's acting like she doesn't know Me again. She's forgetting that she can trust Me.*

It's like if my daughter spent all day at school worrying about whether I'd give her dinner. She'd be distracted, unable to focus on learning and do all she's meant to do there.

I've given my daughter dinner every night for years; she can trust me as her caregiver. Sometimes you and I act like we have no caregiver, or have an untrustworthy one, when in fact we have an *excellent* one.

We belong to a good Father who doesn't abandon His kids. He knows what we need and He provides for us.

Ask Him to take care of you. Live like you actually trust Him.

Thank You, great God, for giving me a new
way to be—trusting and free.

Hot Potato Thought Prayers

In every situation, by prayer and petition, with
thanksgiving, present your requests to God.
Philippians 4:6

I often like to see how quickly I can turn a thought into a prayer. I notice a thought that could hop on the anxiety train but flip it up to God instead.

I wonder why my husband isn't home yet. God, keep him safe in Your care.

Will the upcoming surgery help my dad's condition? I ask for a successful surgery and improved health for him.

I'm saying, *I see that issue . . . but that's Yours, God. Take it away! Do Your thing!* Maybe it's like hot potato thought prayers?

It's kind of like delegating a task, but lightning fast. You look at the thought and say, "Whose name is on this one?" Most of them have God's name on them. Some of them have both yours and His—but He's always ready to help you.

How am I going to tackle this problem? Give me wisdom and clarity. Lead my thoughts and steps. I feel like I'm running on empty! Give me rest and energy. Help me persevere and keep at it. What if I don't have what it takes to do this? Enable me in ways I can't feel yet. Got an issue? Can you make a request out of it? Make turning your concerns into prayers your new habit.

God, train me to keep turning to You with every concern.

Is That a Hamster Wheel?

"Who of you by worrying can add a single hour to your life?"
Luke 12:25

I got a lot done today! I spent three hours worrying about my kid getting hurt, two hours freaked out about my health issues, and a few more hours fretting over my financial issues. Just look at what I have to show for it!"

Well . . . there's nothing to show, actually. Worry accomplishes nothing good. Considering all the energy we put into it, it almost feels like a shame, doesn't it? God presents us with the valuable resources of life, time, and brain power, and we throw it at *pointless worry*?

Charles Spurgeon said, "Anxiety does not empty tomorrow of its sorrows, but only empties today of its strength." When we choose to keep fixating on our concerns, our mental life is the equivalent of a hamster running on his wheel, putting our energy into going nowhere until we're exhausted.

Use your valuable life for the good and worthwhile stuff, like praising God, creating beauty, spreading joy, meeting needs, and building people up. Steer your thoughts in those directions and away from your worries. Live out the peaceful, content, generous character of God. If that seems impossible, ask Him to help you get one step closer to it today. Then ask again tomorrow and the day after that. Don't doubt what He can do!

God, I want to spend my mental energy on what is worthwhile.

You Have Right Now

This is the day that the LORD has made;
let us rejoice and be glad in it.
Psalm 118:24 ESV

*I*f only things would have worked out differently.
I can't believe I made that mistake!
  What if the next setback is worse?
  It's natural for thoughts like these to pop up. But when this becomes where my brain lives, I miss out on so much. I forfeit the present day that God has made, with all of its unique joys.
  God tells us, "Do not dwell on the past" and "Do not worry about tomorrow" (Isaiah 43:18; Matthew 6:34). He knows we can end up here and says *do not do it*. And for good reason. Those bad memories we keep reliving? They've already happened. It's not our job to live them more than once. Those things we're worrying about? They haven't happened—none of them are even real. *Right now* is real.
  We all have experiences we need to process. Let yourself do that, but only for a time, then nudge yourself back to the present moment. We all have things we need to plan for. Sure, prepare, but then give yourself permission to forget about it.
  Practice being present by noticing your surroundings. Describe them to yourself. Then ask God to help you stay in the moment throughout the day and show His little gifts right under your nose.

God, I don't want to miss what You have for me in the right now.

Be Present to Him

See, I am doing a new thing! Now it springs up;
do you not perceive it? I am making a way in the
wilderness and streams in the wasteland.
Isaiah 43:19

I will not worry, I will not worry—especially about that. Repeatedly telling yourself not to think about something usually makes you think about it even more. Sometimes a good way to keep that worry from taking over is simply to pivot. Shift your focus to the present moment.

At any point in the day, let yourself take a pause along with some deep breaths. Notice little things. Be 100 percent all here, right now. Have a spirit of curiosity. What am I experiencing right this second? What's it like exactly?

Ask God to bring something to your attention. Open yourself up to whatever He might be doing. Say, *I want to be present to what You're doing in this place right now.*

Let something beautiful fully capture your attention. Notice when someone smiles at you and linger in that joy for a second. Gaze at the sky. Ask Him to open your eyes to His beauty and presence. And at the end of the day, see how you can answer the question, *How have I experienced His love today?*

God, I want to experience how You are present
and alive and working in this moment.

Just Do Today

*"Do not worry about tomorrow, for tomorrow will worry
about itself. Each day has enough trouble of its own."*
Matthew 6:34

Have you ever tried to make a computer do more than it was made
to do? I'll have maybe thirty tabs and twenty windows open at
the same time, and when my computer crashes, I'm like, *What gives?*

When we're sorting through a bunch of questions about tomorrow, it becomes way too much for our brains. Sometimes we don't
realize we're heading toward system overload, and then, seemingly out
of nowhere, we crash.

Mindfulness can keep us from going there. Research shows that it
can do a whole lot more, such as build immunity, improve focus and
memory, and bring down stress and anxiety levels.[2]

We live one day at a time, and when we're caught up in tomorrow's
problems, it's like we're trying to do more than that. So tell yourself,
Just do today, do right now. Go moment by moment.

When you think about the hard things that are coming, don't try
to conceive of how you'll deal with all of them. Come back to what's
in front of you. Just do the next thing.

Remember it's not your job to control the future; be content with
simply living out today. Drop your concerns off with God and get back
to living fully in the moment with Him.

God, stop me from trying to take on more than I need to.

Listen to the Truth Teller

All your words are true.
Psalm 119:160

How did I end up getting stuck in this impossible situation? *I can't believe she did that—I can't trust anyone. She has a better deal in life than I do.*

In the wide sea of thoughts and feelings we're navigating all day long, we'll come across some negative ones. Many are perception-based—how things look from where we're standing at a particular moment. Many are simply emotional reactions—feelings that can come and go like the tide.

It is as though we are traveling down a pathway in our brain. The more time we spend on that pathway, the wider it gets and the more frequently we gravitate toward it. If we're not planning our route well, our negative thoughts and feelings will generate more negativity in our minds and create a lens through which we view life.

Meanwhile, the Truth Teller is speaking: "Things might look crazy from where you're sitting," He says. "But whatever happens, I will tell you what you can be sure of."

If you listen to the Truth Teller, His words will create new, healthy thought patterns. *Anything is possible with Him. He'll bring me people I can trust. He has love and abundance for me.*

> *God, I believe You always say what's true. I can trust
> You more than my own feelings and thoughts.*

Feed Your Mind with Truth

When your words came, I ate them.
Jeremiah 15:16

When my niece was three years old, she spent lots of time around her parents, who used terms of endearment with each other. Although she had learned to call them *Mom* and *Dad*, one day she started calling them *Babe*. "Can I have more carrots, babe? Thanks, babe." They found this weird, but also . . . understandable.

You really do get out what you put in. The same goes for our thought life. If we put God's truth in our minds, it will come out in our lives. We need a steady stream of new input to lead us into new thought patterns. You can impress the thoughts of God into your mind so you have new thought pathways to travel.

You have to say, *Do I want to change the way I think and live? Yes, I do.* So you'll make listening to the Truth Teller a priority over and over. You'll work with the Spirit to stamp His Word onto your brain.

You'll read your Bible with your coffee. Listen to an audio Bible on your commute or morning walk. Read a prayer book at lunch. Listen to worship music as you make dinner. Pray a psalm before you sleep. Post verses where you can see them. Commit some to memory.

You might have to get up a little earlier or avoid the TV. But you want something new, right? You want a calmer, stronger, freer heart. The only way we get there is by absorbing the Truth.

God, I want to have Your Word stamped onto my brain.

Be Transformed and Renewed

Be transformed by the renewing of your mind.
Romans 12:2

When you put food in the fridge, it just sits there. But when you give it to a child and she eats it, it gives her fuel to grow and develop. It changes her.

If we simply take in Bible knowledge, it's just like putting food in the fridge. But if we engage our heart and mind with God Himself through His Word and open ourselves to Him, we will change.

We're not just trying to receive a knowledge dump; we're going after transformation. We don't want only fresh insights; we want a deeper relationship. We don't want only new neural pathways; we want God's fullness of life in us, which brings purpose, joy, and peace.

It comes only through time spent with Him as our whole focus—communion, connection, relationship-building time. He speaks and you listen. And then He works wonders.

We aren't manufacturing this ourselves. This isn't self-help. This is the Spirit of God making new things and creating beauty.

Come to Him moldable. Come believing. Come receptive to the Potter who has awesome plans and wonderful works in store for you. It'll take guts to trust Him over your own feelings and assumptions, but the newness He'll bring will be so worth it.

I'm listening to You, God, and I believe You.
Change me however You want.

Practice and Train Up

Put on the full armor of God, so that when the day of
evil comes, you may be able to stand your ground.
Ephesians 6:13

Professional basketball players never saunter onto the court after lying on the couch for months. No, they head into a game with sharp focus, go-to strategies, and muscle memory, earned from hours of practice.

We need to do something like that in our life of the mind. We need to be like the psalmist who hid God's Word in his heart and kept it in his thoughts. Repeating Scripture-based mantras can train our brain to jump back to God's reality when we're struggling and also shape how we view life at any given moment. Here are a few examples:

God is mighty and mighty in my life.
Whatever I'm called to do, He'll empower me to do.
He gives me what I need for life and godliness.
He is wisdom, peace, and joy. He gives me wisdom, peace, and joy.
Whatever happens, He is good. He wants goodness for me.
He is what I need, and He is here. He makes me secure.

Internalize God's reality. Repeat it to yourself. You'll be training up for any mental battles ahead and working with the Spirit to have victory.

Create new patterns of thought, God. Prepare me
for jumping back to truth in hard moments.

A Mind That Says Yes to God

We destroy . . . every proud thing that raises itself
against the knowledge of God. We capture every
thought and make it give up and obey Christ.
2 Corinthians 10:4–5 NCV

P aul wrote 2 Corinthians to believers who were facing conflict about the gospel. Some people in the church were sticking to their pride and resisting God. They clung to their own thoughts and elevated them above what God said.

When we cling to our anxious thoughts and stay stuck in them, we do a version of this. But we often don't notice we're doing it.

So we need to stay alert to our thoughts and our navigating options. When a troubling thought comes up, we take a second look at that thought and ask, *Is this true? What's something I know about God that's related to this?*

Once we answer those, we need to give up those anxious thoughts, then decide to trust Him over feelings and let Him redirect our thoughts.

God wants to do a wild, amazing thing in you—to put the mind of Christ in you and remake you, to give you a new way of thinking and a new way of *being*.

God, help me notice and capture my thoughts
and make them line up with Yours.

Present, Prayerful Breathing

He gives breath to everyone, life to everyone who walks the earth.
Isaiah 42:5 NLT

R emember when we talked about slow, deep breathing? Let's do that again today.

Before you begin, prepare to be fully present. Take a minute and acknowledge whatever you've been worrying about. Picture yourself putting it on a shelf out of view and giving yourself permission not to address it right now.

As you start breathing slowly and deeply, think only about the current moment. Notice that breath moving within you. Be a careful observer. *My diaphragm expands and shrinks. It goes out and in.* You might hold your hand near your face. *I feel the breath on my fingers. It's warm and soft. It's breath the Giver of Life gives me.*

You also might like to pick some words to help you meditate in the direction you want your mind to go. Use simple words to ask God to overpower whatever is controlling your internal life. Breathe in what He gives; breathe out what He overpowers.

Inhale. *Calm.* Exhale. *Worry.*

Inhale. *Truth.* Exhale. *Fear.*

Inhale. *Confidence.* Exhale. *Distrust.*

Inhale. *Peace.* Exhale. *Unknowns.*

Inhale. *Strength.* Exhale. *Timidity.*

Reach me where I am, God. Thank You for being closer than my breath.

Tell Yourself the Truth

Steady my steps with your Word of promise so
nothing malign gets the better of me.
Psalm 119:134 MSG

Y ou and I think thousands of thoughts per day, and we choose which ones we focus on or dismiss. Sometimes we need to insert new thoughts—true thoughts.

If the phrase *Don't believe the lie* carries too much negativity, use a more positive one: *Tell yourself the truth*. Here are a few examples.

I am not my mistakes. I am a lovely creation of God and a loved child of the King.

Jesus came to take away the sins of the world—including any sin I revisit and feel shame about. I am forgiven. It is finished. I do not need to keep mulling over something His grace has dealt with.

He gives others grace. He can help me do that too. I can release my resentment and know peace.

Problems in life are par for the course. He equips me to work through each one.

Those amped-up feelings you have? They don't have to be the boss of you. All those scattered thoughts? They don't have to overtake you. Let God's powerful Word steady you.

God, I will keep bringing my thoughts back to Your steadying truth.

Guard Your Thought Life

Stay alert! Watch out for your great enemy, the devil. He prowls around like a roaring lion, looking for someone to devour.
1 Peter 5:8 NLT

What triggers your anxiety? Is it health issues, conflict with others, or problems at work?

Whatever it is, when it prompts a mental battle, remember that you're not in neutral territory. God's enemy wants to pile on the triggers and get you fixated on bad stuff. He's actively working to lull you away from God's peace and sabotage your faith, strength, and steadiness.

God wants us to stay in the moment, fully alive in our purpose. The Enemy wants us to stay fully occupied with trying to solve problems that do not currently exist and will likely never exist.

So guard your thought life by coming back to the essentials. What is God calling you to do with your mind? To love Him all you can. To consume His truth and love and experience His joy and peace. To steer your thoughts toward loving others. To focus on the wonderful works He prepared for you.

Be someone who knows what she's about—who you are, what your mission is, what you know for sure. Stay alert to triggers and persistently tell yourself the truth.

God, You have saved my soul and You can
help me win the battle of the mind.

Call for Help and Cool Your Jets

In my desperation I prayed, and the LORD
listened; he saved me from all my troubles.
Psalm 34:6 NLT

L et's say you start your day with a good moment—then life happens. You find a huge surprise bill in the mail, your kid lies to you, a coworker drops a hot mess at your desk, and your car won't start. You're ready to scream or cry.

Jesus didn't say you'll have it easy; He said you'll have trouble. In those moments, you have to pause and bring your mind back to what is bigger than any earthly problem: the truth and power of God.

You're never alone. You have a guide. He's big and able and can enable you to deal. He gives peace and wisdom for every moment. So breathe deeply. Pray for help. Hold on to a word from Him—any of them. Pray that word. *Cool. Your. Jets.*

Then do the next thing, and focus only on that one thing.

If you need a longer cooldown time, take it. Get Jesus in your view and get His perspective. But don't give up. Don't say, *There's no way. I can never do this. He can't touch my problems or reach my mess of aggravation and fear.*

Expect more from the God who can make people walk on water and bring the dead back to life. He's got *all* the tools.

God, I want to keep turning to You when I need help.

Zoom Out

We are surrounded by a great cloud of people
whose lives tell us what faith means.
Hebrews 12:1 NCV

Have you ever picked up a fancy camera to take a picture, and the lens was zoomed in? Maybe you could see only the lower half of someone's face. But if you zoomed out, you could see lots more.

Sometimes our problems are all we can see; the hard thing right in front of us can take up our whole view and headspace. We don't remember our position in the timeline of history, how countless others before us struggled in similar ways. They chose to trust God, and God empowered them to persevere. That same God can do the same with us.

We can forget the overall arc of our life story and how we've endured through other difficulties. If we think back, we'll find evidence from our past that suggests we can handle the present and the future.

If you can zoom out, you can gain some context for your situation. You can approach it with more engagement and hope: *I'm thankful I've made it through hard times before. I did it ten years ago. I did it last week. I know God can help me do it again today.*

Shift your perspective. There is so much more to the picture.

Help me remember what the evidence from my life and others'
lives shows me. You are our ever-present help, God.

Hiding in Plain Sight

Let perseverance finish its work so that you may be
mature and complete, not lacking anything.
James 1:4

A couple visited a house for sale. Everyone else had looked at it and seen an old run-down building in need of repair. But this couple envisioned a renovated masterpiece, and in a matter of months, it had become their dream home.

What if opportunities are hiding in surprising places in your life? Consider your toughest experiences in the past. In a sense, you've probably walked away from every difficulty as a new you, able to understand new things or do more than before.

So just think: Right now, you're in the middle of difficulties. But you're also in the middle of opportunities. "We are all faced with a series of great opportunities brilliantly disguised as impossible situations," said pastor Chuck Swindoll.[3]

Maybe your challenge is a chance to experience more of God's power. Try reframing your troubles as opportunities to bring more of God's presence and gifts into your life. They'll strengthen your fortitude muscles and equip you with wisdom and skills for the future.

Just imagine: What new things might the new you be able to do?

Help me see new possibilities, God. Through every experience, I
want to grow however You want me to and know You better.

Let Worship Shape Your Thoughts

I will be happy because of you; God Most
High, I will sing praises to your name.
Psalm 9:2 NCV

D o you ever find yourself singing a song you heard hours or days before? Earworms are a thing, right? They're catchy and totally get stuck in your head.

Try using music to your advantage to change your mindset. Sing or listen to a worship song or hymn early in the day and memorize at least some of the words.

Dwell on lyrics that praise the attributes and works of God, like "I Sing the Mighty Power of God."

Think on lyrics that describe what He does for His people, like "How Firm a Foundation." Absorb lyrics that describe how you can respond to Him in faith, like "Be Still, My Soul."

Return to these words throughout the day. Think, *How does this change my perspective? Which idea here can I hang on to and use as a guiding thought?*

It might make you quicker to notice God's presence, to praise and trust Him, and to see possibilities for Him to work. And if you do it day after day, it just might change your patterns of thought.

Lord, may my words and thoughts reflect what
is true and be filled with faith in You.

What You Can and Can't Control

Give us courage to change what must be altered,
serenity to accept what cannot be helped, and
the insight to know the one from the other.
Reinhold Niebuhr

Before a big family gathering, I sometimes get anxious. Do you have the same reaction?

Will someone say something hurtful? Will everyone get along? My husband is even and cool through it all, and I don't know how he does it. He seems to have the whole "if you can't control it, don't think about it" thing down. Meanwhile, I often need to go through a whole mental exercise of what I can and can't control.

Let's do one of those right now, and touch on some of the heavy hitters, okay?

I can't control the actions and words of others, but I can keep showing respect, patience, and love, and set healthy boundaries.

I can't control my past mistakes, but I can learn from them.

I can't control how someone evaluates my work, but I can make my best effort.

I can control my attitude and mindset. I don't decide everything that will happen, but I do decide how I'll respond.

Thinking through all that helps me take a deep breath and release a boatload of tension. Know what I mean?

Lord, free me from spending energy on what isn't mine to control.

Visualize the Handoff

Cast all your anxiety on him because he cares for you.
1 Peter 5:7

God sees us with anxiety and says, "Let Me take that on for you." He stretches out His hand, ready to transfer the weight from our weary shoulders to His strong shoulders. We proceed to keep an iron grip on it, convinced we ought to keep trying to manage every issue on our own.

I like to create visuals of how I'm releasing my cares to God. In college I made a box with a small opening, and when a concern kept plaguing my mind, I wrote it out on a piece of paper and put it inside the box. I imagined that once that paper left my hands, the issue was in God's. *It's not mine to fixate on. It's God's to deal with.*

Think of moments when you hand something to someone—paying money to a vendor, giving a gift to a friend, handing over a project to a coworker. You transfer something, then it's out of your hands. *That's yours. I'm not taking that back.*

Tell yourself you're doing this with God. Then remind yourself who you're giving your concerns to. The God of the universe. Think about His wonders and greatness. Rest assured it's in able hands.

Trade out mottos: Ditch "Every worry is mine to bear; I can't trust Him," and instead go with, "Live carefree before God; he is most careful with you" (1 Peter 5:7 MSG).

I'm handing over all my worries and concerns to You, my able God.

Manna for Problems

*"I will rain down bread from heaven for you. The people
are to go out each day and gather enough for that day."*
Exodus 16:4

T he Israelites were hungry in the desert, so God sent them special
food deliveries. They were to take no more than a day's worth,
and every morning there was more for the taking. He was calling them
to live out a practice of trust.

God provides the resources you need for challenges the same way.
Every day brings a new opportunity for you to receive what you need
from Him. Any moment throughout the day can open up a new way
for you to depend on Him.

Whenever your mind goes to a worrisome place, remind yourself,
If that happens, He'll give me what I need to handle it.

Notice that the Israelites had to go out and gather the manna;
God didn't just instantly make their bellies full. They had their role
to do. Your role is to go to Him with open hands and a trusting heart,
and say, *Give me what I need today. Help me rest in knowing You'll do
it again tomorrow.*

Our God holds us, loves us, and keeps us in His care. Nothing
that will happen in the future could change that; whatever comes,
He's going to keep doing all those things. Do you think the Israelites
dreamed God would rain down bread from the sky?

God, I'm reaching out to receive from You what I need to do right now.

Accept This Season

There is a time for everything, and a season
for every activity under the heavens.
Ecclesiastes 3:1

I f only things were like they used to be. If only I were in the next phase of life. If only I had it as easy as she does.

Do you ever enter into the "If only" space? If we linger with these thoughts too long, they'll likely derail our contentment.

Our life story plays out in seasons, and God has worthwhile things for us in each one. Wherever you find yourself today, try to drop any judgments about how worthwhile this season can be. Try to accept it for what it is. Envision what it would mean for you to fully engage with your present—with people, opportunities, and distinctive aspects of your setting. Imagine how you could make the most of it and open yourself up to whatever rich goodness God might bring through it, even if it is the most difficult season of your life.

You could decide to say, *I won't resent this season for not being something other than what it is. I accept where I am. I won't believe that the future is the only place where I can find peace and happiness. God, open my eyes to how You're working where I am.*

God in His timing will usher you into new seasons, but until then, don't overlook what He has for you right here in this one.

Meet me in this season of life, God. Show me the
worthwhile things You have for me here.

Be Patient with Yourself

Love is patient, love is kind.
1 Corinthians 13:4

I *'m trying and nothing is changing. I'm still all tangled up and quick to freak out.* Have you been feeling this way at all? Sometimes we find ourselves struggling as we work on our thought life. You know what we call that? *Normal.* You're carving new neural pathways and jumping over to them when your instincts want to take the old negative ones. That's no overnight change; it takes time.

You're stepping into the new way of *being* that God has for you. He'll use all the ups and downs to do His thing. Your job is to not give up. Keep the following things in mind during your journey.

Be kind to yourself and embrace a growth mindset. Say, *I can't do this . . . yet. I'm allowed to make mistakes as I'm learning.*

Focus on actions, not results. Think of how fruit grows on a branch (you plant, prune, water, wait) or how a muscle gets stronger (you need repetition and consistency).

Know that positive feelings will eventually follow thoughts and acts of faith.

Remember that God wants this for you, and He's 100 percent committed to you.

God, I'm in this thing for the long haul. Help me sense the patience, kindness, and gentleness You have for me.

~

Hope Is a Driving Force

Hope is to your soul what sunlight and rain are for flowers. It brings you to life and makes you reach up and out, and helps you bloom; without it, you become shriveled and ashen.

When hope is the driving force of your life, it's transformative.

It's also part of worshiping the God of beauty and power. Your trust tells the world, "Just wait till He shows you how good He is. Get ready to be blown away. He's bigger and better than you can imagine."

Hope is available—it's right in front of you. You just have to reach out and grab it.

There's Beauty Ahead

Hope is a passion for the possible.
Søren Kierkegaard, *Fear and Trembling*

All of us need hope right now.

Whether you're stressed or disappointed, upset or restless, grieving or gripped with worries about things not working out—hope can help you. Hope can change how you see what's in front of you and open the door to peace, courage, and resilience.

Hope says that whatever causes our anxiety or pain doesn't have the final word.

Hope says that God can enable us to experience hard things without being permanently overwhelmed by them.

Hope says that God can replace mourning with joy and despair with praise.

Hope says that change is possible and new strength is within reach.

Today you and I can rest in the fact that God ultimately has us in His hands. Our Father, who is infinitely good and whose love is lavish. The Almighty, who is holding our past, present, and future. He says He'll help us through anything and provide what we need.

He has created beauty before. He can create beauty again.

He's told us we should count on it.

God, help me believe in my heart that Your beauty is ahead of me.

The Buoy of Hope

Let your unfailing love surround us, LORD,
for our hope is in you alone.
Psalm 33:22 NLT

When my mom died in our home six weeks after her colon cancer diagnosis, I lifted my face to heaven. I exhaled with a tiny smile.

I look back and think, *How on earth could I have done that?* I was seventeen and losing my whole world.

Hope was possible because God is amazing, and baffling goodness comes from intimacy with Him. I'd been desperately feeding on His Word, singing worship songs over my mom, asking Him to be our Savior and Helper. He met me in all those places and more, and when that moment came, He shared His joy with me: *She's released from the struggle. She ran past the finish line and into My arms.* His joy made me strong. His perspective gave me hope.

He took care of her, and He would take care of me.

He did exactly that throughout my grief. When I thoroughly fell apart, He found ways to buoy me up so the grief didn't drown me. No matter where you are today, dear one, hear this: God can buoy you up too.

Father, give me Your joy that brings strength
and Your perspective that brings hope.

Your Story Isn't Over

[He] is able to do immeasurably more than all we ask or imagine.
Ephesians 3:20

A woman sees no way out of an abusive relationship. An addict curls up on the floor in rehab. An innocent defendant sits in a courtroom as the jury glares at her.

These are dark moments. Each person feels like they've hit a wall. They've come to the end of themselves and the end of their hope.

But these are moments in stories that *aren't over*. The Author isn't done yet. They're like some of the awful moments we see in Scripture.

A faithful man sits trapped with hungry lions. A heroic king ends up sleeping with a married woman and killing her husband. An innocent man hangs on a cross.

Moments when God is still working.

When you're smack-dab in the middle of a timeline, you can't see the whole arc. You don't know that God is weaving together everything in your life to create an amazing story, one that says, "I am her God and she is My beloved. *This* is how I love."

The abused can be rescued, the addict can recover, and the defendant can be freed. Where you are today is just *today*; it's not where you'll land. Your God is on the move and He's got crazy good plans. So put your hope in the God who comes up with the best stories.

God, help me remember there's more to my story.
Fill it with Your glory and goodness.

The God of Good Surprises

Do not be afraid. Stand firm and you will see
the deliverance the LORD will bring you.
Exodus 14:13

L et's say you're watching a gripping movie. And then the plot twists, and you're surprised.

The God holding your future has a taste for the dramatic. He loves a good rescue story. All throughout the Bible, we see people expecting something normal. Then God swoops in and everyone's jaw hits the floor.

A mass of people, collectively about to have a panic attack, saw their captors charging at them on one side and the obstacle of the Red Sea on the other. Then God swooped in.

Three fiercely loyal guys stepped into a furnace full of flames that would consume them. Then God swooped in.

A giant was ready to squish a brave shepherd boy like a bug. Then God swooped in.

We're doing life with a wildly unpredictable yet thoroughly good God. He loves to thrill us with surprises that leave us smiling.

Don't you think He must relish our happy reactions? When our hearts become full of faith in a God like this, we may find ourselves waking up with a whole new mindset. *My God is wonderful. There's no telling what good surprises from Him will show up next.*

God, I want to have a heart that is brave enough to expect goodness.

Remember What Isn't Permanent

For our light and momentary troubles are achieving
for us an eternal glory that far outweighs them all.
2 Corinthians 4:17

W hat were you worried about when you were half your age? How about five years ago? One year ago? Last week?

Things change. What I was experiencing in the past felt all-encompassing, and now it's behind me. God brought me through each hard season—from bad acne to major injuries to heartache I thought would do me in. Our trials are temporary.

When I was in the middle of those things, though, they felt unending, overwhelming, even hopeless. I so wish I could go back to my younger self and say, "You won't always feel like this. Chin up, girl! Things are going to get way better. It's only a matter of time."

I bet you'd say the same thing to your younger self about some stuff too. But since you can't do that, remind your present self that the hard things you're in the middle of today are not permanent. There will come a time when God will bring you out of them. Even if you're facing lifelong issues, one day He'll usher you into His amazing new heaven and earth.

When the trial feels intense, hang on to His helping hand. Say, *I won't feel like this forever. This is just for today, just for a while. And I'm on my way to a home where there will only be the goodness of my God.*

Thank You, God, that all that's hard right now will not last forever.

Remember What Is Permanent

Your beauty and love chase after me every day of my life.
Psalm 23:6 MSG

So you know that a lot of stuff in your life isn't going to be sticking around. What *will* stick around?

God's pursuit of you. His beauty and love in your heart and life. His offer of intimacy. His active, powerful presence. His fountain of true life that He can pour into you. It's all the best stuff.

David was looking at the unknowns of his future, just like you are, and said to God, "Surely your goodness and unfailing love will pursue me all the days of my life, and I will live in the house of the LORD forever" (Psalm 23:6 NLT).

David knew that God's abundant lovingkindness was big enough to cover and saturate and fill up his world forever.

No matter what comes up later for you, the God of love wants to be in your life. He's going to keep offering you His protection, help, peace, comfort, and wisdom. His truth and love and kingdom will remain forever. And He wants to guide you all the way home to heaven.

His beauty and love will chase you every day of your life. You'll need to open your eyes and heart to Him, but He'll always be there.

He and His goodness are here to stay.

God, fill up my world with Your beauty and love, now and forever.

Know Who's on the Throne

"Be still, and know that I am God."
Psalm 46:10

Have you been running yourself ragged trying to fix your problems and answer your biggest questions?

In times of trouble, God was the Israelites' refuge and hope. When they feared their enemies would defeat them, they reminded themselves, "The LORD of armies is with us" (Psalm 46:7 NASB). They'd think back to how He'd overcome their enemies and proved that His power was absolute.

And God said, "Be still, and know that I am God. . . . I will be exalted in the earth." His message was, "Do not panic. Remember that I am the Almighty. I will have victory over all that's wrong."

You've got to have times when you stop your hustle and slow your whirring mind, where you focus on the One who is transcendent. Everything around you might be changing, but He's not. He will make His goodness known as He accomplishes His will. Your job is to humble yourself before Him, let your heart be filled with awe and adoration, and then trust Him.

Once you do that, whenever you notice your limitations, you can lean into them. You can humble yourself and say, *You are God and I am not.* And exhale.

God, You will be exalted in the earth and in my heart. You are the Warrior God and King.

He Lifts Up the Humble

*Humble yourselves, therefore, under God's mighty
hand, that he may lift you up in due time. Cast all
your anxiety on him because he cares for you.*
1 Peter 5:6–7

S cripture says we should cast our anxiety on God—it's in Peter's
letter to believers. But right before that, he said to humble yourself
before the Mighty One, and in time, He will lift you up. God "gives
grace to the humble" (1 Peter 5:5 esv).

We see an extreme picture of this in the story of Job, who experienced multiple traumas and losses. After crying out in confusion,
processing his pain, and questioning God's character, he was ready to
listen to God. He got quiet in His presence.

God reminded Job of His majesty and wonder. He showed him
that His wisdom, justice, and power extend far beyond the limits of
the human mind.

Job eventually humbled himself. "I know that you can do anything, and no one can stop you," he said. "I was talking about things I
knew nothing about, things far too wonderful for me. . . . I take back
everything I said" (Job 42:2–3, 6 nlt).

When we accept our finiteness and God's boundlessness, we open
the door to peace and hope. We can say, "My hope is in You, the One
who is so much greater than I am."

I humble myself before You and honor You, God of the universe.

Hope Is About Trust

Trust in the LORD with all your heart and lean not
on your own understanding; in all your ways submit
to him, and he will make your paths straight.
Proverbs 3:5–6

I hope the weather clears up."

"I hope we don't get lost without a map."

"I hope they like me."

We use the word *hope* to refer to something we want to happen or want to be true. But biblical hope is based on what we already know for sure: the character of God. It is confidence in His trustworthiness.

Hope allows us to say, *I don't get it, but He does.* In the middle of our mess, we can remember His infinite goodness and ability.

When we look at our lives with our limited perspective and try to imagine our future, we can lift our hands up in surrender. *You know what You're doing, God. Whatever it is, whatever You have in store, I'm in. I know Your character and I trust You.*

Your King is trustworthy. You can rest without answers or control. You can put all your confidence in Him. When you do, you'll be like David, who said, "I am like an olive tree flourishing in the house of God; I trust in God's unfailing love for ever and ever. . . . And I will hope in your name, for your name is good" (Psalm 52:8–9).

My hope for the future is based on who You are,
God. Deepen my trust in You every day.

I Have Calmed and Quieted My Soul

I have calmed and quieted my soul, like a weaned child with
its mother; like a weaned child is my soul within me.
Psalm 131:2 ESV

As a college freshman, I felt like I was on a different planet than my peers. They were distressed about friendship dramas; I was still devastated by the loss of my mom. They were dying for Christmas break so they could be back home; I'd sold my childhood home and didn't seem to belong anywhere.

A favorite song at that time had words from Psalm 131, which says, "My eyes are not raised too high; I do not occupy myself with things too great and too marvelous for me" (v. 1 ESV). For me, this turned into: "There's so much I can't understand. I'm giving You all my questions and heartache. Your ways are higher than mine."

I could then say something like verse 2: "I'm calming and quieting my soul. I'm settling into Your care like I'm relaxing into a parent's arms."

Then came the bottom line from verse 3: "Hope in the LORD from this time forth and forevermore" (ESV). I'd repeat that in my head, hanging on to my trust in God. I'd walk back into my dorm more rooted in truth, my soul more at rest. My hope had grown a little more.

When your hope feels weak, come to God with your heavy questions and burdens.

God, my Father and King, my hope is in You.

Not Consumed by Our Troubles

Because of the LORD's great love we are not
consumed, for his compassions never fail.
Lamentations 3:22

There are times our troubles feel all-consuming, draining us of hope.

The Israelites were in this situation—as a result of their own sin, actually. Their city had been destroyed, and Jeremiah wrote Lamentations as an expression of the people's collective sorrow.

But then he turned his attention away from the wreckage and said, "Because of God's steadfast love and unending kindness, we don't have to be consumed by this."

The Hebrew word used to describe God's love in this verse is *chesed*, which is rich with meaning. It can be translated as kindness, lovingkindness, mercy, loyalty, devotion, favor, compassion, goodness, or steadfast love. It's all over the Old Testament, appearing about 250 times, like repeating notes in the song of God's extravagant love.[1]

Jeremiah was saying, "This is bad. *But* we have a covenant-keeping God who won't abandon us. Compassion and mercy keep flowing out of the core of who He is. His love is loyal and He is for us."[2]

It didn't matter that Jeremiah didn't know how God would help them yet. So, dear one, don't let your troubles consume you, even if they're caused by your own mistakes.

God, You always make it possible for me to hope.

Yet This I Call to Mind

Yet this I call to mind and therefore I have hope. . . . I say to
myself, "The LORD is my portion; therefore I will wait for him."
Lamentations 3:21, 24

W ant an example of mind management? Look at Jeremiah. He showed us how he got himself thinking about more than just what he was seeing and feeling. He directed his thoughts toward what he knew about God and told himself the truth. You'll be able to do this more when you build your hope in practical ways.

First, continually absorb God's Word. "The Scriptures give us hope and encouragement as we wait patiently for God's promises to be fulfilled" (Romans 15:4 NLT).

Second, revisit the goodness of God you've experienced and praise Him for it. Think about how He has loved you, provided for you, and helped you throughout your life. Spend time worshiping Him for all of that.

Third, surround yourself with reminders of God's loyal love and other attributes. "Your lovingkindness is before my eyes, and I have walked in Your truth" (Psalm 26:3 NKJV). Post verses on your walls and create rhythms of daily worship.

Now, did you notice what Jeremiah did after he told himself the truth? He saw how he could *respond* to truth, and he resolved to do it. "Therefore I will wait on him," he said. Make that your next step too.

Help me take actions that build my faith and strengthen my hope, God.

Willing to Wait

The LORD is good to those whose hope is in him, to the one who
seeks him; it is good to wait quietly for the salvation of the LORD.
Lamentations 3:25–26

L iving with hope requires a willingness to wait. Shakespeare wrote, "How poor are they that have not patience! What wound did ever heal but by degrees?"[3] Thinking of a wound taking time to heal is a simple reminder of how hope and patience go together.

If we see the wisdom of waiting, we'll be somewhere new before long. The problem is we just don't *like* waiting. Our impulse is to prize immediate gratification, but good things take time: the delicious dinner cooking in the oven, the fruit and flowers growing in the yard.

There's purpose in the waiting. It's not like being on hold on a call with customer service, simply losing time. We're in the space of spiritual development. We're in the hands of the Potter. He works on us, changing the way we think and view life and engage with it, just like He promised He would. As we depend on Him more, He's helping us know Him better and deepening our closeness with Him.

"It is good to wait," Jeremiah said. And "the LORD is good to those who wait for him" (Lamentations 3:25 ESV). We wait because God is our portion—our inheritance, our one true source of goodness, our all in all (v. 24). We trust that He has goodness for us now and later.[4]

I know that transformation takes time. I'll wait
with hope because I trust You, God.

How Will You Wait?

I wait for the LORD, my whole being waits,
and in his word I put my hope.
Psalm 130:5

Once you decide that you're willing to wait, you need to think about *how* you're going to wait.

Will you be angsty and nervy? Joyful and light? There's a difference between surviving the time and actively waiting with expectation.

Sometimes you'll need to take steps of obedience, like the Israelites did when they walked around the walls of Jericho for days before God conquered it for them. Wouldn't you guess their impulse was to knock out their enemies in their own strength, on their own schedule? I'd guess that. But they didn't do that, because God said, "Do it My way and in My time, and I'll be sure to bring you victory in My power."

There also will be times you'll need to make the purposeful decision to rest—rest in God's promises, rest in His present gifts and wonders, rest your mind from fixating on questions and problem-solving efforts. It requires an effort to stick with what's true. It's kind of like standing in front of the ocean, waiting for a boat to arrive. Your soul soaks in the beauty of the sunset as you keep looking at the horizon.

Ask God to help you pursue His way of living right now as you actively look forward to what's coming later.

God, help me wait in a mindful, expectant, and content way.

He Can Use It for Good

You meant to hurt me, but God turned your evil into good.

Genesis 50:20 NCV

A once-favored son found himself working as a slave. His brothers had sold him off like he was property and turned their backs on him.

Next, he was unjustly accused and imprisoned. While in prison, he helped a fellow inmate and asked him to return the favor by helping him get released. But the man forgot about Joseph.

Then, Joseph was able to help Pharaoh directly, so, unbelievably, Pharaoh put him in charge of Egypt—second in command. Joseph enabled the people to survive years of famine.

If you were him, would you have any hope for healing from that family trauma of your past?

One day his brothers showed up, desperate for food, and do you know what God empowered him to do? Joseph showed *kindness* to those brothers who'd treated him like dirt. He said, "Do not be angry with yourselves for selling me here, because it was to save lives that God sent me ahead of you." He kissed them. "You intended to harm me, but God intended it for good" (Genesis 45:5; 50:20).

God turned a nightmare into a grand and beautiful success story. Now, who's to say what He *can't* do in your life?

God, I believe that You intend all things in my life for good. Do an extraordinary work in my heart and accomplish Your will through me.

It's Who You Know

Even though . . . the fields lie empty and barren; even though
the flocks die in the fields, . . . I will be joyful in the God
of my salvation! The Sovereign LORD is my strength!
Habakkuk 3:17–19 NLT

It takes faith to live with hope for something you can't see. It also takes knowing the God you have your faith in.

That's what Habakkuk did when he looked at the dead fields and flocks around him. What he saw could have shattered him. But instead, when there was no sign of goodness around him, he was . . . joyful?

Habakkuk knew about the God who saves, who gives strength, who is able to overpower anything with His goodness. He could say, "God is able. He makes me able. He is all my hope."

When you live with hope, you're not living only in response to what you see and feel. You're living in response to the Great I Am, the One who is and always has been, the One you can always count on. *I am the force that made you; I can sustain you and provide for you. I can care for you and help you. I can make things new.*

When you live with hope, you're living in response to the One who said, "I am the way and the truth and the life" (John 14:6).

What if you lived in response to Him today?

No matter what I see or feel, Lord, I want to say, "You
are able. You make me able. You are all my hope."

Uncertain Yet Certain

*The LORD your God is God; he is the faithful God, keeping
his covenant of love to a thousand generations.*
Deuteronomy 7:9

A nxiety is often a response to uncertainty. Will the news be good
or bad? When will things change? Will we be okay? If you don't
know a good God who's on the throne, it's maddening.

But you and I know the good God on the throne.

That means we can be certain about the biggest stuff—He will
stay with us, care for us, provide for us, and work all things for good.
He'll always be King. There's no question of whether we can trust His
power and wisdom.

Yet we're uncertain of the details. What do we do with that?

Elisabeth Elliot said, "Waiting on God requires the willingness
to bear uncertainty, to carry within oneself the unanswered question, lifting the heart to God about it whenever it intrudes upon one's
thoughts."[5]

This is a practice we'll do over and over, whenever uncertainty
rises. We lift up the questions and the anxious heart. Then we say, *My
trust is in Your character.*

We make the decision not to live in the merry-go-round of questions and angst. We say, *I'll trust Him with the details.*

God, help me think more about what is certain than what is uncertain.

The Faith of Kingdom People

"The kingdom of God is in your midst."
Luke 17:21

Y ou and I have put our faith in Jesus. He pulled us out of darkness and into His kingdom of light. That happened after we did our part and said, *Yes, Lord, I trust You.*

We're all His now and we live by faith in Him. Every day we want to keep saying, *Yes, Lord, I trust You.*

The faith we have in Him for our salvation is the same faith we need to bring into our daily life. We know that if He can do *that*, then He can do *this*. The power He used to save our souls is the power at work in our everyday moments.

When Jesus told the parable of the soils, He was illustrating different responses to God. Some people initially show excitement but then fizzle. They drop their faith as soon as "the emotions wear off and some difficulty arrives" (Matthew 13:21 MSG). Other people embrace His message but then get caught up in other stuff. They let "weeds of worry and illusions about getting more and wanting everything under the sun" become their focus (v. 22 MSG).

As kingdom people, we want to keep receiving and believing God's messages of truth. So have a heart that takes in His Word and is thoroughly changed by it. Have faith that keeps growing and reigns in you, so that Jesus can say of you, "The kingdom of God is within you."

Today I say, Yes, Lord, I trust You.

Do You Believe?

*The blind men came to him, and he asked them, "Do you
believe that I am able to do this?" "Yes, Lord," they replied.*
Matthew 9:28

What seems irreversibly wrong in your life? Maybe it's something
that has been this way for years and feels unchangeable.

I wonder if you're still praying about it. I wonder if the frustration
and heartache has left you so emotionally exhausted that praying and
hoping just doesn't feel doable anymore.

Think about this: two blind men came to Jesus, asking Him to
heal them, and He asked, "Do you believe that I am able to do this?"

For a minute, just try to imagine Jesus sitting with you right now,
looking at your problem with you. He turns to you and asks, "Do you
believe that I'm able to change this?"

What would you say? If you'd say yes, then the next questions are,
Why not pray about it right now? Why not pray about it every day?

Jesus is saying, "Will you trust Me? Will you put this in My hands
and call on My power to touch it?"

We want to have a mind that says yes to God. We do that not only
by capturing our thoughts but also by choosing hope. And when we
choose hope, we bring our whole selves and whole lives to Him and
say, *I believe You're able. Come and touch all of this with Your power.*

*I don't want my weariness to diminish my view of what
You're capable of. You are always all-powerful, God.*

The Signs in Creation

"Look at the birds of the air; they do not sow or reap or
store away in barns, and yet your heavenly Father feeds
them. Are you not much more valuable than they?"
Matthew 6:26

W hat are your favorite things in God's creation? Picture whatever it is that fully captures your heart or fascinates you or
makes you go, *Whoa.*

From forests to mountains to oceans to star-filled skies, God is
taking care of what He made. From chickadees to whales, from wildflowers to watermelons, the Life-Giver is sustaining everything He
created. They receive the nutrients they need, they thrive, and they
put on a show of His beauty and glory.

And Jesus wants you to notice. He wants you to let it build your
hope in your God who nurtures and provides.

"Look at the wildflowers. They never primp or shop, but have
you ever seen color and design quite like it? . . . If God gives such
attention to the appearance of wildflowers—most of which are never
even seen—don't you think he'll attend to you, take pride in you, do
his best for you?" (Matthew 6:29–30 MSG).

Every chance you get, look at the world around you and soak in
all the signs that shout, *His careful attention and provision go on and*
on! Put your trust in Him!

You are worthy of all my trust, my Creator God.

The Benefits of Hopeful Living

We can never give up longing and wishing while we are
thoroughly alive. There are certain things we feel to be
beautiful and good, and we must hunger after them.
George Eliot, *The Mill on the Floss*

Hope plays a crucial role not only in our spiritual lives but also in our mental and physical health. Experts say that hope can reduce our perception of pain and risk for illness. It can improve blood pressure, circulation, and respiration, and lower our chances of having a heart attack, a stroke, and heart disease. Basically, people with hope aren't likely to overwork their nervous systems, and their stress levels won't weaken their long-term health.[6]

Studies also show that hope can lead to more happiness, higher academic performance, and more productivity. One study found that hope resulted in 14 percent of productivity in workplaces.[7]

All of this inspires me to double down on my efforts to live with a hopeful mindset. You with me? Here's a tip from psychologists that will help us: sometimes you have to *act* like you have hope before you become a more hopeful person.[8] Try thinking, *What would the hopeful response be?* Then *do* that. If you keep up that practice, you'll create a habit of hope and establish a hopeful mindset. Before long, you'll really feel that way too.

I am meant for hopeful living, Lord. Lead me into that
way of life and all the gifts You have for me there.

What's Coming Is Mind-Blowing

"No human mind has conceived"—the things
God has prepared for those who love him.
1 Corinthians 2:9

When you're in a crisis and someone mentions the hope of heaven, it may come across as tone deaf or trite. *Yeah,* you think, *but right now I'm suffering, and I'm worried about how I'll cope tomorrow.*

Yet is there ever a bad time to think about the brightness of our future, when we'll get to do and be all that we were meant to do and be? God will fully establish His kingdom of light, remake the heavens and earth, and complete His work of transformation in us. We're talking wholeness—the new, redeemed, eternal humanity, everything He ever intended humanity to be or become.

This mind-blowing awesomeness is our destiny, and it will last forever. That's why Scripture says that "what we suffer now is nothing compared to the glory he will reveal to us later" (Romans 8:18 NLT).

Things here and now will fall apart, and it'll seem like the end of the world. But God wants us to remember it's not. Anything we suffer will not win out over the resurrection and the new life to come, and He's always at work in us, making us new. Nothing will stop God from making things right and beautiful.

God, it's only a matter of time until I get to experience
the new life You'll create. Fill my heart with joyful
anticipation for all the beauty ahead.

You're on Your Way Home

We are citizens of heaven, where the Lord Jesus Christ lives.
And we are eagerly waiting for him to return as our Savior.
Philippians 3:20 NLT

H ave you ever been squinting hard to read a book and then realized the lights are dim? *Well, that would do it.*

This is kind of like when we remember that earth is not our home; heaven is. Things feel off for a legitimate reason.

There's an unrest in our souls, a desire for more, a recognition that things aren't as they should be, a sense that we don't quite belong here.

We see the goodness of God and we receive the gift of His presence here and now—but we know we're meant for His perfect heaven. He's put eternity in our hearts.

It's helpful to recognize that sometimes our anxiety and ache of dissatisfaction is rooted in our longing for our true home. We can go to God with our grief and unfulfilled hopes. We can remember that Jesus Himself stepped into the brokenness and made it possible for us to go home.

Let the recognition of all this drive you into hopeful prayer. He's come for us. He has a home for us. We're not there yet, but we're on our way, and He'll be with us throughout the entire journey.

Thank You for sending Jesus, the Way, and for making heaven my true home. Be with me in the waiting, God.

The Difference a Savior Makes

"His name will be the hope of all the world."
Matthew 12:21 NLT

What difference does Jesus make in our lives? Think about the difference between jumping on a trampoline—floating then landing onto a bouncy surface—and falling off a roof with nothing to catch you.

The whole world was in a nightmare situation like falling off a roof. But God loved us *so* very much that He sent His Rescuer, His Son, the hope of all the world.

When anxiety grips me and controls me, my mind operates like Jesus never showed up, or like His love never found me. I think I'm headed into a future with no Helper, that everything is riding on limited Carrie, and that basically I'm doomed.

But when I wake up to who is right there with me, I have relief and safety and peace. I know His strength and support. He frees up my heart to be light and happy. He sings me a song of hope that I can't stop singing back to Him.

Jesus is the hope of all the world. He came to earth radiating love and spent His life conquering death. His light won over the darkness, and He can do the exact same thing in our hearts and lives today. Whatever comes later, He can do it then too.

He makes all the difference.

Jesus, help me live like You make all the difference in my world.

Make Faith Lead Your Thoughts

We live by faith, not by sight.
2 Corinthians 5:7

Have you ever noticed that the more you think about problems, the bigger they get in your mind? *How* do they grow like that? Well, I give them more power the more I fixate on them.

How about I strengthen faith-filled thoughts instead? Want to do it with me? Here are some ideas to get us started.

Challenge yourself to start your thoughts with faith every morning. Create a few go-to statements or prayers. During a season when I was fighting thoughts of despair, I regularly prayed, *You can do anything, God. I'm looking for Your wonders. I'm waiting in hope.*

Start associating daily routine moments with awareness of God's presence. For instance, when you turn on a light switch, you could remember He's the Light of the World and think, *You're the Light of my world and my future.*

Post three powerful verses or Scripture-based mantras—ones that build up your faith—in places where you'll see them every day. At the end of the day, write out three ways God fulfilled His word and showed His character to you.

We want faith leading our thoughts. Chase after it. Grab ahold of your faith every day and put it up in the front of the pack.

Keep me awake to my thought options, God. Help me
strengthen faith-filled thoughts, not worries.

Acts of Hope

Commit your way to the LORD; trust in him, and he will act.
Psalm 37:5 ESV

S he'd had the major health problem for twelve years and no doctors could help her. The bleeding and suffering kept on and was getting worse. She could have despaired, but instead she hoped. She could have stayed home, but instead she went after Jesus.

If I can just touch His clothes, I'll be healed, she thought as she reached out her hand. She touched Him, and she was healed. This brave woman took action because she had hope, and the power of Jesus changed her life (Mark 5:25–34).

What are the acts of hope you can take today? Maybe it's going to counseling. Maybe it's making a doctor's appointment. Maybe it's writing out your prayers, telling Him what you're hoping for and how you trust in His character.

Bring your brokenness and needs to the Healer. Open your hands to Him and ask Him to fill them with good and beautiful things only He can provide. Take action with immense belief in your heart.

Will you see the results you want? We don't know.

We can't predict the wonderful ways of our wild but good God. That's okay. We know who He is, so we'll keep courageously offering our whole selves to Him, fully entrusting them to His power and wisdom.

Lord, help me have the guts and wisdom to put my faith into action.

Create Happy Anticipation

No temper could be more cheerful than hers, or
possess, in a greater degree, that sanguine expectation
of happiness which is happiness itself.
Jane Austen, *Sense and Sensibility*

What are you looking forward to right now? When we're anxious, our worries steal the show in terms of our focus. But when we shove them offstage, guess what's sitting right there? All kinds of great stuff—or open space ready to be filled up with great stuff.

Research has proven that we experience happiness not only from having positive experiences but also from *anticipating* them. Those bright spots we can see coming up on the calendar can do wonders for our state of mind.[9] Why not get super intentional?

Fit something you love into your daily routine, like reading with coffee, journaling, exercising, or listening to an audiobook or podcast on your commute. Every week, have a standing time you talk with friends or family, join a group with a common interest, try a new recipe or restaurant, visit a farmers market, or get active outside. Go to the theater or a concert, host a game night, invite friends to visit a bookstore with you, or throw a party for a friend.

If none of this is your jam, zero in on what is! Build your own bright spots into your life and enjoy looking forward to each one.

Help me build more happy anticipation into my
life and brighten my everyday perspective.

Use That Imagination for Good

"With God all things are possible."
Matthew 19:26

I've heard that worry is the negative use of imagination and is like praying for what you don't want. It's basically using your time and energy to envision a worst-case future. Why would we do this?

Well, our brains have a bent toward negativity. But if we're self-aware and intentional, we can absolutely change our focus. What we focus on informs our imagination and view of the future.

What would happen if the following things took up more of your thought life?

- a list of dreams and hopes, big and little, for the rest of your life
- a vision board of what you want to be in your future
- miracles in Scripture
- the actions or mantras of people who inspire you

Just imagine all the bright possibilities! He has a beautiful future for you. What if you let yourself spend more time imagining how awesome it is? What if every day you decided to hold a vision for that beautiful future?

*God, make me brave enough to dream up wonderful
new things for my future with You.*

Make Hope the New Default

May the God of hope fill you with all joy and peace
as you trust in him, so that you may overflow
with hope by the power of the Holy Spirit.
Romans 15:13

G od wants His kids' hearts to be joyful and peaceful. Our part is trusting. His part is empowering us to overflow with hope, which can become our default mindset.

We don't have to amplify the negative and downplay the positive. We can choose hope instead of pessimism. We can notice and soak in God's goodness and let His love and words of promise fill our hearts. We can respond to Him by saying, "'My hope is in you all day long' and at night, 'my body also will rest in hope'" (Psalm 25:5; Acts 2:26).

In this mindset, every day is a clean slate and fresh start, full of possibilities and potential good surprises.

Henri Nouwen wrote, "Our spiritual life is a life in which we wait, actively present to the moment, expecting that new things will happen to us, new things that are far beyond our own imagination or prediction. This, indeed, is a very radical stance toward life in a world preoccupied with control."[10]

Consider some new leading thoughts today: *God is preparing amazing things. His abundant goodness sparks anticipation and joy.*

Give me the courage and faith to make hope my default
mindset. Holy Spirit, make my heart overflow with hope.

Loyalty and Confidence

I am confident I will see the LORD's goodness while
I am here in the land of the living. Wait patiently
for the LORD. Be brave and courageous.
Psalm 27:13–14 NLT

W hen a solar eclipse occurred in ancient times, people freaked out. The world had gone dark—were they facing a tragic end? They didn't know the sun was still there, even though they couldn't see evidence of it, and it was only a matter of time before they'd see its bright light again.[11]

There will be times when our world goes dark and we can't sense evidence of God's presence and light. So we need to try to respond to that reality even when we can't see or feel it. Someone once said, "Learning to weep, learning to keep vigil, learning to wait for the dawn. Perhaps this is what it means to be human."[12]

When you choose hope, you're deciding not to give up waiting on the One who never gives up on you. *I'm counting on Your goodness. I'm confident You'll bring beauty, light, and power into my world, because You are the God of all those things.*

Stay open to possibilities beyond what you can imagine. Your life points to His goodness and glory, saying, *Get ready to be blown away.*

I want my heart attitude to show loyalty to You, Lord.
Make me brave enough to live with confident hope.

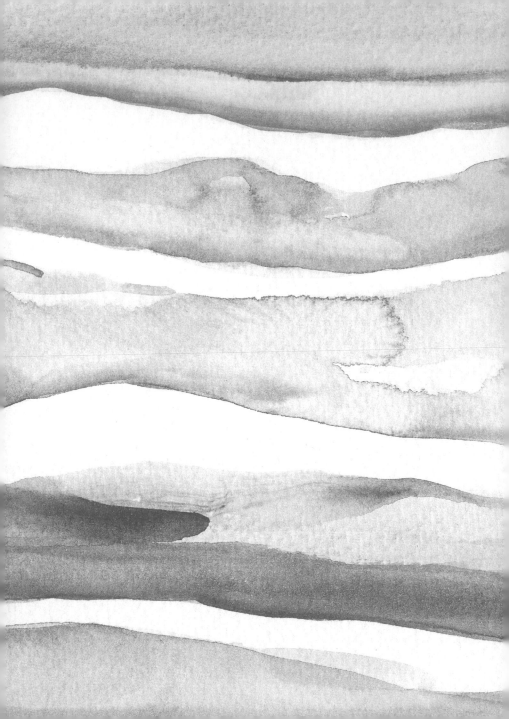

~

Pursue Balance and Wellness

Want to change your thoughts and feelings? Try changing what you're doing. Every choice you make holds a lot of power.

This month we're getting super practical. What are some actions that set us up for anxiety, and what are actions that steer us away from it? How can we take better care of ourselves, have more nourishing experiences, and holistically grow into our strongest selves?

God has wired us to need certain things for wellness and provided lots of ways for us to have anxiety-reducing, mood-boosting, life-giving experiences. We just need to choose to bring them into our lives.

Make Balance the Norm

Can a man scoop fire into his lap without
his clothes being burned?
Proverbs 6:27

P acked schedules. Mile-long task lists. A breakneck pace of life. We are a society of overloaded and tense people, trying to keep up with everyone's demands and expectations. We barrel through our days overwhelmed, tired, and anxious.

It comes down to cause and effect. We *go, go, go*—we don't *go, rest, go*. When our minds and bodies are imbalanced, conditioned to stay in overdrive, we experience the results of that. It's like how neglecting to change your car's oil will eventually land you on the side of the road.

Now, can you single-handedly change our crazy never-let-up culture? No. But can you carve out a healthy way of life for yourself? Yes.

You can figure out how to have more restful and life-giving experiences. You can lean into God's design of humans and experience the restoration and strength that comes from wisely taking care of yourself.

You're in charge of you, and the best version of you is within reach. Are you ready to prioritize balance and wellness, and see what it's like to feel steadier and more energized?

God, I want to make choices that will make me
healthier and stronger, just like You designed.

Self-Care Is Not a Bad Word

Our bodies are our gardens, to which our wills are gardeners.
William Shakespeare, *Othello*

S ome people bristle at the term *self-care*. Maybe it sounds self-absorbed and indulgent to you.

But you know what? It's really about honoring the way we're made—and the One who made us and lives in us. It's about coming to terms with what it takes to be healthy, strong, fully functional human beings.

If you have a hard time with the idea of self-care, think of it as receiving care from God. *I believe Your love is extravagant, God. You pour it over me. I'm receiving it with open arms as I eat healthy food and nestle into my cozy bed.*

Or think of it as a way to love and honor Him. *This body and mind and heart You gave me? I'm going to nurture and strengthen them. I'll give them what they need to be their best in this season.*

You may feel self-absorbed and guilty, like you can't do right by the people you love if you prioritize your own care. But that's not true. You're filling up your tank so you have fuel to spend on them. You're bringing new strength to your life, which flows into theirs.

It is up to you to do this—for God, for others, and for yourself. No one except you can make it happen.

God, help me acknowledge my needs and prioritize meeting them.

A Sacred Temple

*Do you not know that your bodies are temples of the Holy
Spirit, who is in you, whom you have received from God?*
1 Corinthians 6:19

You've been given a job with some high-level responsibility. You
are a steward of God's special creation—*you*.

Your body has been designated a sacred place, one to be treated
with the utmost respect. You are a temple in which the living God
dwells. He makes His home in you. It's an incomprehensible honor.

The key to success in this role of Temple Caretaker is remembering that simple things done regularly are important. Calming and
life-giving habits that nurture, protect, and build resilience look oddly
ordinary: sleeping enough, eating right, exercising, spending time in
nature, connecting with people, enjoying plants and animals, relaxing
more often, meditating and praying, doing more of what you love,
having more mindful experiences, and scaling back responsibilities to
what's truly manageable.

It takes consistency, but when you desire to do the best with what
He's given you, you'll be driven and committed. And when you nourish yourself with the experiences you need to be well, you can flourish
in the directions He wants you to go.

*Lord, I want to commit myself to honoring You by caring
for the body You gave me, the body You live in.*

The Mind-Body Connection

As he thinks in his heart, so is he.
Proverbs 23:7 NKJV

H ave you ever been put on the spot and started sweating? Or have you ever sat quietly watching waves and felt calmer?

How we think affects our bodies. Negativity has been linked to having fewer antibodies, and positivity has been linked to having more antibodies.[1]

What we do with our bodies affects our brain too. Exercise, sleep, social connection, productivity, and relaxation all carry a neurological impact.

While we can't change how we feel directly, we *can* change our actions, which is like changing our feelings indirectly.[2] In other words, we can't control what feelings pop up, but we can do things to generate *new* feelings.

Jesus said, "Do not let your hearts be troubled" (John 14:1). His words acknowledge our agency. Manage your mind so that faith, hope, and praise are forefront. Avoid the propensity toward an anxious mindset by nurturing your body and brain so they can be as healthy as possible, in a better position to manage fear and anxiety. There is a lot of power in every choice you make.

Heavenly Father, I want my mind and body to work together to make each other strong. Help me make choices that foster that.

Carve Out Time to Be Calm

The true strength of a man is in calmness.
Leo Tolstoy

Had any stressful moments lately? You got through them because God designed you with a *sympathetic* nervous system. It's the "fight or flight" response, the equivalent of a car's gas pedal.

He's also given you a *parasympathetic* nervous system, which allows the body to calm down. It's the "rest and digest" response, the equivalent of a car's brake pedal. In this state the body reduces inflammation, repairs tissues, and digests food.[3] You feel nice and relaxed.

You can guess what happens if we're in the high-stress zone too much, right? It's genuinely terrible for the brain and the body.[4] So we need to be intentional about relaxing regularly. Over time, it will make us healthier and stronger, giving us a "'buffer' for stress" and helping us "stay calm and present in challenging situations."[5]

There are lots of ways we can let our parasympathetic nervous system do its thing: breathing deeply, meditating, praying, getting a back rub, doing yoga, taking a walk, laughing, singing, and spending time outdoors with pets and with loved ones.[6]

So know that every time you relax, you're accessing a part of yourself that God gave you to make you strong. You're giving yourself what you need in the moment as well as investing in future calmness.

I respect how You designed my body to function. Help me choose relaxation. Create more calm in my body, God.

Unplug Already

Adopt the pace of nature. Her secret is patience.
Ralph Waldo Emerson, *Lectures and Biographical Sketches*

D*ing! Beep! Ding! Beep!* Are your screens running your life? Write that email. Check out that news article. Scroll through social media. Return that text. *Eesh.* As digital engagement is taking over our lives, our nervous systems are overstimulated and crying out for relief.[7]

When we spend a ton of time in front of a screen, "the brain has no time left with which to process the world, chunk information, and form long-term memories." We also become more distractable and have a harder time focusing.[8]

If we want to be healthy people, we've got to figure out a healthy balance here. We have to insist on breaks so we're not constantly in high gear and on high alert.

Having less screen time brings tons of benefits: better sleep and posture, less eyestrain and fewer headaches.[9] It also can improve focus, lower chances of weight gain, and reduce anxiety.[10]

So set boundaries that work for you. Decide you'll check email or notifications only a certain number of times a day, not constantly. If you work in front of a screen, take breaks throughout the day. Step away from social media for significant amounts of time. Let yourself really and truly unplug.

God, help me steward my brain well by having smart boundaries with screens.

Rhythms of Relaxing

Keep good company, read good books, love good things
and cultivate soul and body as faithfully as you can.
Louisa May Alcott, *Rose in Bloom*

I f we want a balanced life, we've got to make room for enriching experiences. We can't just hope they happen; we've got to make plans for them. Schedule them like important meetings and show respect for their value by protecting that time.

Establish rhythms of relaxing. Make a list of ways you can relax and find times you can do them regularly—daily, weekly, and monthly. Soak in a bubble bath every Saturday. Light a candle and listen to calming music for twenty minutes in the evening. Take some slow, deep breaths on a work break. Do things that help you process, like journaling or opening up to a friend. Block out time when you have no agenda and simply enjoy being present. Remember that you have to rest in order to recharge.

Establish rhythms of life-giving experiences, where you're engaged with others in uplifting ways, your mind is stimulated, your body is invigorated, or you experience a sense of purpose. Good meals, good conversations, good laughs.

Build these kinds of experiences into your life regularly, and you'll be cultivating the wellness and strength of your mind, body, and soul.

God, help me prioritize having relaxing and enriching experiences.

Rhythms of Communion

Be still in the presence of the LORD.
Psalm 37:7 NLT

You'd never have much of a relationship with your best friend if you never spent time with her. The same goes for your relationship with God.

Establish rhythms of communing with Him. Have times when you are still in His presence. Get up a little earlier. Get alone on your lunch break. Set aside time in the evening. Whenever it is, get intentional about engaging your heart and mind with your Life Source. Focus on the One you want to love with all you've got. Let your heart be filled with praise and adoration. Open up and share what you need to. Let Him remind you of His character and love and of your identity and value. Let Him fill your cup with peace, wisdom, calmness, and strength.

Have times when you're with His people. You connect with the Spirit alive in them, and they connect with the Spirit alive in you. Make yourself an active part of a spiritual community.

And do whatever else makes you feel close to Him, like serving in some way or spending time in nature.

Make a plan for how these things can happen in your life regularly. These experiences are so important—they feed your soul. They restore, replenish, and fortify you. They make the light in your life stronger.

I want to draw near to You, God. Meet with me and change me.

The Positive Effects of Meditation

"Fix these words of mine in your hearts and minds."
Deuteronomy 11:18

W e do the spiritual practices of prayer and meditation because we love God and they help us come close to Him. But it turns out they have positive physiological effects too.

Meditation has been shown to lower blood pressure, tension, stress and anxiety, and perception of pain and to help people sleep better.[11]

Meditation also changes the brain's shape and enhances its function.[12] Brain scans reveal significant differences between the brains of those who are committed to prayer and meditation and those who aren't.[13] When we meditate, we activate the frontal lobe,[14] which is mainly responsible for attention, reasoning, memory, impulse control, and other high-level functions.[15] And it's like building a muscle—whenever we activate it, we make it stronger.[16]

Remember that Christian meditation is not like other types of meditation. We're not emptying our minds; we're filling them with God's truth.

So read God's Word and spend time with your sustained focus on it. Linger with it and let it sink in and become a part of you. After you meditate on His Word, ask Him to show you the difference He wants the Word to make in your perspective and actions.

Lord, come change the way I think and live as I
fix Your words in my heart and mind.

The Importance of Sleep

It is a common experience that a problem
difficult at night is resolved in the morning after
the committee of sleep has worked on it.
John Steinbeck

When I don't get enough sleep, everything feels harder. Focusing, problem-solving, exercising, remembering, communicating, being patient.

Sleep researchers will tell you all this and more is to be expected because, yep, getting sleep is super critical for wellness. Adults need at least seven hours a night.[17]

Getting enough sleep makes your brain and body work better. You're quicker to concentrate, remember things, and be productive. Adequate sleep boosts immunity, reduces inflammation, and regulates hunger hormones, which can prevent overeating.[18]

There's a strong link between sufficient sleep and mental health. Our brains do important things for our mental health while we're asleep, including "the consolidation of positive emotional content." Not letting our brains do enough of that can negatively affect our mood and emotions while we're awake.[19] We're literally working with fewer resources as we strive to have a positive mindset. So if we want to fight off anxiety, we'll get serious about going after those seven-plus hours of sleep!

God, I respect that You designed sleep to be important for my body.

Tips for Good Sleep

A well-spent day brings happy sleep.
Leonardo da Vinci

How about we take a look at some tips for getting our all-important sleep?

First, don't take naps or consume caffeine later in the day; it can actually remain in your body for up to twelve hours.[20] Avoid eating a heavy dinner shortly before turning in since digestion can keep you up, and scale back on spicy and fatty foods.[21] Also, skip the nightcap, since alcohol can disrupt your sleep. Don't exercise within a few hours of bedtime, and avoid screen time at least an hour beforehand.[22]

Next, set up your bedroom. Keep it dark and cool, around sixty-five to sixty-eight degrees.[23] Try using a calming scent, like lavender.[24] And make your bedroom a place for sleeping—not a place for work or for screen time. Get your brain associating that bed with rest.[25]

Try to stick to a regular schedule with the same bedtime and waketime. Schedule in wind-down time before sleeping. Create some bedtime rituals that will cue your brain that it's time for rest, like relaxing with a book or music, lighting a candle, or doing some stretches.[26]

Last, manage your mind. Turn concerns into prayers and leave them with God. Ask Him to guard your heart and mind with His peace and to help your body relax in His care.

I want to prioritize sleep and reap the benefits! Help me, God.

Move Your Body

Exercise not only changes your body, it changes
your mind, your attitude, and your mood.
Anonymous

W ho's up for a natural mood changer, a reliable way to reduce anxiety? Sign me up pronto.

Ah, the power of exercise. It builds muscles and bones, benefits the brain, and protects us from diseases. It improves sleep, lowers anxiety, and boosts mood and energy.[27]

Okay, so we get that exercise is important, but still we struggle to actually do it. It helps to see it as an essential thing, like food and sleep, and to emphasize the fact that it's rejuvenating. It's not meant to be a punishment or a chore.

See it as therapeutic, remembering it's awesome for your mental health and hormone levels. You get a mood boost from serotonin, a good feeling from dopamine, and stress relief from endorphins.[28] View it as a way to have fun and enjoy what your body is able to do.

So walk, bike, or swim. Dance or do yoga. Check out different classes or online videos. Join a team or club. Work in the garden. Exercise with a friend or a pet. You can listen to music or a podcast as you do it. But do something every day. Remember that anything is better than nothing, and every little bit helps.

God, I want to celebrate what You make my body able to do and
receive the benefits You designed for me to receive through exercise.

Drink More Water

Drinking water is like washing out your insides.
The water will cleanse your system . . . and
improve the function of all your tissues.
Dr. Kevin R. Stone

T rue or false: Hydration is related to anxiety. The correct answer
is *true*. Really.

The brain, just like every other body system, needs water to work
properly.[29] Research shows that when we're dehydrated, normal tasks
seem more difficult and the brain has to work harder to do them.
Unsurprisingly, we can end up with a headache, a bad mood, or less
energy. Here's one more scientific fact you may find horrifying, like I
do: dehydration actually *shrinks* the brain.[30] Yikes all around.

While dehydration isn't a sole cause for anxiety, it can definitely
be a contributor; it's stress on the body and brain. Drinking water can
have a calming effect.[31] It also improves focus, increasing the speed of
mental abilities by 14 percent, according to one study.[32]

So drink water when you first wake up, and keep drinking liquids
throughout the day. Women need about nine cups a day and men need
about thirteen.[33] The next time you fill up your glass and start swal-
lowing, remember you're taking excellent care of yourself and helping
yourself be calmer and stronger.

Thank You, Lord, for the difference drinking
water can make in my wellness.

Choose Healthy Food

All living things look to you for food, and you
give it to them at the right time.
Psalm 145:15 NCV

Y ou wouldn't try to drive your car with an empty tank. So don't try to do life without the fuel of nutrient-dense food or try to live on calories with few health benefits. Give your body what it was made for—give it the good stuff.

Remember that healthy food not only gives you energy but also affects neurological function and mood.[34] It's definitely related to our mental health.

As much as you can, stick with whole foods. Fill up on lean proteins, high-fiber carbohydrates, vegetables, and fruits. Enjoy treats, but be moderate with sugar intake, as too much sugar can increase stress and anxiety levels.[35] Seek out nutrient-dense options like salmon, eggs, nuts, seeds, beans, blueberries, leafy greens, broccoli, oats, and sweet potatoes.[36]

Spend more time at the farmers market and the perimeter of the grocery store, where you'll find things like produce. Minimize eating out, high-calorie frozen meals, and boxed foods with preservatives.

Your generous Father is providing you with food that nourishes and replenishes you.

Thank You, Father, for providing me with the
food I need to be strong and healthy.

That Won't "Feel You Better"

Discernment is not a matter of telling the difference
between right and wrong; rather it is telling the
difference between right and almost right.
Charles Spurgeon

When my daughter was two, she had a head cold. While I was bathing her, she grabbed her dad's shampoo bottle, squirted out a handful, and started rubbing it on her belly. With confidence she said, "This will feel me better," which my toddler-translator mind understood to mean, "This will make me feel better."

We grown-ups aren't that different. How often do we reach for things that won't help us? When I find myself feeling convinced that I should have that extra treat or watch another episode, the visual of my kid's attempt at shampoo therapy comes to mind. And I think, *No, this won't "feel me better."*

We need to avoid using good things in a way that ultimately affects us negatively. Establish smart boundaries that will free you up to enjoy things but protect you from immoderation.

When you don't feel like doing the right thing for your body, remind yourself you don't want to jeopardize what you need long-term for a short-term indulgence. Choose the thing that your future self will benefit from later.

Holy Spirit, give me self-control and wisdom
as I work toward a balanced life.

Declutter and Organize

Rid yourself of anything that distracts from your best life.
Joshua Becker

D o you have more stuff than you know what to do with? Do you keep passing over clothes in your closet you never wear? Is your home setup stressful or functional?

The physical aspects of our lives impact our mental state more than we usually realize. If our home is orderly and clean, we feel calmer and think more clearly. But if we're surrounded by clutter, we're setting ourselves up for more stress.[37]

The next time you have some free hours, do an overhaul of one of your rooms. Clear out as much stuff as you can. Recognize that you have limited real estate and give only the essentials and favorites a spot.

Create a place for things to belong instead of letting them pile up somewhere. Set up some new storage options. Pick a spot to put your keys and wallet every day, and keep your priorities and schedule in one spot. Make it easier for yourself to keep up with what's going on in your life.

Freeing up space in your home is going to free up space in your mind and make you feel lighter overall. It will energize you, give your whole mindset a lift, and probably inspire you to spend more of your energy on life-giving experiences. It's worth the effort!

Lord, help me see how I can manage my home
in a way that supports and frees me.

Shed the Old and Find the New

Every moment is a fresh beginning.
T. S. Eliot

D on't you love the way you feel after a haircut? Your ends feel all clean and crisp, not straggly or split. There's a nice swish and a new shape. There's nothing quite like it.

When my daughter was five, she asked me to chop off a bunch of her hair, more than ever before. After I did, she beamed at herself in the mirror. "I love it!" she said. "It's the new me!"

Sometimes we need to take some action to feel like a new version of ourselves, and even simple things like haircuts can remind us that we can change in good ways. New beginnings are possible.

Think about this the next time you clip your nails, or when you exfoliate or brush off dry skin. You're shedding old layers to make room for something new that wants to shine. Those shiny parts are still *you*; they just need some help to be seen.

Taking action to bring out that newness can remind us of our agency. We may feel powerless in some areas, but we actually have control over quite a bit. As you take care of yourself in one way, remind yourself that you have the power to do a lot more for yourself too. New possibilities are available to you if you want them.

God, I want to discover new possibilities and step into fresh beginnings.

Simplify Your Life

Let us strip off every weight that slows us down. . . . And let
us run with endurance the race God has set before us.
Hebrews 12:1 NLT

M any of us are anxious because we have an overly complicated life or because there's no room in our lives to do the things we were made to do. Most often it's both.

We need to decide to let go of some things so we're not so weighed down and spread thin. We have to prioritize doing things that inspire us, keep us grounded, and help us grow into our best selves.

Try taking an inventory of everything you're giving your time, energy, and focus to. Mark which ones are life-giving, which ones are causing stress, and which ones are neither yet are still adding to the pile-up.

Next, work through a few questions. Are you investing yourself in the wrong pursuits? Can any of your non–life-giving activities be adjusted? How can you carve out time for replenishing and fulfilling experiences?

Be honest about your limitations. Learn to say no and start getting intentional about creating a life with a healthy balance—one where you're not always overwhelmed, your needs are met, and you do more of what brings you joy.

Help me, Lord, to evaluate, simplify, and build
a life that leads me to my strongest self.

Nourishing Experiences

The purpose of life is to live it, to taste experience
to the utmost, to reach out eagerly and without
fear for newer and richer experiences.
Eleanor Roosevelt

I magine clearing out an entire room in your house, and then the reward that would follow: the fun task of deciding what to put in it. Picture yourself carefully choosing just the right colors, objects, furniture, and art. It's whatever *you* want.

Once you've created more room in your life, the big question is what you want to fill it with. You get to build and design your life. You get to choose the positive experiences you'll bring into it: the people who cheer and inspire you, the work that fulfills you, your favorite flavors and colors and textures, the sounds of nature and music, the new things to try, the ways you'll commune with God, the activities that calm and energize you. Whatever nourishes your soul, helps you grow into your best self, and flourish in the directions God wants you to go.

Think on these questions: What has brought you joy in the past? What are five things you absolutely love doing? What opportunities around you pique your interest?

God, help me build a life with nourishing experiences. Show me what
will strengthen me and help me grow in the ways You want me to.

Get Outside

To sit in the shade on a fine day and look upon
verdure is the most perfect refreshment.
Jane Austen, *Mansfield Park*

L ying in the grass in the sunshine. Walking along a river. Seeing
sunlight sparkling on water. Hiking a hilly trail. Listening to
birds chirp. These kinds of moments are so calming, aren't they?

Our fast-paced, screens-obsessed culture isn't exactly steering us
in this direction. As our society is getting increasingly disconnected
with nature and more connected to electronic media, we're losing out
on a ton of benefits.

Research shows that taking in the beauty of nature helps us
relax—even after only *five minutes*.[38] It helps us sleep better, builds
immunity, and improves memory.[39] It prompts similar brain activity
as meditating—the kind of attention that frees us from a hyper-alert
state of mind and lets us reflect.[40]

One study found that exercising outdoors made people feel less
tense and more revitalized than exercising indoors.[41] Another showed
that people's stress hormone levels went down after walking in nature.[42]

What are we waiting for? Let's get out there and receive the gifts
God has waiting for us right outside our front door.

God, thank You for making my time spent in
nature such a healing experience.

Bring on the Levity

A merry heart does good, like medicine.
Proverbs 17:22 NKJV

L aughter is the most beautiful and beneficial therapy God ever granted humanity," said pastor Chuck Swindoll. We definitely need to put humor in our toolbelt for dealing with anxiety. It wields some heavy-duty power.

Laughter releases tension and relaxes muscles, which can last for up to forty-five minutes afterward. It boosts energy, improves immunity, reduces stress hormones, and produces endorphins, which relieves pain and stress.[43] There's no question it relaxes us. And "the calmer we are, the more we remain in a rational or positive mind."[44]

Laughing about something other than our circumstances can bring us relief simply by capturing our attention. Humor can also give us a new view of our life situation; finding a way to laugh about our worries and struggles can make them seem less threatening and heavy.[45] *Levity* does mean "lightness," after all.[46]

So seek out people who will laugh with you. Get goofy with friends and family. Watch silly animals on YouTube and silly people on TV shows. Tell stories and revisit memories that make you smile. Quote funny movie lines. Be playful and quick to lighten things up. See the humor in life, and you'll make yourself more resilient.

You are the God of joy and You want joy for me. Help me bring more humor and levity into my everyday mindset.

Spend Time with Animals

O LORD, what a variety of things you have made! In wisdom
you have made them all. The earth is full of your creatures.
Psalm 104:24 NLT

I f you've had pets, you know the fun and joy they can bring. But
did you know that they actually boost our mental and physical
health too?

They provide constant companionship, which can bring comfort
and prevent illness. When we're with them, we feel less alone and
anxious, and needed as their caregivers.[47]

Humans benefit from interacting with animals whether or not the
animals are their pets. The interaction can lower our heart rate, blood
pressure, and stress hormone levels.[48] Time with them shifts our focus
away from our worries and prompts us to be engaged, active, and silly.
Being playful with them can produce the happy hormones serotonin
and dopamine.[49]

We can even benefit from just watching footage of animals. One
study examined a group of stressed-out people before and after watching a video of cute animals, and every person had a lower heart rate,
lower blood pressure, and less anxiety afterward.[50]

So call over that pup to play with or that cat to cuddle. Fire up
some fluffy critter videos. Watch fish swish around a tank. Let the
delightful creatures God made calm and relax you.

Thank You, Lord, that I get to enjoy the wonderful creatures You made.

Don't Underestimate Hobbies

To be really happy and really safe, one ought to have at
least two or three hobbies, and they must all be real.
Winston Churchill

There are times when hobbies feel like a luxury, nice options for people who aren't stressed. But hobbies are in fact an important part of wellness.

One study proved that hobbies can reduce stress and prompt people to feel happier not only while they're engaged in the activity but also for hours or days afterward.[51] Another one showed that physical leisure activity can lower the risk of experiencing fatigue.[52]

We need to make room in our lives to do things just for the joy of doing them. They not only energize us and boost our mood but also strengthen our sense of self, reminding us there's so much more to who we are than the tasks we do.[53]

We need to get real about what makes us happy too. It doesn't matter if nobody else gets why you like to do something; it just matters how the activity affects you. Be true to who you are and your own uniqueness. What do you have a genuine interest in? What did you like to do when you were younger?

Pick a hobby and preserve some time and energy for it regularly. Don't see it as a luxury; see it as a stress reliever that is one more way for you to step toward wellness.

Lord, thank You for activities that relieve stress and bring joy.

Be Curious and Discover

Isn't it splendid to think of all the things there
are to find out about? It just makes me feel glad
to be alive—it's such an interesting world.
L. M. Montgomery, *Anne of Green Gables*

Getting caught in anxiety results in a pretty monotonous thought life; we keep rounding the track of the same concerns over and over. It's terribly dull. Sometimes we need to get into a different mindset by discovering new things.

Think back to times in your life when you've been curious. What new experiences did your curiosity lead you to have? How did they make you feel? Discovering new things impacts our thought patterns and mindset.

So seek out some new mental stimulation. The world is wide and full of possibilities. Go on a road trip. Explore a new place. Take a cooking or dancing class. Join a rowing club. Take guitar lessons. Read silly kids' poetry that gives you a giggle. Listen to new music. Grow new plants. Hike a new trail. Try a new flavor.

Pick something and go for it. Be willing to step away from what's familiar and keep an open mind. You just might find something you love that shifts your perspective in wonderful ways.

Thank You, God, for filling this world with
interesting things to discover and delight in!

Get Creative

*If you hear a voice within you say "you cannot paint," then
by all means paint, and that voice will be silenced.*
Vincent van Gogh

My daughter and I are all about dancing, cooking, painting, and coloring with sparkly gel pens together. What forms of creativity do you like? When was the last time you did them?

When we're busy, creative experiences tend to fly out the window, but they really do contribute to our overall well-being. They help our brains work better, bring down our anxiety and stress levels, and improve our mood.[54]

When we're creative, we stop focusing on our worries and get fully engaged with the present task. This can calm us in a way that's like meditation, drawing us "into a physical state of deep relaxation that alters [our] physical and emotional responses to stress."[55] And when we see the results of our labor, our brains produce happy dopamine.[56]

Even if your results aren't awesome, that's okay! Still create something, knowing the experience itself is valuable. Build and bake and craft and write. Draw something following a YouTube video. Make origami or bracelets. Just experiment with childlike freedom and have fun. Why not? Work with your hands, give it your full attention, and enjoy the positive effects.

*Almighty God, thank You for giving me the
happy experience of creating.*

The Sense of Sight

I believe the world is incomprehensibly beautiful—
an endless prospect of magic and wonder.
Ansel Adams

I've never seen anything like it!" When have those words come out of your mouth? Maybe you saw an Olympian accomplish an incredible feat or a purple-pink-orange sunset that filled the sky. What you saw fully captured your attention and made you totally present in the moment.

God gave us five senses. When we are mindful of them, we have a richer experience of life. We'll start with the sense of sight and explore how it can soothe or bring joy.

From gazing at a waterfall or mountain to examining intricate butterflies and leaves, there's a whole world full of shapes and designs to observe. So step outside or check out photos and documentaries that show the gorgeous landscapes that cover the planet.

Look at happy things like flower bouquets and twinkle lights. Surround yourself with colors so they can give you an emotional boost: yellow, orange, and red can prompt "happiness, optimism, and energy," while purple, blue, and green can be "calming and soothing."[57]

Change your thoughts and feelings by simply changing what you look at.

God, calm and lift my spirit through what I choose to see.

The Sense of Hearing

Life seems to go on without effort when I am filled with music.
George Eliot, *The Mill on the Floss*

As the youngest of three girls, I was always the first one to head to bed as a kid. And I just knew a party was going on without me. My mom blanketed the noise of whatever they were doing (and the fun I was missing) with harp music. And you know what? It totally worked. I would lie still in my bed with my eyes closed, just listening, and before I knew it, I was drifting off to sleep. The music totally relaxed me.

People have used sounds for therapeutic effects and health benefits for ages,[58] and today music therapy is a discipline and profession.[59] Research has proven that music can calm the nervous system. If you search online for songs that will reduce anxiety, you'll find music that's been shown to "lower heart rate, slow breathing, and decrease levels of the stress hormone 'cortisol' in the blood."[60]

You can also find tons of recordings of rainforest sounds or waves or other ambient sounds. Look for calming tracks with an acoustic guitar, a piano, or soft vocals. Why not make a playlist? Add to it whatever other songs have soothed you in the past. Then set aside time regularly to be still and listen and be fully present. Let your sense of sound usher in peace and positive emotions.

God, help me experience more calmness through what I choose to hear.

The Sense of Smell

Smell is a potent wizard that transports us across a
thousand miles and all the years we have lived.
Helen Keller

What are some of your favorite smells? Cookies in the oven, curry on the stovetop, fresh flowers in a vase? Smell has a powerful effect on us, impacting our mood, concentration, and anxiety and stress levels.[61] A number of scents have been proven to relieve stress or anxiety: bergamot, geranium, sweet basil, frankincense, clary sage, rosemary, and peppermint. And others have been shown to help calm and relax us: lavender, chamomile, vanilla, lemon, jasmine, rose, cinnamon, vetiver, and ylang-ylang.[62]

Our sense of smell is connected to memory and emotion. You can find yourself thinking of a memory you haven't thought of in years because of something you smelled.[63] So you might think back to some of your most comforting or calming memories and see if any scents are associated with them.

Use your sense of smell to your advantage. Whether you diffuse oils, light candles, whip up something in your kitchen, walk in an outdoor area scented by plants, or get a whiff of something lovely another way, take some moments to really enjoy those smells. Notice how different scents affect you and continually come back to the ones that calm you.

God, help me experience more calmness through what I choose to smell.

The Sense of Touch

To touch can be to give life.
Michelangelo

You can't get a back rub or take a bath without feeling different afterward. Whenever you come into contact with something or someone, there's an effect.

Researchers have found that sports teams that habitually give each other high-fives and hugs perform better. Student participation improves when teachers give an encouraging pat on the back or arm. And people in stressful situations have had their blood pressure and heart rate go down because of a loved one holding their hand or hugging them.[64] Touch makes a difference. And it's no wonder—our skin is our body's largest organ. It's our super receptor to the world around us.[65]

We also benefit from nonhuman contact, like squeezing a stress ball or silly putty.[66] We feel the impact when we walk outside and feel fresh air on our face, grass under our feet, and sunshine warming our skin.

Be intentional about using your sense of touch to relax and be calmer. Do back and foot rubs with your family. Take a bath or go for a swim. Pull on a soft sweater and grab a fuzzy blanket. As your skin experiences these things, your brain and body will respond.

God, help me experience more calmness through my sense of touch.

The Sense of Taste

If more of us valued food and cheer and song above
hoarded gold, it would be a merrier world.
J. R. R. Tolkien

I f you could go to any restaurant, market, or kitchen and taste anything right this minute, what would it be? Freshly picked strawberries, handmade pasta, your grandma's warm bread, dark chocolate from Belgium?

God brings us joy through food. While we don't want to use it for anxiety relief to an unhealthy extent, mindfully savoring and celebrating different flavors and textures can be the calming and mood-boosting experience we need.[67]

Enjoy the go-to soothing options of hot soup and warm drinks, like milk with honey and cinnamon, or teas like chamomile and green tea. Create a list of all your favorite foods and drinks and make a point to enjoy them on a regular basis. Also be adventurous and try out new foods and drinks.

Whenever you put something in your mouth, make an effort to make it a mindful experience. Chew slowly. Think of how amazing God is to come up with all the different flavors in the world, and how some of them combine to create unique tastes. Thank Him for your thousands of tastebuds and all the gifts of the present moment.

God, help me experience more calmness through my sense of taste.

Sing Your Way to Calm and Happy

Sing to the LORD, all the earth. Sing to the LORD and
praise his name; every day tell how he saves us.
Psalm 96:1–2 NCV

I f there's a song in my head for a while, my family will inevitably hear me singing it. Sometimes I'll keep it in because I think it could be annoying, but then it's only a matter of time before I burst out with it at top volume. Their usual response is either laughing or joining in, bless them.

Did you know that singing can make us happier, more relaxed, and less anxious? Singing stimulates the vagus nerve, which activates relaxation.[68] Studies have shown that it lowers stress hormones and produces endorphins. It can be a form of meditation and a way to express our emotions, which often relieves stress. Overall, it has a "calming yet energizing effect."[69]

As if that weren't enough, it brings even more health benefits: it's good for our lungs, diaphragm, brain, circulation, and immunity. And when we sing with others, it builds our bond with them.[70]

So make a point of changing your brain and mood through singing. Don't just sing in the shower or under your breath. Sing with the people you hang out with. Join a choir. Belt out a song in the car. Find more times to use your voice and receive all those healthy effects.

Thank You, God, for making singing a way for
me to become healthier and happier.

~

Face Down Fear

Everybody has fear. And everybody gets to decide how they respond to it.

Fear wants to own you and cage you. Are you going to let it? God gives you the keys to the cage locks—the tools to fight back and knock down the barriers fear creates.

Name the fears that have been blocking your path to a freer life with more joy and strength. Identify truths to replace those fears as you put your trust in the God who is bigger than anything you'll ever face.

Fear Is Not from God

There is no fear in love. But perfect love drives out fear.
1 John 4:18

Adam and Eve were happy in the garden—totally content, at peace, and close with God. Then sin entered the picture.

They made clothes for themselves and hid from God. So He called out to them; He wanted them to come close. Eventually Adam explained, "I heard you in the garden, and I was afraid because I was naked; so I hid" (Genesis 3:10).

Sin opened the door to debilitating problems: self-consciousness, insecurity, fear. Adam and Eve felt scared of the world and God and didn't think they could be close to Him.

That fear became the template for every human's experience. When we become aware of our weakness, our sin, and external dangers, we become afraid. But there's something we must remember: Fear doesn't come from God. It's a result of our distance from Him and lack of trust in Him. Scripture shows that God repels fear: "God is love. . . . Love drives out fear" (1 John 4:8, 18).

Dear one, God didn't create you to be a slave to fear. He has something far grander and more beautiful for you. He's calling out to you now, beckoning you to come closer. *Let Me bring you out of fear and into the light with Me.*

God, I'm so grateful that You do not intend fear for me.

Calm, Freedom, and Strength

Where the Spirit of the Lord is, there is freedom.
2 Corinthians 3:17

Apart from God, we have reason to fear. But with Him, it's a whole different story. His power is greater than anything we face and His good gifts overwhelm every threat and fear. *He is the game-changer.*

Picture Jesus standing on the boat telling the wind and waves, "Quiet! Be still!" (Mark 4:39). He can do the same for your heart. If you let Him, "He will calm all your fears" (Zephaniah 3:17 NLT).

Jesus gives freedom and strength. He provided a spirit not of fear but of "power and love and self-control" (2 Timothy 1:7 NCV). And He gives peace. He told His disciples, "I am leaving you with a gift—peace of mind and heart. And the peace I give is a gift the world cannot give. So don't be troubled or afraid" (John 14:27 NLT).

You are human—so yes, you've made mistakes and have limitations. You live with uncertainty and potential dangers. But none of those things keep God from being who He is or from giving what He gives.

He is the Almighty who makes peace possible. So run to Him and trust Him so He can calm and steady you.

I praise You because You and Your gifts change everything, God.

A Fortress of Stability

God is in the midst of her; she shall not be moved; God will help
her when morning dawns. . . . The God of Jacob is our fortress.
Psalm 46:5, 7 ESV

You know those moments when you feel unsteady—those times when the foundations of your life are changing? How about the moments when you fear that you'll never feel steady again?

Psalm 46 was written for those moments.

It's all about God's stability, how it never changes and how He gives it to His people. The world, your life, and your heart will experience huge ups and downs, but He will remain firm and constant. When you turn your awareness to His presence and give room for Him to dwell in your heart, like He dwelled in Jerusalem, you will know Him as the great protector and provider. It could be said of you, "God is within her, she will not fall." "God will help her at break of day."

Mountains could slip away. Nations could rise in uproar and fall apart. The structure of your life could collapse. What then? The Lord Almighty will be your fortress.

Listen close here. No matter what is happening around you, God can make your heart strong and your mind steady. He can release the grip fear has on you and bring you relief, stability, and hope.

He's right here, right now, ready to be your all in all.

Almighty God, I want to live in the stability of Your presence
and let the awareness of Your power overcome my fear.

"Don't Be Afraid"

"Don't be afraid," he said. "Take courage. I am here!"
Matthew 14:27 NLT

The disciples were out on a boat at night without Jesus when they saw a figure headed toward them, walking along the surface of the water. "It's a ghost!" they cried out in fear. But Jesus calmed them. "Don't be afraid," He said. "Take courage. I am here!"

In the Sermon on the Mount, Jesus said, "Don't be afraid; you are worth more than many sparrows" (Matthew 10:31), reassuring His listeners that they were known and valued. "Have courage, son! Your sins are forgiven," He told a paralyzed man just before healing him (Matthew 9:2 NET). And time after time in Scripture when an angel of the Lord appeared to someone, the angel said, "Don't be afraid."

This is a constant message from our God. Often after He says, "Don't be afraid," He gives a reason—Himself. "I'm here. I'll be with you. I'll provide. I'm what you need." He sees what we're up against, and He knows His own capabilities and love. His conclusion is: "Fear is not necessary, nor is it My desire for you."

His message hasn't changed, dear one. It wasn't just for earlier generations, because He doesn't change. He knows we get afraid, so He directs us away from it. "Trust in Me," He says. "I'm right here, and I'm not going anywhere. Let Me help you live with courage."

Make Your words settle into my heart, Lord.
Lead me out of fear and into courage.

Courage and Peace

"Why are you frightened?" he asked. "Why
are your hearts filled with doubt?"
Luke 24:38 NLT

After Jesus' resurrection He appeared to the disciples, and they were terrified. When He saw their fear, He asked, "Why are you filled with fear and doubt?"

It was similar to His response to their fear on the boat in the wild storm. After He calmed it, He asked, "You of little faith, why are you so afraid?" (Matthew 8:26).

Behind His words I hear, *Just how good and powerful do you think I am, anyway? How small have I become in your mind?*

Jesus makes it clear that we have more reason to be full of courage and peace than we do with fear and doubt. He proves Himself as the good, loving King over and over.

Our fear is saying, *I know what I can sense, and I sense trouble. I'm not sure I can trust God to be good, to be present, to help. I'm not even sure He's in control anymore.*

What does Jesus tell us to do instead? "Don't let your hearts be troubled. Trust in God" (John 14:1 NCV). Remember that "with God all things are possible" (Matthew 19:26).

I believe and trust You, God. Fill my heart with courage and peace.

A Child of God, Not a Slave to Fear

The Spirit we received does not make us slaves again to fear; it
makes us children of God. With that Spirit we cry out, "Father."
Romans 8:15 NCV

W hat if the worst happens? What if there's failure or suffering
ahead? What if people see the real me and reject me? What if
God rejects me?

When thoughts like these guide us, we put on masks and become
isolated. But God's message throughout Scripture is, "Don't be afraid.
I know you and love you. I've made a way for us to be close forever.
Come into the light." There was a broken relationship, but His love
reached across.

We think our biggest problems are what we fear, but they're
actually a lack of trust in His love and power, and a belief that our
brokenness keeps us from Him. His arms of acceptance and strength
are open wide. He is always there for us and loving us.

That's why it's our job to follow Hebrews 10:21–23: "Since we
have a great priest over God's house, let us come near to God with
a sincere heart and a sure faith. . . . we can trust God to do what he
promised" (NCV).

Whatever you face, face it *with* Him and *believing in* Him.

Father, I believe You've made me Your child and freed
me from fear. So now I draw near and trust.

Stare That Fear Down

You want me to be completely truthful.
Psalm 51:6 NCV

W hat are your fears? Is it easy for you to name them? Or do you generally try not to look directly at them?

Be brave. Be brutally honest. Try listing them.

Next, try to understand why you fear them. Do they have links to your past? How do they connect to any of your assumptions or beliefs about yourself, the world, or God?

Many of us are living with unresolved pain or old mindsets that have been passed to us from others—family, friends, teachers, society, media. Maybe you're carrying secrets or shame. Know that you get to choose what you do with those things. You can say, "It stops here. It stops now. I will seek healing and fight for a new mindset."

When we name our fears and the issues associated with them, they often feel less powerful—especially when we do it with others. They might say, "I get that. I've felt that way too." They might even look at Scripture with you. God can use them to show you His acceptance and grace, His comfort and care, His power and truth.

So get honest with yourself, with God, and with others. Bring all your fears and unresolved issues into the light. Open your heart to God's transformative power and His Spirit of healing.

Lord, give me the courage to name and understand my
fears and listen to what You have to say about them.

Pray About Your Fears

The LORD is close to everyone who prays to
him, to all who truly pray to him.
Psalm 145:18 NCV

W hen the time for the cross was coming closer, Jesus was "deeply distressed and horrified"—so He "fell to the ground" and prayed (Mark 14:33, 35 HCSB).

He began with "Abba, Father," showing honor for God and inti-macy with Him. Jesus expressed trust: "Everything is possible for you" (v. 36). Then He made His request and submitted to the Father's will.

Jesus is our model, our example to follow in everything. When we're afraid we can run to our Father and press into Him, like we're burying our face in His neck. "Because we are his children, God has sent the Spirit of his Son into our hearts, prompting us to call out, 'Abba, Father'" (Galatians 4:6 NLT). We can come to Him with abso-lute vulnerability and trust; this is part of what it means to be His children.

So when fear pops up, don't sit back and let it take over. Run to your Helper. Face it with Him! He's ready and able to help you. "When his people pray for help, he listens and rescues them from their troubles. The LORD is there to rescue all who are discouraged and have given up hope" (Psalm 34:17–18 CEV).

Whenever fear comes up and I'm looking at something
daunting, Lord, I'll face it with You.

God Helps Us Move Through Fear

"I am the LORD your God who takes hold of your right
hand and says to you, Do not fear; I will help you."
Isaiah 41:13

E lijah was a courageous guy; he had no problem confronting leaders who'd turned Israel against God. He'd showcased God's power when He threw down fire from the sky and the false god Baal didn't. But when the evil queen threatened to kill him, as she had so many others, Elijah fled—and spiraled into despair. "'I have had enough, LORD,' he said, 'Take my life'" (1 Kings 19:4).

God didn't say, "If you say so . . ." and turn His back on him. He took care of Elijah and helped him move through his fear. God gave him food, drink, rest, and time.

After Elijah took a forty-day journey to God's mountain, God invited Elijah to open up. He listened and revealed Himself to Elijah in a gentle whisper. He made it clear that Elijah was not in this alone and that He would guide him. He gave Elijah clear next steps—anoint and activate two people who would help remove Baal worship. He revealed there were seven thousand people in Israel who were still loyal to Him. And so Elijah started moving in this new direction.

When fear made Elijah run and shut down, God restored, empowered, and redirected him. He'll do the same for you.

God, You're so gentle and caring, so strong and wise. I'm
counting on You to help me move through my fear.

Don't Let Feelings Be the Boss

We live by what we believe, not by what we can see.
2 Corinthians 5:7 NCV

How are you feeling right now? And yesterday and last week? Odds are you didn't feel exactly the same all of those times. Feelings come and go. Acknowledge and move through them, but don't put them in charge. They're fleeting reactions, not guiding truths.

Anchor yourself to what God says is true, and know that's not always going to line up with what you see and feel. Live by what you *believe*. Keep your heart from being troubled by believing Him. He's working to protect, help, and provide for you. You can't see all the good He's doing, but you can trust He's doing it.

There was a time when a massive army was positioned to capture the prophet Elisha. When his servant saw them, he got really scared. But Elisha told him, "Don't panic. Our army is way bigger." This made no sense to the guy—until Elisha prayed for the servant's eyes to be opened. Then he "saw the hills full of horses and chariots of fire all around Elisha" (2 Kings 6:17). God's army stood ready to fight on their behalf.

If your circumstances have you bouncing from confusion to anger to fear, remember that God is working in invisible ways. Hold on to His promises and truth instead of just what you see and feel in the moment. Trust Him to be your powerful, ever-present Helper.

Lord, I want what You say—not my feelings—to guide me.

Focus on Truth

Take the sword of the Spirit, which is the word of God.
Ephesians 6:17 NCV

God's Word is a weapon He gave us to overcome all the crazy stuff we encounter. So when you're facing a fear, meet it with truth.

It feels like I'm on my own. "The Father . . . will give you another Helper to be with you forever" (John 14:16 NCV).

What if something terrible happens? "Neither death nor life . . . neither the present nor the future, nor any powers . . . will be able to separate us from the love of God" (Romans 8:38–39).

I can't handle how hard this is. "We overwhelmingly conquer through Him who loved us" (Romans 8:37 NASB).

I'll never recover from what I've been through. "The people who trust the LORD will become strong again" (Isaiah 40:31 NCV).

Darkness is taking over the world. "The God of peace will soon crush Satan under your feet" (Romans 16:20).

God is holding out on me. "Don't be afraid, little flock. For it gives your Father great happiness to give you the Kingdom" (Luke 12:32 NLT).

Don't go in circles dwelling on your fears. Focus on what you know is true and put your hope in God. Keep looking at and listening to the Mighty One. He's with you and always will be.

Spirit of God, use the Word of God to overcome my fear.

The Wrong Focus Sinks Us

Peter got down out of the boat, walked on the water and
came toward Jesus. But when he saw the wind, he was
afraid and, beginning to sink, cried out, "Lord, save me!"
Matthew 14:29–30

When Jesus walked on water toward the disciples' boat, He invited Peter to join Him. Brave Peter, believing Jesus' power, raised his foot out of the boat and bore all his weight down. He started walking on water too, taking one step after another toward Jesus.

Then his focus changed. He noticed the wind. He looked at the waves around him. He became afraid—and began to sink.

This is what we do. We see the danger that could overtake us and fix our eyes on its power. We sense our own lack of power, get overwhelmed, and just lose it.

Peter cried out to Jesus, and He immediately caught him. "'You of little faith,' he said, 'why did you doubt?'" (Matthew 14:31). Jesus' power had been right there, on display, yet Peter looked away from it.

Peter's act of belief is our goal. But his wavering focus? That's our warning.

No one and nothing has power like our God. If we keep looking at problems and threats, we're going to sink. But if we fix our eyes on the Powerful One, we'll get to live and move in His power.

Help me, Lord, to live with big faith—with
my eyes on You and Your power.

Stick to Facts and Faith

"Don't be upset, and don't let all these doubting questions
take over. Look at my hands; look at my feet—it's
really me. Touch me. Look me over from head to toe.
A ghost doesn't have muscle and bone like this."
Luke 24:38–39 MSG

Sometimes we put our imaginations to work creating a terrifying future for ourselves. We have to stop ourselves from magnifying our fears and instead stick to facts and faith.

What is good and right in your life? What are some ways you're strong and supported right now? Notice what's in front of you.

Jesus prompted the disciples to do something like this when they were freaking out about seeing Him after the resurrection. They thought they were seeing a ghost, so He turned their focus to facts: "Here, look at My hands and feet. Touch Me. See for yourself that I'm real and alive." They could have just closed their eyes and backed away, determined to believe they were in a horror movie. But they let Jesus lead them away from that.

Don't live in an imagined worst-case scenario. Live where you are today. God will give you the resources you need for tomorrow.

He says, "Be brave, not afraid." So don't let bleak imaginings take over your mind. Keep trusting.

Lord, anchor me in the present, in reality, and in You.

Shift from Fear to Trust

I cry out to God Most High, to God who
will fulfill his purpose for me.
Psalm 57:2 NLT

David had a target on his back. Saul was out for his blood. When Saul sent men to stake out David's house so they could kill him, David turned to God: "Protect me from those who rise up against me. . . . O my Strength, I will watch for you. . . . My God in his steadfast love will meet me. . . . I will sing praises to you, for you, O God, are my fortress" (Psalm 59:1, 9–10, 17 ESV).

Later David fled from Saul and found himself in Philistine territory, Goliath's homeland—yet another dangerous place for him. He prayed, "When I am afraid, I will put my trust in you. . . . You keep track of all my sorrows. . . . This I know: God is on my side! . . . You have rescued me from death; you have kept my feet from slipping. So now I can walk in your presence, O God, in your life-giving light" (Psalm 56:3, 8–9, 13 NLT).

The Spirit consistently directed David's heart away from fear and into trust, praise, and closeness with God. And it all started with David opening up to God and responding to who He is. Follow David's lead. Ask the Spirit to lead you into trust.

God, help me open up to You, hear You, respond to You, and trust You.

When You're Afraid, Praise Him

I will always trust in God's unfailing love. I will praise you forever,
O God, for what you have done. I will trust in your good name.
Psalm 52:8–9 NLT

W hen fear rises up in you, praise your God.
Pick a worship song and sing to Him. Talk to Him. Tell Him
how faithful, how mighty, how glorious He is.

When you don't know what to do, when you feel lost and afraid,
you raise your voice to Him. You tell Him how good He is. You say
how much you trust and love Him.

If you feel shaky or unsteady or as though you need to cry, then
turn your face to Him. "Let your tears flow. . . . Pour out your heart
like water in prayer to the Lord. Lift up your hands in prayer to him."
And then say, "The LORD's love never ends; his mercies never stop.
They are new every morning" (Lamentations 2:18–19; 3:22–23 NCV).

No matter where you are, bring your heart to Him. Think about
how beautiful and strong He is. Thank Him for all He's done. You
may be fearful, but you've got reasons to praise Him and hope in
Him. Remind yourself of His trustworthiness. Focus on connection
with Him.

You're always good and beautiful, God, so I
can always trust You and praise You.

Imagine Your Good God with You

Be strong and courageous. . . . The LORD himself goes
before you and will be with you; he will never leave you nor
forsake you. Do not be afraid; do not be discouraged.
Deuteronomy 31:7–8

H ave you ever noticed that in our worst-case scenarios, we're usually alone and helpless? We've morphed into a version of ourselves with no God-given resources, and God is nowhere to be seen. It's silly and ridiculous. Yet in our imagining, it feels awfully realistic.

Try to stop yourself from doing this. If you entertain negative possibilities for your future, don't leave God out of them. Think how He'd equip you with the resources you'd need—like He has for His people throughout history. Imagine how He'd carry you, strengthen you, and guide you, how He'd come close and walk you through each moment.

Help yourself do this by continually soaking in who He is and remembering what He's done. Praise Him and enjoy Him instead of freaking yourself out. Focus on His promises more than your fears.

You don't have to make the unknowns of your life dark or assume you can't bear what they hold. Think who is holding your future! The God of good surprises, the God of beauty and power. There's plenty about the future we don't know, but we do know this: He's making it bright, and He's not going anywhere.

Who You are today is who You'll be tomorrow. I'm
so grateful that You'll never leave me, God!

Rehearse Trust in Your Deliverer

When I am afraid, I will put my trust in you. I
praise God for what he has promised.
Psalm 56:3–4 NLT

B ree was stuck in a pattern of fear. She had been in a terrible car accident, and months later she still felt scared every time she drove.

After she talked with friends about it, they prayed with her and reminded her that God didn't want her to be controlled by fear. "Pray like David when he said, 'Rise up, O God, and scatter your enemies. . . . Blow them away like smoke' [Psalm 68:1–2 NLT]. Keep turning to Him for help!"

So when Bree felt calm, she began rehearsing what she'd do when the fear popped up. She said things like, *When I'm afraid, I'll trust in You. You steady me and counsel me with Your loving eye on me (Psalm 32:8). My hope is in You, God. Come blow away my fear like smoke.*

Practicing the mindset of trust *before* the fear kicked in helped Bree; soon she was calm behind the wheel again.

Think about how you can rehearse trust like this. Envision what the calm, trusting version of you would look like. Pray about it all and connect with God *now* so you can more easily reconnect to Him later, when fear shows up.

Deliver me from a spirit of defeat and fear, Lord. Lead
me into a mindset of faith, resolve, and courage.

A Mighty Rock and a Steadfast Mind

Those of steadfast mind you keep in peace—in peace
because they trust in you. Trust in the LORD forever,
for in the LORD GOD you have an everlasting rock.
Isaiah 26:3–4 NRSV

Sydney lost her job. Jake was diagnosed with cancer. Ruby's son is battling an addiction. Simon's seeing signs of what could become another pandemic.

These difficult moments, when the foundation of our lives starts to crack and tremble, are part of life. But when our eyes are on God and we trust Him completely, it's as though a mighty rock comes up out of the shaky ground and gives us a stable surface where we can plant our feet.

This is why David said, "You make my lot secure. . . . I will praise the LORD, who counsels me. . . . I keep my eyes always on the LORD. With him at my right hand, I will not be shaken" (Psalm 16:5, 7–8). And, "When besieged, I'm calm as a baby. When all hell breaks loose, I'm collected and cool. . . . Stay with GOD! Take heart. Don't quit" (Psalm 27:3, 14 MSG).

Even if things get really bad, God can be our rock, peace, and hope. He's always loving, powerful, and present. He'll lift us up and stabilize us as we trust in Him.

Lord, make me steady and strong as I stay close to You and trust You.

Strengthened by Love to Endure

Anyone who meets a testing challenge head-on and manages
to stick it out is mighty fortunate. For such persons loyally
in love with God, the reward is life and more life.
James 1:12 MSG

J esus said we'll have trouble in this world, but we often forget that. We feel thrown when hard stuff shows up out of nowhere.

But God doesn't want us paralyzed in fear. He wants us moving forward with full confidence in His ability to help us.

And don't forget that God makes trials function as transformers: "The testing of your faith produces perseverance" and spiritual maturity (James 1:2–4). Every time you turn to God and depend on Him, your faith gets stronger.

Helen Keller said, "We could never learn to be brave and patient if there were only joy in the world."[1] And John Bunyan wrote, "Afflictions . . . make the heart more deep, more experimental, more knowing and profound, and so more able to hold, contain, and bear more."[2]

Keep exercising and growing your faith as you confront fear and endure difficulties. Say, "My God loves me, and he goes in front of me" (Psalm 59:10 NCV).

God, I believe You're able to strengthen me
to endure anything in my future.

Why Be Afraid of People?

I trust in God, so why should I be afraid?
What can mere mortals do to me?
Psalm 56:4 NLT

C orinne feels as though she can never win with the people in her life. Her siblings criticize her. Her friends exclude her. Her coworkers are cold. She's always bracing herself for the next time she'll feel slighted and wondering how she can change these dynamics.

People can intimidate us, put us down, and belittle us. They can size us up and decide not to accept us. Their behavior can influence how we live and how we see ourselves. Before we know it, we can find ourselves controlled by the fear of what their reactions to us will be.

People are going to do what they're going to do, but they don't decide who you are. They don't determine your worth. You are not living unto them; you are living unto the One who created and designed you with joy, who accepts you in His grace.

He says, "I am the one who comforts you. So why should you be afraid of people, who die? . . . Have you forgotten the LORD who made you? . . . I will cover you with my hands and protect you" (Isaiah 51:12–13, 16 NCV).

Don't forget your Comforter. Make Him the authority and guide of your life.

God, I'm defined by what You say, not what others
say, and by how You love, not by others' choices.

Push Away Fears

If we did all the things we are capable of, we
would literally astound ourselves.
Thomas A. Edison

D o you ever think that your weaknesses and failures will keep you from doing what you're meant to do in life? One man had reason to feel that way.

He didn't do well in most school subjects and failed college entrance exams twice. After working with a tutor, he tried a third time and passed.[3] He dealt with depression and had a lisp but still pursued a career in politics.[4] He lost five elections.[5]

Did any of these issues shut him down? Nope. Even with these shortcomings and setbacks, Winston Churchill became one of the most successful political leaders of the twentieth century.

Fear will say you're not good enough. But you have to say no to fear with confidence—refuse to let it diminish your view of who you are and who you can become.

God made you so you could pursue the works He's called you to. Some failure along the way isn't going to change that.

God is able to empower you to grow and be resilient. Don't underestimate Him! So push fear out of the way and be brave.

Empower me, Lord, to say no to fear and to grow and be persistent.

Be One Who Says, "God Can"

God is looking for those with whom He can do
the impossible—what a pity that we plan only
the things that we can do by ourselves.
A. W. Tozer

G od promised to give the Israelites a new homeland, rich with resources and beauty. He was super clear: "I'm giving the land of Canaan to you."

He sent twelve spies to check out the land so they could report back to the group. Ten of them said, "The land is amazing, but there's *no way* we could defeat them. The cities are fortified, and the people are big and powerful—too strong for us!"

The other two spies, Caleb and Joshua, disagreed. They saw the same things the others did, but they added more to it: *God.* "We should attack now and take the land; we are strong enough to conquer it" (Numbers 13:30 GNT).

All of Israel was gripped with fear, crying, "If only we'd died earlier! Why is God sending us into battle to die? We should just go back to Egypt!" It grieved God's heart. The people chose doubt and fear, so they didn't enter the promised land; the next generation did, with Caleb and Joshua.

Are you facing something scary? Don't just think of what you can do. Think of what God can do.

I want to follow my faith, not my fear, God.

Money Is a Bad Master

*"No one can serve two masters. Either you will hate the one
and love the other, or you will be devoted to the one and
despise the other. You cannot serve both God and money."*
Matthew 6:24

Money is one of life's biggest stressors. Do we have enough? How will we use it? How will we get more? It's essential in life—we must earn and steward it—yet it can really mess with our priorities.

The problem comes when we treat money like a master, not a tool. Money doesn't love you or have good purposes in mind for you. It can't satisfy you. If you pursue it, you'll never feel as though you have enough. It's unpredictable and it lets you down. If we're relying on something so fleeting, then we have a lot to be fearful about.

But Jesus pointed us toward the Good Master—the One who loves us, has good purposes in mind for us, and satisfies us. "Do not worry about your life. . . . Is not life more than food, and the body more than clothes?" (Matthew 6:25). Put your trust in God, Jesus was saying. Don't let money issues distract you from what matters most.

In Hebrews we read, "Keep your lives free from the love of money and be content with what you have, because God has said, 'Never will I leave you; never will I forsake you'" (13:5). We belong to the God who reigns over money and *the whole world*. He is with us and taking care of us.

God, You reign over all things and You are my good provider.

Stubborn Much?

"The minds of these people have become stubborn. They do not hear with their ears, and they have closed their eyes."
Matthew 13:15 NCV

M argo was reeling from a painful breakup and hearing rumors that her employer would be downsizing. Her emotions were running to the extremes—panicked, heartbroken, hopeless.

"You'll find another job, and you'll meet someone else," her family told her. But Margo shut her ears to their words. And she couldn't bring herself to think about Scripture or talk with God. Withdrawing from everyone, she kept envisioning a future of being alone and jobless.

We can understand how she got there, right? But even when we're hurting and afraid, we get to make choices, and those choices have results. If we're stuck on our own perspective and feelings, we'll close the curtains on the light of God's Spirit.

Jesus experienced anguish and fear, but there's no account of Him saying, "Not now, Father. I can't talk to You or hear from You. My feelings are too overwhelming." No—He'd actually run to His Father with those feelings.

You do the same. No matter how bad your situation or feelings are, don't stubbornly close yourself off from Him. Listen to Him and let Him take care of you.

I want to keep my heart soft and open to You, Father.
I'm listening. I trust You more than my feelings.

Moses' New Job

"Now go; I will help you speak and will teach you what to say."
Exodus 4:12

When God told Moses his new job was to bring the Israelites out of Egypt, Moses was *all fear*. Their conversation from Exodus 3:11–4:7 went something like this:

MOSES: "Who am I to do this? I'm one hundred percent unqualified."

GOD: "I'll be with you. I'm all you need."

MOSES: "Who would I say sent me? How would I even go about this?"

GOD: "Tell them I AM sent you."

MOSES: "What if people don't believe me or take me seriously?"

GOD: "I'll show My power through you."

MOSES: "I'm always tripping over my words. Again—totally inadequate!"

GOD: "Again—I'll be with you. I'll help you and guide your words."

Moses came up with every excuse not to leave his comfort zone. But God turned this timid man into Israel's bold leader.

Are there hard things ahead of you? God can empower you to do them. Say yes and rely on Him as you move forward in His direction for you.

Lord, I don't want my fear to keep me from saying
yes to You. Do Your will through me.

Put Him Above It All

*"These are the people I am pleased with: those who are
not proud or stubborn and who fear my word."*
Isaiah 66:2 NCV

Over and over God tells His people not to be afraid. But there is one fear He says we *should* live with: the fear of Him.

Jesus said, "Don't be afraid of those who want to kill your body; they cannot touch your soul. Fear only God" (Matthew 10:28 NLT). This is a mindset that elevates God over all of it and takes Him most seriously.

When we are seized with fear, we need to get honest about a few things: *Have I blown up this thing I'm fearing so much that it has become bigger than God in my mind? What does He say about it?*

At the burning bush Moses displayed a lot of fear about things *other* than God—his own inadequacy and worst-case scenarios. But after more encounters with God, Moses changed. He became more focused on God's power and perfect will and began revering Him most. Moses went on to do extraordinary things as God worked in and through him.

As our view of God and reverence for Him increases, we'll care more about exalting Him than avoiding difficulty. We'll be quick to say, *Come, Lord, have Your way and Your glory in my life.*

God, You are more powerful and important than anything I fear.

Surrender

*I trust in you, LORD; I say, "You are my
God." My times are in your hands.*
Psalm 31:14–15

Audra lives with an illness that puts her life at risk. With the
help of her doctors, she's currently doing well—she's busy and
productive as a working mom. But she lives with the possibility that
the illness could get the better of her at any point, with no warning.

Henry's parents died in a plane crash, and every time his wife steps
on a plane, he thinks, *I might lose her too.*

Zeke's job is in danger of going away because of a recession.

Many things in our lives are out of our control, which can drive
us *nuts.* Our fear about those things can rule us—or it can make us
aware of our need for God, who can handle the big things we can't.
We need to pray about those things we can't control and then resolve
that we won't obsess and stress over them anymore.

Okay, but how do we get there?

We remind ourselves: God is on His throne and trustworthy. He
will work things out for good, even in ways we can't imagine. And no
matter what happens, He's our ever-present Helper.

Because of this we can say, *I don't have to know what's coming. I
will trust the One who is running the universe.*

*I'm alive to love, trust, and worship You,
God—help me make that my focus.*

Bravery Means Doing It Afraid

When we are called to obey, the fear does not
subside and we are expected to move against
the fear. One must choose to do it afraid.
Elisabeth Elliot

S erena is about to initiate a difficult conversation with a family member. Jack's on his way to his seventh chemo treatment. Addie's gearing up to confront her bullyish coworker.

Each of them is feeling fear. Each of them is moving forward anyway.

Eleanor Roosevelt said, "You gain strength, courage, and confidence by each experience in which you really stop to look fear in the face. . . . *You must do that which you think you cannot do.*"[6]

If you have to do a good thing afraid, that's okay. That's called bravery.

When in your life have you done this? Think about that brave version of yourself and remember that you can be brave again—even if you don't feel that way right now.

Whatever hard thing you're looking at, think about why you're doing it. If it's the right thing, it's worth it. Go ahead and do it afraid.

I won't insist on staying comfortable, God. Even if I'm
afraid, I'll do the hard, right thing to honor You.

Fight and Throw Off Fear

Fight the good fight of the faith.
1 Timothy 6:12

I magine a woman on an important mission. After traveling through mountains and crossing rivers, she is now facing a dark, dangerous forest.

She steps in and looks around, alert and on guard. Moving swiftly, she makes good progress, hearing only the sound of her own footsteps. And then she hears hissing. Ten snakes come flying out of the trees and wrap themselves around her body. Instead of panicking, she methodically grabs each one and hurls them away.

Then a hooded figure seizes her. She wriggles herself free, ninja-kicks him several times, then runs as fast as she can out of that forest and all the way to her destination.

Fear is something we have to fight. We need to grab it and hurl it far away from us. We have to ninja-kick it and escape it. We have to say, "No way. You are not stopping me from living out my purpose. God, who's alive in me, is more powerful than you."

This is part of our life of faith, and we have an active role in it: "Let us throw off everything that hinders and . . . run with perseverance the race marked out for us, fixing our eyes on Jesus" (Hebrews 12:1–2). Be resolute. Decide that fear won't get the better of you today.

God, give me the courage and power to fight and throw off fear today.

A Spirit of Confidence

My heart is confident in you, O God.
Psalm 57:7 NLT

A re you dreading the future or anticipating it with hope and joy? If you imagine difficulties ahead, is it with a spirit of defeat because of a lack of resources, or a spirit of confidence because you know who will be with you?

Fear will rear its ugly head, but you decide what you do with it. You can think, *Nothing is too hard for Him (Jeremiah 32:17). Nothing can overpower His love. Whatever happens, nothing will come between us. "The LORD is with me; I will not be afraid" (Psalm 118:6).*

Fight your fears so you can step into the abundant life God has for you. Make every effort to give Him your attention. Ask the Spirit to give you a strong and peaceful heart that has confidence in Him.

"The person who trusts in the LORD will be blessed," Jeremiah wrote. "The LORD will show him that he can be trusted. He will be strong, like a tree planted near water that sends its roots by a stream. It is not afraid when the days are hot; its leaves are always green. It does not worry in a year when no rain comes; it always produces fruit" (Jeremiah 17:7–8 NCV).

Put your trust in your Creator and Sustainer. He's at work now and He'll be at work later.

*I can live with courage and confidence because
I'm with You. You are amazing, God!*

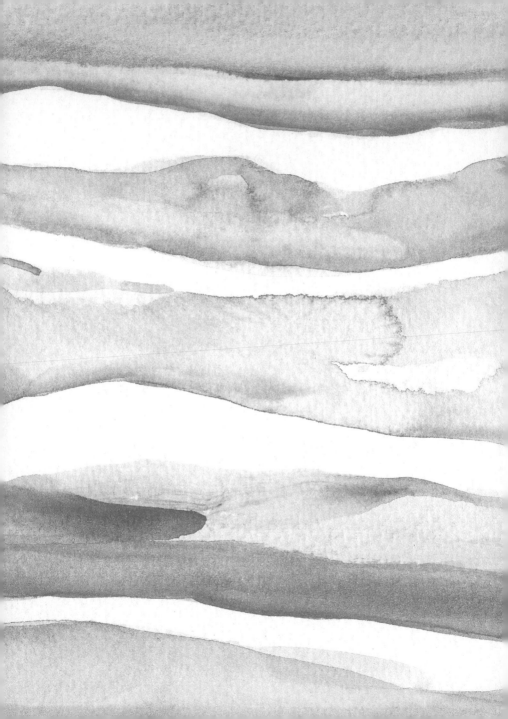

~

Be with Your People

God designed you to need other people.
Yes, relationships are hard. Yes, people are flawed. But God still works through them. So don't push people away; keep them close.

Find people you can count on and be open with, people you can learn from and experience the love of God with. Bring them into your life and build your connection with them. Be present and available. Encourage and build each other up. Hope and pray together. Draw near to God and live in His love together.

Made for Relationship

God said, "Let us make mankind in our image, in our likeness."
Genesis 1:26

Y ou were not created to live in isolation. And is it any surprise? Think who designed you—a God who is Father, Son, and Holy Spirit. The Trinity is eternally joyful and loving in Their relationships, and you were made in Their image.

It wasn't long after God created Adam that He said, "It is not good for the man to be alone" (Genesis 2:18). And after this we see story after story in Scripture of people in relationships: marriages, families, communities, nations. People doing life together.

God created a people for Himself and gave them a whole way of life that would reflect His character. He came to earth Himself to build His kingdom and bring more and more people together in His love. He set up the church as His own body, a way for Him to be present and move and work in the world.

Even though relationships bring challenges, you know in your soul that it's not good for you to do life alone. In a culture that is increasingly pushing us toward isolation, we have to remember this and prioritize living in connection with others.

So the next time you have a chance to connect with someone, say yes. Put the time and effort in. Remember you're made for connecting.

God, thank You for making me in Your image! Show
me how to live the way You designed me to.

God's Spirit via Community

If we love one another, God lives in us and
his love is made complete in us.
1 John 4:12

When in your life have you felt most known, accepted, and loved? Take a minute to remember exactly what you experienced and how it made you feel.

The heart of God was in those experiences. He was using other people to help you receive His love and strength. The God of the universe could choose to live only in fancy temples, but instead He lives in flawed people. He works through messy relationships. He uses a network of them to reach our hearts and work among us. He makes them pathways of grace.

You need people because they help you experience God. As God lives in us, we help each other grow and transform, becoming emotionally healed and spiritually mature. He uses us to pull each other back into the light when we find ourselves in darkness. We are His body on earth, and "as each part does its own special work, it helps the other parts grow, so that the whole body is healthy and growing and full of love" (Ephesians 4:16 NLT).

Do life with people who love God and who accept and love you. God wants you to be able to look at others and sense, *I am loved. I am not alone. God gives me grace, freedom, and joy.*

God, help me build relationships that become pathways of Your grace.

When You're Not Alone

Refuse to give in to [the enemy], by standing strong in your faith.
1 Peter 5:9 NCV

There's something about isolation and staying in our own heads that messes with our perspective. Questions feel heavier, shame taunts louder, and fear grips tighter. Pain seems permanent and problems look impossible.

But when we bring other people into it, we see things differently: our issues aren't nearly as dark and hopeless as we thought.

The Enemy wants to get us isolated so that we forget all about God. After Peter told believers, "Cast all your anxiety on him because he cares for you," he said, "Be alert and of sober mind. Your enemy the devil prowls around like a roaring lion looking for someone to devour. Resist him, standing firm in the faith, because you know that the family of believers throughout the world is undergoing the same kind of sufferings" (1 Peter 5:7–9). This is absolutely related to issues of anxiety. We need to draw near to God with other believers and stand firm in our faith together.

Reach out for the support of God's family. Trust Him to work through your relationships to make you courageous, guide you with truth and wisdom, and strengthen you with His presence.

God, help me stay close to people who connect me to
truth, and help us stand firm in our faith in You.

Friendship Refreshes the Soul

Just as lotions and fragrance give sensual delight,
a sweet friendship refreshes the soul.
Proverbs 27:9 MSG

When I'm stressed and anxious, I sometimes have an instinct to distance myself from people. I am totally worse off when I withdraw. I need people, perhaps even more so when I'm stressed and anxious. They refresh my soul and bring me strengthening joy.

You don't have to be outgoing, love parties, or have forty friends. A few close friends and family members can make all the difference in your overall health and joy levels. People help us feel lighter and give us perspective and a break from our thought patterns. The truest friends support us, validate us, build us up, and steer us toward truth and wisdom.

So let people in. Have regular rhythms of connection, recurring touchpoints that keep you close. Put up pictures of their faces where you'll see them when you're apart, so you can remember the joyful, strengthening bond you share. Think back to the moments with them that have been the sweetest and most encouraging to you.

Also, get intentional about being someone who refreshes other souls. Be fully engaged with the people around you. How can you make people feel seen, valued, and special? How can you help them feel supported and celebrated?

Thank You for all the sweet gifts You give us through friendship, God!

Aaron Held Up Moses' Arms

Aaron and Hur held his hands up—one on one side, one on
the other—so that his hands remained steady till sunset.
Exodus 17:12

I t was time for battle: Amalek versus Israel. Moses stood at the top of a hill nearby with the staff that had been an instrument for God's miracles. He lifted it up as a sign of reaching up for God's strength on the Israelites' behalf, knowing they could win only with God's power working through them. As long as his arms were up, the Israelites were winning, but whenever he rested them, they were losing.

So Aaron and Hur set up a stone for Moses to sit on. Then they stood on either side of him and held up his hands. Aaron and Hur shared their strength with Moses, and they stood united, appealing to God together for a bunch of desperate soldiers immersed in battle. They kept his arms steady until sunset, until the Israelites won.

There will be times when you run out of strength, and you're going to need your own Aaron and Hur to hold you up—to step in and do things to help, to pray for you and encourage you. There may be times when you need to lean on their faith when yours feels weak. This is part of being human—Scripture shows us that. So go ahead and receive support from people. Reach up to God together and ask for more of His power in your lives.

Help me accept support from others and
help us rely on Your power, God.

We Need People to Help Us See

You're going to wear yourself out—and the people, too. This
job is too heavy a burden for you to handle all by yourself.
Exodus 18:18 NLT

M oses found himself consumed with the work of a judge, listening for hours to the Israelites' issues and discerning how to
handle them. It was way too much for one person to do, and it was
keeping him from his calling: teaching the people about God's way
of life. Moses' father-in-law, Jethro, said, "This is nuts! Delegate that
work to other leaders." Moses needed someone else to help him see the
problem and the solution.

When Esther was in a position to save the lives of countless Jews,
her uncle said, "Who knows but that you have come to your royal
position for such a time as this?" (Esther 4:14). It triggered in her a
sense of purpose and courage.

We need others to help us see problems to solve, opportunities to
step into, and areas where we need to repent and be healed. Others
help us see both the good in ourselves or our situations and the areas
where we need to grow.

Remember you can't see everything you need to see on your own.
Keep your ears open to the trusted people around you. Listen for God's
leading through them.

Through the help of others, Lord, enable
me to see what You want me to.

Who Are Your People?

*Let us consider how we may spur one another
on toward love and good deeds.*
Hebrews 10:24

Y ou know you're made for relationship and you need to live life close to people. Today let's think through who your people are.

- Who helps you feel the love of God when you're around them?
- Who would you describe as positive and emotionally healthy?
- Who is responsive to your efforts to connect?
- Who listens well and is truly attentive?
- Who is authentic and vulnerable with you?
- Who offers you help, gives encouraging words, and makes you feel stronger?

The people who came to mind are probably good candidates for building connections. These are the kind of folks you want to be doing life with. If you're not close to them now, reach out.

Also consider the nature of your current closest relationships. How would you describe them—healthy or dysfunctional? Mostly uplifting or draining? Let answers to those questions dictate whether you set boundaries or maintain a strong connection in those relationships.

*Reach me through my relationships, God. Help me
see who I should surround myself with.*

God Provides People for Us

God sets the lonely in families.
Psalm 68:6

Maybe you were born into a strong support system—a tight-knit family, where everybody helps each other out. Or maybe you've developed a solid group of friends that have become like a family. Or maybe not.

It could be you've taken inventory of who you know and who you want to build connections with and have come up dry. If you feel disconnected or alone and you need a support system, run to God. He is in the business of connecting us to the people we need! He's the God who takes in the orphan, defends the widow, and sets the lonely in families. He knows you need people—He designed you that way—and He knows the people who need you.

Ask Him to provide, and look around you. Get involved at church or join a community activity, and depend on Him to lead you to new people to be close with.

If you do already have strong relationships in your life, keep an eye out for people who need a support system. Who knows, maybe they need to be part of your group of friends, and your group needs them too.

Thank You, God, for connecting me to the people I need.

Ruth and Naomi Stuck Together

Be devoted to one another in love.
Romans 12:10

N aomi, Ruth, and Orpah were grief stricken and poor. They'd all lost their husbands, and as widows they'd have a difficult time surviving. Naomi, the mother-in-law to the other two, decided to return to her homeland of Bethlehem to see if she could survive better there. She told her daughters-in-law, "Go to your mothers in your own homeland. May you find stability in a second marriage."

Orpah agreed, but Ruth didn't budge. "No. I'm sticking with you and doing life with you until I die. I'm making *your* people and God *my* people and God." Ruth could've gone her own way, but instead she committed herself to Naomi and her God. As these women stayed together and hung on to Him, He led them in rebuilding a life.

Naomi encouraged Ruth's marriage to Boaz, who also bought back land that belonged to Naomi's family. He took care of her and Naomi, and had a child with Ruth (Ruth 1–4). And it happened as the women stuck together and trusted in Him.

Whatever your situation is, remember to stick with your people. If you're not close to them right now, change that. Reach out and reconnect. Then maintain a commitment to them and to God.

God, I want to stick with my people. Help me keep them close, love and honor them, and trust You together with them.

Do Life Together

They devoted themselves to the apostles' teaching and
to fellowship, to the breaking of bread and to prayer.
Acts 2:42

The early church did life together in a big way. They hung out *a lot*. They prayed together and kept regular rhythms of worship and fellowship: "They followed a daily discipline of worship in the Temple followed by meals at home, every meal a celebration, exuberant and joyful, as they praised God" (Acts 2:46–47 MSG).

The early believers were super generous, sharing their things with each other and going out of their way to take care of people. Barnabas sold a field he owned and offered the profit to the disciples to distribute to the needy. Lydia, Priscilla, Nympha, Mary, and Philemon all invited people into their homes. Tabitha made clothes and helped the poor. They worked together to meet people's needs.

Our individualistic culture stands in stark contrast to their togetherness and others-oriented approach to life. We could do with some more of what they had, couldn't we?

Ask God how you can take a step in that direction. Invite someone to a meal. Decide you'll meet some people weekly to talk about your lives and pray. Get more involved at church. Open your home to people. Focus on God and enjoy Him with others.

Lord, help me do life with others and invite
Your Spirit to work good through us.

Benefits of Connectedness

How good and pleasant it is when God's
people live together in unity!
Psalm 133:1

I f there's anything we gained from the COVID-19 pandemic, it was a deeper understanding that isolation isn't good for us. It hurts our overall health. And the same is true in nonquarantine circumstances, when we're around people but don't feel connected to any of them.

Studies have shown something you likely know from experience: having strong social connections makes you happier.[1] But they've revealed a slew of other benefits too: connection boosts immunity, improves the ability to manage emotions, and reduces the likelihood of feeling anxious.[2] It lowers stress and helps build resilience.[3] It often causes people to be more active and avoid unhealthy behaviors like smoking.[4] It's huge for our overall health!

Here's something that won't surprise you: more and more people are experiencing loneliness due to the high use of social media. Technology is great, but be sure it doesn't keep you from getting enough in-person social time.[5]

Feeling known and supported by others, and knowing and supporting them in return, goes a *long* way toward wellness. So experience how good it is when God's people do life together.

Thank You, God, for using my relationships to
help me grow stronger and healthier.

We Carry Each Other to Jesus

They went up on the roof and lowered him on his mat through
the tiles into the middle of the crowd, right in front of Jesus.
Luke 5:19

A paralyzed man had four amazing friends—the super strong and faithful kind. One day, they did the best thing they ever could've done for him: they carried him to Jesus.

Jesus was teaching inside a building, and the crowd listening was so huge that there was no way in. But that didn't stop these guys. They got innovative, climbing up to the roof and then lowering their paralyzed friend down into the room, right in front of Jesus.

Quite the bold move! But they were motivated by compassion for their friend and by belief in Jesus. They knew he needed Him, so they did everything in their power to get him close.

"When Jesus saw their faith, he said, 'Friend, your sins are forgiven. . . . Get up, take your mat and go home'" (Luke 5:20, 24). Jesus responded to the faith of the friends.

There will be times in life when you need to carry a friend to Jesus and other times you'll need friends to carry you. Be willing to take actions of faith for others, and be honest when you need their help. We're made to need each other.

God, bring me people who will carry me to You,
and show me who I need to carry to You.

We Free and Nourish Each Other

"Take off the grave clothes and let him go."
John 11:44

L azarus was dead and in his tomb. But Jesus wanted to bring him back to life. So He told Lazarus's mourners, who were standing by the tomb, "Take away the stone" (John 11:39). Then after Lazarus walked out, He said, "Take off the grave clothes and let him go." He could have just done it all Himself, but He involved these people. They played a role in Lazarus's extraordinary experience.

Jesus did the same thing when the disciples came to Him with a big problem: thousands of hungry people in the middle of nowhere. "Send them away, so they can go buy themselves food," they told Him.

"We don't need to do that," He said. "You give them something to eat." He took the five loaves of bread and two fish they had, looked up to heaven and broke them, then gave them back to the disciples. And the disciples handed out the miraculously multiplied food to all the people (Matthew 14:15–19).

God gets people involved in what He's doing. He wants to use you to work in other people's lives and use other people to work in your life. He uses us to free and nourish each other.

So position yourself for this to happen. Be willing to get involved with others' growth and let others get involved with yours.

Lord, keep me close with others and make us alert
to Your Spirit. Use us in what You're doing.

Be Authentic and Vulnerable

If I must boast, I will boast of the things that show my weakness.
2 Corinthians 11:30

P aul talked about boasting in *weakness*. How often do you see that? Why would he do this? Because it highlighted God's strength.

It takes guts to be vulnerable and say, "Here's where I'm weak. This is how I struggle." But when we acknowledge those things, we open the door for God's power to meet us exactly where we are.

We need to do this with God in private prayer and also in our closest relationships. We need to open up and let people in so the Spirit can work through them to reach us.

Are you authentic and transparent with others? Do you invite vulnerability from them by being available, present, and accepting? The quality of your relationships depends on what you put into them. If you have the guts to be real and vulnerable, you'll be making more room for the Spirit to work.

Remember that everyone has weaknesses—you're not supposed to be free of them. You're supposed to identify them, bring them to God, and ask Him to work in and through you. Bring other people into this process so you can sense His acceptance and support. He wants to use them to help you experience His grace and power in new ways.

Help me, God, to acknowledge my weaknesses and struggles
so I can experience You more deeply with others.

Rely on Prayer

We constantly pray for you.
2 Thessalonians 1:11

W hen Jesus was preparing to face the cross, He prayed. He told His disciples to pray too.

"My heart is full of sorrow, to the point of death," He said. "Stay here and watch with me. . . . Stay awake and pray for strength" (Matthew 26:38, 40–41 NCV). He wanted their support and directed them to prayer.

God wants us to rely on prayer and make it a huge part of our lives. James told believers, "Pray for each other so that you may be healed" (James 5:16). Paul said he prayed for the Thessalonians constantly. Peter said that God has chosen us to be His people who do His holy work of connecting people with Him—"a royal priesthood" (1 Peter 2:9).

This is a key part of your life in Christ. So pray for other people *all the time.* Doing this will not only keep you from focusing on your own stress and anxiety but also train your mind to turn to God with problems. You'll start doing it for yourself more often.

Pray for people you know well, for people you don't know well, and for people you've never even met. Ask other people to pray for you. Call on your all-powerful God to work and help and show His might in your lives.

Thank You, Lord, for inviting us to talk to You and
depend on You and for working through our prayers.

I See You and I'm with You

Great is his steadfast love toward us, and the
faithfulness of the LORD endures forever.
Psalm 117:2 ESV

There's a simple little practice I like to do with my daughter to build our bond. It's something I do after I've sat and listened to her, when we're just cuddling, or at bedtime.

Taking one of her hands, I trace each of her fingers and thumb, one at a time from base to tip, and as I do, I say a statement for each one:

"I see you."

"I hear you."

"I like you."

"I love you."

"I'm with you."

This is the kind of warm acceptance, togetherness, and steadfast love we receive from our Father God, and I want to be a vessel of His love for her the best I can. My aim, of course, is not only to say those words but to live them out.

Bring this heart attitude to your close relationships. Offer God's steadfast love to them. Say it. Exemplify it. Pray they'll feel it from you. And when you do, you just might find that they will do the same with you.

Fill my relationships with Your steadfast love, God.

Share Each Other's Joys and Hurts

If one part suffers, every part suffers with it; if one
part is honored, every part rejoices with it.
1 Corinthians 12:26

The body of Christ is interconnected, like the human body is. One part depends on another. So when one part hurts, other parts hurt too.

Whenever you're hurting, look for someone to be with you. Don't be alone. We're meant to hurt *with* each other. The same goes for when you're happy. Look for someone to share it with.

Join other people in their highs and lows too. "Rejoice with those who rejoice; mourn with those who mourn" (Romans 12:15). Be present with them. Be willing to be a conduit of God's strength and comfort for them. Paul talked about receiving comfort from God in our troubles "so that we can comfort those in any trouble with the comfort we ourselves receive from God" (2 Corinthians 1:4). Let your compassion move you to pray or find ways to help.

Don't forget that God has connected you to the other parts of His body. There's never meant to be a time when one part exists in isolation. So come alongside each other. Share in one another's joys and hurts and everything in between. Pass along the strength, comfort, and help the Spirit gives.

Lord, keep me from living isolated and help
me build bonds with Your people.

Ask for Support

The eye can never say to the hand, "I don't need you."
The head can't say to the feet, "I don't need you." . . .
All the members care for each other.
1 Corinthians 12:21, 25 NLT

As a part of the body of Christ, you are meant to rely on the other parts of the body. All the parts are designed to be connected and care for each other. This means that *you* need to receive support from others and offer it too.

Now, our individualistic culture isn't really down with this; it's all about self-sufficiency and arm's-length living. "I'm just fine over here, thanks!" we always want to say. But maybe we're not okay. Maybe we need to ask for support and help. That's healthy and wise.

Sometimes you need concrete help: somebody to watch your kids or give you a ride, a friend to go with you to that daunting doctor's appointment. Maybe you have too much on your plate and you need to delegate a bunch of stuff. Other times you might need prayer, emotional support, or just more connectedness.

You're not supposed to be able to do it all on your own. We all have troubles and problems, and we're all meant to help each other with them! We do life *together*, so we share burdens just like we share joy.

God, give me courage to ask people for support and help.

Find the Good Instead of Grumbling

*Do not grumble, as some of them did. . . . These things happened
to them as examples and were written down as warnings for us.*
1 Corinthians 10:10–11

W hen the Israelites were in the wilderness, they did *a lot* of grumbling. It became their pattern of relating. And the more they murmured and complained to one another, the more discontent the group became.

There was a lot of fear, discontentment, and impatience. There was a lot of forgetting, not believing, and not trusting. There was a lot of focusing on themselves, their problems, and their negative feelings.

Paul told believers to learn from the Israelites' poor choices. "We must be on guard so that we never get caught up in wanting our own way as they did. . . . We must never try to get Christ to serve us instead of us serving him. . . . We must be careful not to stir up discontent" (1 Corinthians 10:6–10 MSG).

When you're with others, don't default to complaining. Yes, we need to get honest and process hard stuff with one another. But our main aim as God's people should be to listen to Him and cling to Him in faith. We're to be people who seek His truth, goodness, and peace, who wait on Him in hope and give Him thanks.

Seek out people who will do this with you and help cultivate this dynamic in your relationships.

Lord, help me stir up faith and peace, not discontent.

Listen, Believe, and Hope

Let us hold unswervingly to the hope we profess, . . . not giving
up meeting together, . . . but encouraging one another.
Hebrews 10:23, 25

G rumbling can grow in a group. But so can hope.
Have you ever found that it's hard to be hopeful when you're alone? It's possible; it's just harder than hoping with others. It's one reason we're meant to do life together and regularly focus on truth together.

We see it in the disciples—they stayed together and talked about the experiences they'd had with Jesus (Luke 24:14). Paul wrote to communities, guiding them in how to do the Christian life together. Believers continually gathered to worship Jesus, to remember His example and teachings and build their trust in Him.

We need to do the same. What's likely to happen when we do? What Paul told believers in Romans 15:13: "May the God of hope fill you with all joy and peace as you trust in him, so that you may overflow with hope by the power of the Holy Spirit."

Hope. Joy. Peace. That's what God wants to give His people!

God of hope, thank You for filling us up with Your peace, joy, and hope.

Faith-Building Conversations

I long to visit you so I can bring you some spiritual gift
that will help you grow strong in the Lord. When we
get together, I want to encourage you in your faith,
but I also want to be encouraged by yours.
ROMANS 1:11–12 NLT

What we focus on in our thought life becomes our reality as it shapes our perception. The same is true for what we focus on in our conversations with others. One simple way to magnify God's goodness in your life and to build your faith in Him is by talking about these things with others.

When you hang out with friends, talk about how beautiful and amazing He is. Talk about what He's rescued you from, the identity He gives, and how lovingly He treats you. Marvel over all His spiritual and physical gifts. Take joy in Him together. Ask each other questions that get you discussing your day-to-day experiences with Him.

For example: "How do you sense God's love for you?" "What makes you feel His joy?" "What helps you feel close to Him?" "What are you praising and thanking Him for?" "What difference does He make in your life?" "What has God shown you through hard times?"

Make your focus the goodness of God and see how the Spirit works in your hearts.

God, I offer You my conversations. Use them
to build my faith and others' faith.

Pass the Peace

The God of peace be with you all.
Romans 15:33

I n some church services, there's a time when people "pass the peace" of Christ to each other. They lock eyes, grasp hands, and say something like, "Peace of Christ." It's an ancient Christian tradition that reminds us of the peace Jesus gives us and prompts us to extend it to others, including forgiving as we've been forgiven.

That's a simple practice that points us toward a way of life: pursuing and experiencing God's peace and spreading it to others.

Do you know any believers who make you feel calmer? Somehow just being in their presence puts you at ease. Maybe the peace of God is super strong in them, and when you're around them, you get a little bit of it yourself.

Seek out these people. Go to them when you're struggling to experience God's peace. If you don't know anyone like that, ask God to provide. Maybe He'll even make you and your friends that kind of people, and you can take turns passing His peace to one another throughout your ups and downs in life. Draw near to Him, trust in Him, and invite Him to fill and overflow your heart with His peace.

Help me, God, to receive Your peace and pass it on to others.

Encourage Each Other

Encourage one another and build each other up.
1 Thessalonians 5:11

W hen you notice the strengths of others, what do you do? Do you think, *Why don't I have that strength?* or maybe, *Wow*, but keep quiet? Do you say anything to the people you're noticing?

Everybody has different strengths, so don't bother comparing yourself to others. Most of the time when we think about how we don't measure up to others, we assume people are thinking the same thing. And most of the time they're not.

We need to shift our focus because God's given us an important job: to encourage and build each other up. Paul told believers, "Look for the best in each other, and always do your best to bring it out" (1 Thessalonians 5:15 MSG). When you see a strength in someone, tell them about it. Say how great it is! When you see someone discouraged or hesitant, bolster them up with a good word.

You need to receive this support and help from God through others, and you need to offer it too. So make it your mission to lift people up and point them to God. Surround yourself with people who focus on God's truth and on their job of being an encourager—and if you don't know anyone like that, ask God to direct you to them.

Heavenly Father, thank You for designing Your family to be one that supports and encourages each other.

Strength in Weakness

In Christ we, though many, form one body, and
each member belongs to all the others.
Romans 12:5

A young girl felt crippled by anxiety. When it came time to go to school or a friend's house, she'd start spiraling. She couldn't see the light, only darkness. Her parents gave her tools to deal with these moments, but she still struggled to wield them. And so her dad started saying, "Let me believe for you that what God says is true. Let my faith in Him help you. Lean on my faith."

She'd look in his eyes and they'd steady her. His confidence calmed her. As she felt connected to his belief in God, she took steps of belief and, eventually, she developed her own.

A boy who used a wheelchair never knew the thrill of running. So his dad ran behind his wheelchair in a race, pushing him into the wind, and helped his boy experience a new adventure and joy.

We are not self-sufficient beings. We're not designed to be completely strong on our own and separated from one another. We are parts of His body—we belong to each other, find purpose in helping each other, and carry His power and grace to each other. So let other people bring strength where you need it and do the same for them.

I open my heart to the strength You want to
bring me through others, God.

Peter's Friends Prayed Him Free

Peter was kept in prison, but the church was
earnestly praying to God for him.
Acts 12:5

P eter was put in prison for following Jesus and building the church. How did his believing friends respond? They started praying and kept at it—we're talking constant, fervent, earnest prayer. Their faith was in the Mighty One, and they persisted in calling on Him to act on Peter's behalf.

And act He did! He sent an angel to escort Peter out of prison, striding right past the guards. One minute Peter was bound up in chains and the next he was knocking at his friend's house, where people were praying for him. They were ecstatic to find him standing there, free and safe and back with them again.

It's a perfect picture of what Scripture tells us: "When a believing person prays, great things happen" (James 5:16 NCV).

Got a huge problem? Ask someone to pray for you. Pray for people you know who are facing hard stuff. Turn to the Mighty One with all of it and ask Him to act and help and provide. Pray with belief and pray with perseverance.

Lord, I put my trust in You to act and work
in my life and in the lives of others.

Gain Wisdom from Others

Walk with the wise and become wise.
Proverbs 13:20

Have you ever known anyone who emanates wisdom? Whenever you're around them, there's always a moment when you're like, *Whoa. Insight.* You grab that nugget of wisdom, tuck it into your heart, and let it guide you later.

These people are treasures, and you need them in your life. It's not enough just to listen to a pastor teach once a week. You have to be around spiritually mature people regularly. You need to watch their choices, listen to their reactions, and hear them share about their thought processes.

This is how believers have been growing for generations. Paul told the Philippians, "Keep putting into practice all you learned and received from me—everything you heard from me and saw me doing" (4:9 NLT). He told older believers to show and teach younger believers how to live out love, self-control, and wisdom (Titus 2:2–7).

Here are some truths you might truly *internalize*—not just understand—by spending time with wise people: Doing the right thing is rarely easy. Mean what you say and follow through on it. Prioritize your marriage by setting boundaries in other relationships. Have compassion for people who've hurt you; they've acted from their own hurts.

God, help me get close to wise people and open my heart to the wisdom You've given them.

Take Initiative Like God Does

Do not be interested only in your own life, but
be interested in the lives of others.
Philippians 2:4 NCV

W e love because God first loved us. He took the initiative. And He says to us, "Love others the way I've loved you."

We need to take the initiative with others. We can't just sit around and wish we felt closer to people. We have to step out and reach out. Make contact and suggest activities and invite people to join us. Welcome people into our lives and make effort in our relationships. Show care and interest. Help and honor people. This goes for both forming new bonds and deepening existing ones.

We also need to initiate grace. God has lavished it on us. He's offered it when we didn't even ask for it. So pour grace out on people. Be quick to forgive. Be the first to apologize.

As you live in the way of God's love, you'll find a calming strength. You'll be inviting the Spirit to bring His peace, patience, and joy to your heart.

God, make me strong and intentional about connecting
with others. Use me to reach them with Your love.

Bonding Activities

There is nothing in the world so irresistibly
contagious as laughter and good humor.
Charles Dickens, *A Christmas Carol*

Sometimes we bond through just sitting down and having great conversations. Other times we bond through shared experiences. As you take the initiative in building relationships, find activities that bring you and others closer. Here are some ideas:

Stories—Watch a movie or read a novel or memoir and then talk about it.

Food and drink—Share a snack, meal, coffee, juice, or smoothie. Savor the flavors and notice the textures together.

Music—Play instruments or sing together. Go to a concert. Crank up the stereo with a favorite song.

Adventures and outings—Go on a walk or hike. Jump on your bikes or in a boat. Visit a museum. Take a trip.

Hobbies—Whether you're creating, exercising, learning, or discussing some other shared interest, connect over what you get excited about or something new you're trying.

Volunteering—Join a church or community project where you can serve alongside each other.

Games—Go to a basketball game. Pull out cards or a board game. Get playful and have fun.

Lord, lead me to the experiences that can build bonds with others.

Availability and Presence

There are companions who harm one another, but
there is a friend who sticks closer than a brother.
Proverbs 18:24 NET

For weeks after Josie's dad died, Josie kept finding herself crying in her office. Her coworker and friend Victoria would come sit with her—just sit with her in silence, in her grief, on the office couch. The first time, Josie said, "I'm sorry, I don't know what to say."

But Victoria gently replied, "That's okay. I'm just here to be with you." And Josie eventually melted into her silent presence and just received the gift of it. There was no agenda. No solutions. No questions, even. Just her presence. And that meant the world to Josie.

Melissa, a woman in her forties, reached out to Annie, who was in her twenties. "Want to start meeting for tea every Tuesday night?" she asked. Annie agreed, and it was the first time someone built her up through encouraging conversations so regularly.

They supported each other and helped each other connect with God, and it happened through presence—just showing up and being available over and over.

Ask God for availability and presence from others and be willing to offer it. You never know what kind of healing or strengthening work He might do through it.

Keep me from underestimating the power of availability
and presence, God. Help me prioritize them.

Let Negative Stuff Roll Off

Do not become angry easily, because anger will not
help you live the right kind of life God wants.
James 1:19–20 NCV

A slip of the tongue, a careless act, a negligent silence—people do stuff that can make us bristle, turn away from them, and resent them. Sometimes we're so wounded we don't know how to be any other way. But as we become healed and loved in God, we have a new way to be. He gives us new strength, contentment, and capacity for grace.

Everybody has their own issues, and even as other people are doing the best they can, they're going to do stuff that doesn't feel good to us. What will we do with that? Will we give it so much power that it spoils our relationships or steals our peace and joy? Will it become our focus, pulling our attention away from God's extravagant love?

We get to choose.

How about deciding not to absorb that negative stuff? Let it roll off you. You're not alive to nurse hurts and live in angst. Anger won't lead you into the goodness God has for you. Ask Him to help you let it go and enable you to have peace and choose love.

God, I don't want to spend my energy on nursing hurts and
resentment. Make me slow to anger and quick to love.

Peace and Unity

Strive for full restoration, encourage one another, be of one mind,
live in peace. And the God of love and peace will be with you.
2 Corinthians 13:11

S ometimes it doesn't feel all that hard to be at peace and do good—
and then we get around people. Their actions frustrate us. Our emotions get stirred up.

But God gives us a new way to *be*, remember? He gives us a new mindset and attitude: tenderness, compassion, humility, patience, forgiveness, encouragement, and love. Every time we live out these things, we move closer to our full restoration in Jesus. God is working through us to build us up "until we all reach unity in the faith . . . and become mature, attaining to the whole measure of the fullness of Christ" (Ephesians 4:13).

Jesus intends for us to be unified. He prayed, "May they experience such perfect unity that the world will know that you sent me and that you love them as much as you love me" (John 17:23 NLT). How tragic would it be if we let petty issues and frustrations keep us from the amazing destiny He has for us?

Remember it's God who enables you to live in the new mindset. Reach for His help every time you need it. Don't walk away from what you're made for. Keep giving yourself to connectedness and love.

Lord, help us all live from the new mindset and attitude
You provide and give us a spirit of unity.

~

Listen to the Voice of Love

God is the One who knows you best and loves you most. Nothing in the universe is a mystery to Him. He is your guide, your biggest supporter, your ultimate helper, your most intimate friend. He is your source of hope, peace, joy, and strength.

What is He saying to you? Get still and get close to Him day after day so you can hear and remember His voice. His love really changes everything.

You Can't Earn God's Love

His loyal love endures.
Psalm 106:1 NET

L ove is the core of who God is, always and forever. His love for you flows out of the essence of who He is and is not based on fickle moods.

You are loved as you are, right now.

God doesn't love you more when you're on top of the world, when you achieve your goals, or when you receive praise from people.

God's love for you is settled and final. It never wavers. It is infinite, just as He is infinite. It is a force that takes action and never fails.

Your ups and downs won't change who God is or what He has decided, and He has decided to make you His beloved. He surrounds you with His love and makes it your identity and your future.

I love You back, God. Help me grasp more of
how deep and wide Your love is.

You Are His

I have called you by name, and you are mine.
Isaiah 43:1 NCV

The life you live is unpredictable and full of change. People draw near, then drift away. Places feel familiar, then foreign.

Sometimes you feel as though you have nowhere to belong. But you can be comforted to know you belong with God.

Long before you knew God, He knew you.

Long before you loved Him, He loved you.

He created you in joy. He watched over you, delighted in you, and reached out to you.

Your Father in heaven pulled you into His love and placed you in His family. He's your safe place, your home, where you're known and supported and free from fear.

God called you into your purpose, to join Him in His work and show His heart to the world.

He's made you His own. So when you feel lost or start to forget who you are, remember: you are His.

Your great love makes me who I am, God. I belong with You.

God's Love Pursues You

There is no God like you in the skies above or on
the earth below who . . . relentlessly loves.
1 Kings 8:23 MSG

There have been times when you have walked away from God, and He has pursued you.

You've hidden from Him, like Adam and Eve. And He has called out your name and sought you.

You've wandered away from your Lord, like a sheep. He's made it His mission to find you and carry you home.

You've betrayed Him and fought for getting your own way, like the people who put Jesus on the cross. But He's said, "Father, forgive her. She is worth My life."

You have set your heart against God, like Saul. He's found you in the darkness, shined His light on you, and asked, "Why are you fighting Me? I have so much for you, a life full of gifts and purpose and joy" (see Acts 9:4).

Our God's love is a pursuing love.

It's powerful yet tender, persistent but not rude, relentless and patient and unfailing.

You're His beloved. He's intent on pouring out mercy and grace to you. And He'll keep pursuing you with His love and goodness every single day.

God, I am blown away by Your powerful, pursuing love.

Know the Lord's Voice

*I am the good shepherd. The good shepherd lays
down his life for the sheep. . . . My sheep listen to
my voice; I know them, and they follow me.*
John 10:11, 27

D o you know God's voice? You'll find it is not accusing or shaming. It's not condescending or condemning. It's not tempting or
lying. It doesn't point your attention to sins He's already forgiven and
released you from. It doesn't say you're unlovable or inadequate or call
you a failure or nothing special.

He calls you lovely and loved. He reminds you that He made you
wonderfully and marvelously, that He delights in every detail of His
design. No, you're not flawless, but you're accepted.

The Father's voice builds you up, speaks truth over you, and calls
you into new beauty. His voice tells you to live into the bravery, virtue,
and purpose He made you for.

Be like Jesus' disciples who did life with Him. Come close every
day so you can hear Him better. He'll keep speaking, and you'll learn
to know His voice.

"Do not be afraid. Have courage; I am here."

"Do not be anxious. I will help you overcome."

"I love you. I'll never leave you. I've got you."

God, I want Your voice to be the loudest thing I can hear.

Abide in God

Abide in Me, and I in you.
John 15:4 NKJV

God wants you to live in His love, to remain in it, to make it your home wherever you are.

He wants you to abide in *Him*. And He wants to abide in you.

He is the life source, so let Him fuel your life.

He is abundance and beauty and truth. Let Him fill you with it.

He is the One who knows you best and loves you most. Let Him love your soul.

God is inviting you to intimacy as you've never known. He's calling you into the very closeness you were made for.

Spend time with the Word and with other believers. Join God in His work wherever you are. Stay awake to His constant presence. Keep believing in Him.

Submit to the Father: "Not My will, but Your will. I want whatever You want." God's grace will always cover your sin, but obedience is the path to close relationship. There is so much sweetness and strength for you there.

My amazing God, I want to live in intimacy with You.

Complete Joy

"If you keep my commands, you will remain in my love, just as I have kept my Father's commands and remain in his love. I have told you this so that my joy may be in you and that your joy may be complete."
John 15:10–11

For all eternity, the Trinity has perfect joy. God wants to bring you into that.

He came to earth so you could know and enjoy Him forever.

He came so you could have real life—life that keeps going, life with richness, fullness, and abundance—and the joy that comes with it.

He wants you to have the most joy you can possibly have. It comes from abiding in the Father's love and having sweet closeness with Him.

It doesn't come from an ideal life situation, a pain-free existence, or what the world values. It comes from the joyful One Himself.

Every time you choose the way of life, the way of love, whatever the Father calls good and right and beautiful, you take another step toward that big joy.

God wants your joy to explode in a life of happy adoration, worship, and dependence. So keep coming to Him with an open heart, full of faith, ready to submit and discover. Let His joy be in you.

Jesus, I want to have Your joy in me. Lead me in the life of Your love, truth, and joy.

The Rescue Mission

*Nothing now, nothing in the future, no powers, nothing
above us, nothing below us, nor anything else in the
whole world will ever be able to separate us from the
love of God that is in Christ Jesus our Lord.*
Romans 8:38–39 NCV

God came after you with His love. He set out on a rescue mission, and He completed it absolutely and with far-reaching results. Now He has you in His arms and He fully, *permanently* embraces you.

He's left no possible way for you ever to be away from His love. It is forever in you and with you. It's a sturdy barrier surrounding you, like a bulletproof vest. No darkness, however powerful, can pry you out of His care and protection.

No trouble, trauma, anxiety, danger, sin, loss, or suffering of any kind can pull you away from God's love. If you imagine the worst-case scenario for tomorrow, don't forget also to bring His love into it. It's never going away.

Nothing can win out over His powerful love that defines you and protects you. No one can snatch you away from Him.

He's made sure of it.

He's got you. You're with Him now, right where you belong, and you will be forever.

God, I am so grateful that absolutely nothing can come between us.

Do Not Be Afraid

"Do not fear, for I am with you; do not be dismayed,
for I am your God. I will strengthen you and help you;
I will uphold you with my righteous right hand."
Isaiah 41:10

D o not be afraid."
God said it over and over to humans, and He'll say it over and over to you.

He says it for good reason: *He* is with you. *He* is for you. *He* is your God.

He knows all things. He knows what's ahead, and He can handle it. He's so much greater than what you fear.

Do not panic. Do not agonize. Do not worry. Do not despair.

Look at God's power. Sense His nearness. Let Him calm your fears with His love.

Move forward with faith in God, and He will go with you, directing you and strengthening you. He's not leaving! Even in the darkest places, He'll be there with you. His power and help will be all you need.

Keep holding on to God. He's holding on to you.

God, I believe that You are greater than my fears.

God Sings Over You

He will take great delight in you . . . [and]
rejoice over you with singing.
Zephaniah 3:17

G od sings over you, the one He made, the one He saved, the one
He chose for His family.

Not only does He take delight in you, but He's made you His
treasure.

Like a mother singing her love over her newborn.

Like a bridegroom whispering his adoration to his bride.

Like a warrior chanting his joy over the victory for his homeland.

God's heart is bursting out love for you.

Will you come closer? Will you draw near and stay? Hear His song
of love and let it resound in your heart.

Abide in God and walk with Him so you can receive and know
and share in His delight.

God, I'll let Your song of love resound in my heart
and sing my adoration back to You.

Rest for the Weary

"Come to me, all you who are weary and
burdened, and I will give you rest."
Matthew 11:28

You are exhausted and weary. You're carrying heavy burdens and concerns. You're trying to do too much. Your soul needs a sanctuary. Go to God.

Let His presence be your shelter and refuge, the place where you recover and feel safe and secure. Breathe deeper there. Rest there. Let Him replenish you.

You are spending energy on things you don't need to. You think some things are important when they're not. You have worries about things He's already taking care of.

He will help you.

Let Him guide you into a freer, fuller way of life where there is so much more goodness for you. Keep slowing down and coming close so you can see more and more of what He has for you.

I want my soul to find rest in You, God. I'll
linger here, close to You, right now.

Forgiveness and Freedom

If we confess our sins, he is faithful and just and will forgive
us our sins and purify us from all unrighteousness.
1 John 1:9

You've missed the mark, and you know it.
God knows it too.

But be assured that He is greater than every wrong thing you've done.

Be brutally honest and talk it over with Him. Confess it all and grieve the consequences. And then, be brave. Get back up. Turn around and step forward with Him.

It's your choice: You can beat yourself up and wallow. You can replay it in your head and agonize. You can let it ruin you.

Or you can believe what God tells you: He forgives you. He is faithful and just. He purifies and cleanses and clears out all that's wrong. He throws your sins into the sea and makes sure they're not yours anymore. *He makes you new.*

God loves you. He didn't give up His life for you to obsess over mistakes and get swallowed up in regret. He poured out His life so you could live forgiven and free and healed.

Receive this love gift He's offering you. Confess and believe Him, and He'll do what only He can do in your heart.

I say yes to what You offer, Lord. I believe You're greater
than all my mistakes and that You make things right.

God Is for You

The LORD is with me; I will not be afraid.
Psalm 118:6

Y ou are in a battle zone. But you have not been left alone.
God's not standing opposite from you. He's standing by your side. He's not against you. He is for you.

You are His precious creation, and He calls you wonderful and lovely. He sent His Son to give up His life for you. God went to great lengths to make you right with Him, to bring you back into His arms, to ensure that you're both on the same team. And He's given you His Spirit of power to live in you, to guide you, to help you in every way.

Your Father wants what's best for you: freedom in your mind, strength in your heart, and light overcoming darkness in your life. He wants wholeness and abundance and purpose.

So you can trust Him. Align yourself with Him every day, let His Spirit reign in you, and you'll go after the victory and the life of beauty together.

Heavenly Father, I'm so grateful You made a
way for us to be on the same side.

When You Struggle

*The LORD came down in the cloud and stood there with him and
proclaimed his name, the LORD. And he passed in front of Moses,
proclaiming, "The LORD, the LORD, the compassionate and
gracious God, slow to anger, abounding in love and faithfulness."*
Exodus 34:5–6

God revealed Himself to Moses on Mount Sinai as the God of
compassion and mercy. He's the same God today as He was then.
He sees exactly where you are. Your life is messy, and you're
struggling, even as you do your best. You're dealing with strong feelings and battling discouragement. You're unsure and weak and weary.
You're human.

But God is not ashamed of you or embarrassed by you. He's not
put out or tired of you. None of this is too much for Him.

Even when you think He might walk away, He won't. He'll stand
by you, loyal and patient and beaming with love for and pride in His
child.

God's love isn't just for people who don't struggle. It's for you,
right where you are today. He knew all about these struggles when
He made you.

So keep on. You'll make it through. Lean on God, and He'll see
to it.

God, Your acceptance and support are my lifeline.

He Will Wipe Away Your Tears

"He will wipe every tear from their eyes. There will
be no more death' or mourning or crying or pain,
for the old order of things has passed away."
Revelation 21:4

T he pain of this world is not forever. It's not the final word. And God will make sure it will not ruin you. He will redeem you.

Remember He is the Overcomer who has taken the sting out of death.

He is the Savior and will defeat sin and all that's brought His people anguish. He will wipe the tears from every face.

God is the Creator and Good King. He'll bring you into His glorious new heaven and earth. No sorrow. No suffering. Instead, love and unity. Peace and wholeness. Joy and worship. Perfection and utter fullness of life forever.

Hold on and get ready. The glory of what's coming will outweigh all you'll endure on earth. God is coming for you! He is making all things new and right and beautiful!

I praise You, God, for overcoming all Your people's
pain and making all things right.

God's Heir

If we are children, then we are heirs—heirs
of God and co-heirs with Christ.
Romans 8:17

God is the Great and Mighty One, the God of power, glory, and majesty. Everything in the universe is His. He has all the resources.

He's also the extravagantly generous One who has decided to share His resources. Jesus is His heir, and, as God's adopted child, *so are you.*

This is astronomically bigger and exceedingly grander than any earthly inheritance. This is joining in God's reign over all things, stewarding and harmonizing His universe, enjoying absolute peace and perfection. This is forever life with the King.

What He has for you won't spoil or fade, and it starts during your time on earth. He shares His resources with you now through His Spirit, who lives in you and provides for you. He is God's sign guaranteeing what will be yours later.

He loves you so much that He's qualified you to be a coheir with His Son. He's sharing His power and glory with you. He's making Himself your reward.

The Lord is your portion now and forever. He gives you all you'll ever need—and *more.*

Gracious God, I want to receive the resources You give. I'm
amazed I get to live in Your glorious presence now and forever.

Every Hard Place

"When you pass through the waters, I will be with you;
and when you pass through the rivers, they will not
sweep over you; when you walk through the fire, you will
not be burned; the flames will not set you ablaze."
Isaiah 43:2

God parted the Red Sea so His people could be free. He dried up the Jordan River so His people could go to the promised land.

He kept Shadrach, Meshach, and Abednego safe in the furnace.

He was their God, and He is your God.

He was with them then, and He is with you now.

You are in the thick of it here—processing the past, dealing with the present, gearing up for what's next. There are troubles in your story, yes, but take heart; He is the God of all power.

In the illness, the job loss, and the separation, He'll be with you. In the betrayal, the loneliness, and the grief, He'll be there too.

When there is no way forward, God will make a way. When you come to the end of yourself, He'll provide and give you peace and wisdom and strength. He'll protect you, guide you, and care for you.

God loves you and will never leave you. Stay aware of Him and invite Him in. Let Him give you the power you need for each moment.

Thank You, God, for bringing Your power
into every hard place of my life.

I Give You My Peace

"My peace I give you. I do not give to you as the world gives."
John 14:27

G o in peace," Jesus told people after He healed them (Luke 7:50; 8:48).

"Peace be with you," He said to His disciples when He first appeared to them after His death (Luke 24:36).

"My peace I give you," He had said to them days beforehand (John 14:27).

He is the God of Peace, and He wants you to live with His peace in you.

You have frustrations and hurts and questions. He can meet you where you are. In the midst of all those things, let Him be your peace.

You're living with unknowns. Your view is limited and dim, but it won't be later. You'll understand more in time—there's so much God is going to reveal to you! Until then, let Him be your peace.

God's peace is different from anything else you've known. It's a power that steadies you, a force that guards you, a sense of calm strength that stays with you.

Set your mind on God. Open yourself up to Him. Let Him work in you. Receive His gift of peace and let it rule in your heart.

I want the peace of the eternal Trinity to reign in my mind,
my heart, and my life. Come and work in me, God.

The Ever-Present Sustainer

He is before all things, and in him all things hold together.
Colossians 1:17

God lives and acts from eternity, so He is eternally the Creator. From your perspective you can be sure that in the beginning He created life, today He creates life, and tomorrow He will create life.

God did not set the world in motion only to sit back and disengage. He holds all things together, lovingly sustaining His creation.

He is not a faraway God, a too-arrogant-to-care or too-distracted-to-notice God.

He is the always-working, ever-present, intimately involved God. He orchestrates the galaxies wheeling through time and space. In every heartbeat of every living creature, He is present. It's in Him that you live and breathe and have your being (Acts 17:28).

He holds *you* together.

It's what He's done before and it's what He'll do later.

Trust God to be who He is, eternally your Sustainer.

I am in awe of who You are. I will rely on You,
my ever near and sustaining God.

God Doesn't Get Weary

The LORD is the everlasting God, the Creator of the
ends of the earth. He will not grow tired or weary.
Isaiah 40:28

You are worn out from all that life throws at you. But God is different. He never gets worn out.

You are familiar with impatience. He is endlessly patient.

You get tired after working and helping or simply being awake for a number of hours. He runs the universe and never gets tired.

God is always vibrant and fully alive, always active and alert. He is the One who watches over your coming and going, guarding you and helping you. He is your keeper who won't sleep on the job, your helper who won't grow weary.

He sees you. He is here for you and available to you. He doesn't get tired of being your all in all, and He always has more power to give. He will keep rescuing you and carrying you every day of your life.

From the beginning to the end, He is your God and will take care of you.

I am amazed by Your power and persistent care. Thank
You for being my active Guardian and God!

Nothing Is Impossible with Me

Sovereign LORD, you have made the heavens and
the earth by your great power and outstretched
arm. Nothing is too hard for you.
Jeremiah 32:17

The almighty God has no limits.

He set the boundaries between water and land and keeps the world turning.

He designed every creature and causes crops to grow.

He makes the sun rise and the whole sky glow.

He thunders His power and the earth trembles.

The wind and waves obey Him.

Armies of angels stand ready to do His bidding.

Is there something in your life you think He can't handle?

You're thinking of your limits; you're projecting them on Him. He is greater than all things—any threat, any enemy, any brokenness. No problem or wound or sin is too hard for Him to overcome. His love is bigger than anything you face and anything you fear.

Believe God and entrust all you are to Him.

The almighty God has no limits.

Almighty God, I believe You can handle or
accomplish or conquer anything in my life.

Nothing Surprises or Stumps God

His understanding no one can fathom.
Isaiah 40:28

Your life is complicated. Sometimes you feel overwhelmed by tangled webs of problems and need after need you don't know how to meet. Sometimes you feel shocked or confused.

But nothing ever surprises God. He knew about the things you would deal with when He said, "I will be your helper and provider."

Nothing stumps Him. He always knows what to do. He always knows what's right and does what's right. There is always a way forward, and He knows the way. He knows the solution.

Remember: God is generous, so come ask for help. He will give you wisdom and will guide you! There's no limit to how many times you can ask. Come to God believing, with a heart full of faith and confidence in Him.

Live with the deep peace that comes from knowing you will never be lost in a mystery God can't help you with.

Anything that throws me doesn't throw You, God.
I'll run to You again and again for wisdom.

Nothing Is Wasted

God causes everything to work together for the good of those
who love God and are called according to his purpose for them.
Romans 8:28 NLT

W hatever you've endured or will endure, God will redeem. He
will use it for good and will bend it toward His purposes.

He is resolute and determined. He will accomplish His good,
pleasing, and perfect will and won't let anything get in His way.

God weaves and orchestrates and transforms. He heals and renews.
He shows justice and brings in His overpowering goodness. He builds
up His kingdom of light. He makes you stronger and wiser and pulls
you closer to His heart.

Your Father is working for your benefit. He's showing the world
who He is through your life.

So remember who He is and what He does.

He overcomes darkness and brings in beauty.

God, I can't understand, but I believe. Work Your
good and Your glory in and through my life.

The One Sure Thing

He is the Rock, his works are perfect, and all his ways are just.
Deuteronomy 32:4

Almost everything you know is changeable. People come and go. Circumstances come and go. Money, jobs, possessions, houses, accolades, and good health all have limits. They will seem reliable and sure, but at some point they will fade.

God is the only constant One.

He is the eternal One, the I AM.

His truth is what counts. His glory and works and kingdom will remain, and His presence is infinite.

You need security, stability, and strength. God is the only reliable source for you, and He is right here.

Build your life on what is firm and unmovable. Anchor yourself to what is unchanging and permanent. Make God your solid-rock foundation.

Come closer to Him every day. Choose more dependence and more worship.

Live as though He is the one sure thing in your life.

My God the Rock, I choose You.

God Listens to You

*"You will call on me and come and pray
to me, and I will listen to you."*
Jeremiah 29:12

H annah asked for a baby, and Solomon asked for wisdom.
Moses appealed for mercy on behalf of Israel.
Elijah called for fire to fall from the sky.
Paul needed contentment and the strength to persevere.
God listens to His people, and He listens to you.
He's never too busy or far away. He's always attentive and near.
He works through your prayers to accomplish what is good and right.
So talk to Him. You won't always hear or understand His response,
but He will respond.

Call on God's name. Lift up your heart. Put every problem, need,
and concern into His hands. Turn every heartache, longing, and
dream into prayers.

The more faith-filled you are, the more effective your requests will
be. The closer you're living with Him, the more powerful your prayer.
Remember, nothing is impossible for God.
Come believing.

*I want to come to You with anything and everything in
my world. You're my go-to, God, not my last resort.*

Your Worth

*"Five sparrows are sold for only two pennies, and God
does not forget any of them. But God even knows how
many hairs you have on your head. Don't be afraid.
You are worth much more than many sparrows."*
Luke 12:6–8 NCV

God's love has a nature and power unlike yours. His love does not simply appreciate worth in you; it *gives* worth to you.

His love isn't contingent on how good and beautiful you are. His love is what *makes* you good and beautiful.

He doesn't look for perfect people to appreciate. He pronounces what is good.

He created you and called you good.

He revealed your worth by sending His Son to die for you and making you like Him.

Your worth doesn't rise with your salary or people's praise. It doesn't fall with failure or rejection. You don't have to strive and battle for your worth, either to gain it or to keep it. God has given you His love, so He has given you worth—it's fixed and determined and unchanging.

So live in the reality that God's love names you and defines you.

Thank You, Father, for Your worth-giving love.

Be Brave

Be strong and courageous.
Deuteronomy 31:6

When God says, "Be strong and courageous," He has something important for you to do.

He has prisoners to free, orphans and widows to care for, and people to feed.

He has relationships to mend, traumas to heal, people to build up and love—and more.

And He wants you to join Him.

He will enable you to do hard things. So be brave. Be who He made you to be. Go after the good, worthwhile works He prepared for you. Do what He made you to do. Make the world more beautiful, spread His light, and build His kingdom. Show people His character.

God gives you a spirit of power, not fear. Let that spirit of power drive your thoughts and actions. Throw yourself at the things He cares about and has caused you to care about too.

He's equipped you, positioned you, and called you, and now He says, "Go." Go with great faith in what He can do through you. Think of His power, then be brave.

Because of who You are, God, I will choose to be brave.

Lose Your Life and Gain *God*

"Anyone who holds on to life just as it is destroys
that life. But if you let it go, reckless in your love,
you'll have it forever, real and eternal."
John 12:25 MSG

The life God gives is "real and eternal." But you have to choose it. You have to say yes to His good reign.

He invites you into His kingdom life—a kingdom that seems upside down to the world. The last are the first. The servants are the greatest. Those who let go of what they have receive abundantly more. Those who lose their lives for His sake find them.

When you live with God as your King, you don't have to keep grasping for control. You can fully depend on Him. He lifts up the humble who say, "Everything is not up to me. I give myself to my King. I love Him and live for His agenda." They sacrifice themselves and then find their true selves.

The doors of the kingdom remain open to people worn out from trying to conjure up their own stability or glory, to those who realize they are not God.

Join God in the kingdom life. Know the freedom of letting go and accepting His good reign. Receive the joy of His presence and His real, eternal life.

I love You, Lord. I trust You. I give myself to You,
my King, and say yes to Your good reign.

Transformation

Those God foreknew he also predestined to be
conformed to the image of his Son, that he might be
the firstborn among many brothers and sisters.
Romans 8:29

God is the One who creates, sustains, and *transforms*. He turned humble fishermen into mighty healers.

He turned the one who denied Jesus into the one who founded His church.

He turned a villainous persecutor into a faithful preacher.

And you think you might be too far gone?

You are still in the midst of changing from one way of being to another. You are still in this world getting ready for the next. Throughout the ups and downs, God keeps transforming you. You are His work in progress, and He's making you more beautiful every day, more and more like His Son.

Your flaws and failures will not keep Him from finishing what He's started. Don't let discouragement keep you from running the race. Recommit yourself to Him every day. Obey with faith and reverence and love. Trust Him to do what He's promised, and know that He'll be with you every step of the way.

I open my heart and my life to You, God. Have Your way in me.

Your Story

As in Adam all die, so in Christ all will be made alive.
1 Corinthians 15:22

In the beginning, just after God created His perfect world, darkness arrived.

But He wouldn't let that stand. Sin would not be the author of the story of His creation. So He walked on the earth Himself to live a new story. And now it can become your story too.

There was the first Adam. Jesus became the Second Adam. The old and the new. The way of death and the way of life.

Jesus lived out perfect faith and obedience. He lived out perfect love and service. He lived out perfect union with the Father. He overcame evil and conquered death. He brought heaven to earth and built the kingdom of light.

Come live it out with Him.

Experience parts of it now and know its entirety later. Join His body and His story and His future. Let Him fully claim your life, and know that He gives you far more than He asks.

God's story has more beauty, freedom, and love than you've ever known. He will make it yours too.

I want to live out Your story, Jesus. Envelop me into the way of life.

Your Future

*"If I go and prepare a place for you, I will come back and
take you to be with me that you also may be where I am."*
John 14:3

Y ou belong to Jesus and you always will.
He's preparing His Father's house with many rooms and will
make it your forever home.

He'll fully establish the kingdom of light, and you'll live there
with Him always.

He'll reign forever and you'll reign with Him.

The One you're made for, the One your soul hungers for and fits
with perfectly, will be with you in the life to come.

He will be your infinite joy.

So fill your world with Him now, and celebrate what's coming!
Practice the songs you'll sing with the angels. Shout out His praises,
how His victory and purity and love will reign forever!

Jesus, I'm bursting with excitement over my future with You!

Come and See His Wonders

Come and see the wonders of God; His acts for humanity
are awe-inspiring. He turned the sea into dry land, and
they crossed the river on foot. There we rejoiced in Him.
Psalm 66:5–6 HCSB

Waters turning dry and water turning into wine. Come and see God's wonders.

Fiery bushes not burning and fire falling from the sky. Come and see His wonders.

The Word becoming human, choosing humility and suffering, then rising as King and Conqueror. The Son proving to be the One who takes away the sins of the world. Come and see His wonders.

Hear the astonishing stories again and again. Listen to the broken He's healed and the faithful who've been His hands and feet. Marvel at His works throughout the centuries and in your time now. He's replacing despair with praise, fear with courage, and death with life. He's revealing and building His kingdom. He's waking up His children and pulling them into the light.

You are busy. You're doing so many things yet missing the important things. Look beyond what's directly in front of you, the immediate tasks and concerns.

Look up. Seek God.

Almighty God, I am awestruck. May I live my life giving
You my attention, devotion, and praise—my all.

~

Find the Good

When our anxiety is on the rise, everything can start to look bleak. But the reality is that there are always good things right in front of us. They might be sitting behind a veil of fear, sadness, or worry, but they're there.

If we look for the good, we'll find it. If we see the good, we can be grateful. And if we're grateful, we can be happier.

The even better news is that the more we look for bright spots, the more we'll find. And before long, that will snowball into more lightness, peace, and joy.

Celebrate the Sweet in the Bittersweet

*Rise up, O LORD, in all your power. With music
and singing we celebrate your mighty acts.*
Psalm 21:13 NLT

Autumn is my favorite season. The gorgeous mix of new colors, the leaves dancing in the wind and slowly floating down to the ground, the crispness in the air—I love it all. If I can get a hot drink, a sweater, and a scarf, I am one happy girl.

Of course, I could instead fixate on the fact that the leaves are coming to the end of their life cycle. With less sunlight the tree stops making its food through photosynthesis, which causes the leaves' chlorophyll and its lively green to go away. Those pretty leaves even make scars on the tree when they fall.[1] That's all pretty sad stuff.

The changing leaf colors is bittersweet, but what do we usually do? We celebrate the sweet parts of it. We dwell on the beauty of it.

This is good practice for what we need to do in more areas of life.

Think of one bitter thing you're dealing with. Can you find any sweetness in it at all? Once you spot it, see if you can dwell on it and savor it. How is it unique? How does it affect you? Try to focus on the beauty you can find and treasure it. See how it affects your perspective and experience.

God, help me see and enjoy the sweet parts of bittersweet things.

A Way to Lightness

Come, let's sing for joy to the LORD. Let's shout
praises to the Rock who saves us. Let's come to him
with thanksgiving. Let's sing songs to him.
Psalm 95:1–2 NCV

When someone does something kind and helpful for you, how do you feel? When someone gives you a gift, what are your thoughts and what do you say? "Wow. This is wonderful! Thank you!"

You feel gratitude. Your thoughts and words are positive. You smile. You're not worried or upset. You're calm and happy.

These are special moments; no one has them constantly. However, it is possible for us to have more of them if we're quick to look for and dwell on good things. This mindset will lead us to spend more of our mental energy delighting than worrying. And the more we delight in good things, smile, and say "Thank you," the lighter we'll feel.

I wonder if you can imagine retraining your thought patterns so that, more and more, you are finding fun, choosing cheer and gratitude, and embracing humor and adventure. What would that version of you look like?

You can start taking steps that way today. Right this minute, God has surrounded you with gifts. Which ones can you spot?

God, help me have a lighter, more grateful, more joyful heart.

Your Focus Shapes Your Perception

A man is what he thinks about all day long.
Ralph Waldo Emerson

Jess had a physical illness that brought intense challenges to her life. As a single parent living on a low income, she often felt overwhelmed with stress and anxiety.

Then she met a coworker who had even more hardships in her life and—to Jess's shock—had an immense amount of joy. Watching this woman made Jess realize, *I have a choice in how I see my life, how I live, and who I become.* She realized she'd been dwelling mostly on the hard parts of her life: how she struggled, what she lacked, what she feared.

She started to make a change in her focus.

A year later, Jess was a much happier person. Her circumstances hadn't changed, but now she celebrated the closeness she had with her kids, how she got to love and care for them, the ways she was healthy, and the ways God loved and provided for her.

Our focus shapes our perception and how we experience our circumstances. We can choose sadness and fear and walk around bummed out about all that's wrong. Or we can choose gratitude and peace and walk around joyful about all the goodness and beauty we're noticing and experiencing with God.

What will you choose today?

God, lead me in focusing on Your goodness
and experiencing it more fully.

Talk About the Good

Rejoice always . . . give thanks in all circumstances;
for this is God's will for you in Christ Jesus.
1 Thessalonians 5:16, 18

L ife is always handing me a raw deal. Just look at the mess in my life."

That's one way to look at things. Here's another: "God is always taking care of me. Just look at all His goodness in my life."

We create an environment for ourselves with our words. It's almost like we're choosing a room in a hotel—the dank basement that keeps getting darker and smellier or the penthouse full of fresh flowers, lamps, and gold treatments. The basement perpetually bums us out. But in the penthouse, our eyes keep lighting up as we notice delightful things.

We choose what room we live in by choosing our focus. What we think and talk about creates the environment for all our new experiences.

So talk about the bright parts of life more than the difficulties. Yes, acknowledge problems and do what you can about them, but don't make them your focal point. Look at what's going right, what delights you, all that is a gift to smile about. Share your joy about those things with other people and brighten up their environment too.

God, help me cultivate a bright and joyful
mindset by choosing gratitude.

You Find What You Look For

The unthankful heart . . . discovers no mercies; but . . . the
thankful heart . . . will find in every hour some heavenly blessings.
Henry Ward Beecher, *Life Thoughts*

If someone tells you to walk in a house and try to find imperfections—chipped paint, shoddy workmanship, worn-down furniture—what will your mind do when you walk in? Focus on the flaws. But if you'd been told to find what's beautiful and delightful to you? Your eyes would have been drawn to those things instead.

Have you ever noticed that we do something similar in life? If we're set on finding roadblocks, excuses, or reasons to keep feeling bad, we'll find them. If we're set on finding open doors, good things, and reasons to be happy, we'll find those instead.

Whenever you find yourself doing this, steer your mind another way—toward thankfulness and hope. Practicing gratitude can help you start noticing more good things throughout your day.[2]

You get to do life with *a good God.* "Good and upright is the Lord" (Psalm 25:8). "The Lord is good to all; he has compassion on all he has made" (Psalm 145:9). So "give thanks to the Lord, for he is good; his love endures forever" (1 Chronicles 16:34). Be someone who keeps saying *wow* and *thank you*, who sees good things in the present and bright possibilities for change. God's put them all around you!

God, I want to spend my life looking for
Your goodness and enjoying You.

What's Your Narrative?

*Let all that I am praise the LORD; may I never forget the good
things he does for me. . . . He fills my life with good things.*
Psalm 103:2, 5 NLT

I recently had a chance to listen to a lot of people's stories—people from all walks of life. Many of them endured crushing difficulties, heartbreak, and loss, and there was a variety of responses and conclusions drawn from their hardships. Some people were bitter; others were at peace. Some were in despair; others were resolved to live with hope and praise.

Hard times come to us all. But how we respond to them, how we interpret them, and what attitudes we settle into—those are the choices we get to make. That's what we can control. I found myself thinking, *What narrative am I constructing for my life? How will I interpret what's in front of me and where I've been? Will I let the hard parts bring me down and keep me from delighting in the good?*

The story you tell yourself about your life will dictate how you view God, your own capacity and potential, and your future.

Consider the narrative you're creating and what you're believing about yourself, the world, and God. Are you seeing Him alive and powerful?

*God, help me tell myself the story of Your love,
power, and presence in my life.*

Let the Spirit Bring Your Mind Peace

Letting your sinful nature control your mind leads to death. But letting the Spirit control your mind leads to life and peace.
Romans 8:6 NLT

When we say yes to Jesus, we start a whole new life in the Spirit. We naturally drive our thoughts to darkness, but the Spirit directs our thoughts into the light.

That sounds amazing, but what do we *do* exactly? Well, Paul got very practical in Philippians 4 about how to handle our thought life. First, he said to focus on celebrating and taking joy in God, turning every worry over to Him in prayer, and thanking Him. The result? God's peace will guard your heart and mind (vv. 4–7).

Next, he said to think about what's true, honorable, right, pure, lovely, admirable, excellent, and worthy of praise. *Practice* what you've seen the wise and faithful do. The result? "The God of peace will be with you" (vv. 8–9).

This is what it means to do our part in inviting the Spirit to reign in us. We turn to God and say, "I want Your way. I want to live by the Spirit" (Galatians 5:25). We follow His practical steps, and eventually we'll see the fruit of His Spirit—including goodness, peace, and joy (v. 22).

I want You to reign in my mind so You can lead me to life, strength, and peace.

Fix Your Thoughts on *This*

Fix your thoughts on what is true, and honorable, and
right, and pure, and lovely, and admirable. Think about
things that are excellent and worthy of praise.
Philippians 4:8 NLT

I magine Jesus is sitting right next to you. You're both quietly thinking. What might you be thinking about, and what might He be
thinking about?

The mind of God is beyond our grasp, but Scripture tells us about
it: He is truth, peace, joy, goodness, love, beauty. He generates and
celebrates these things because He is perfection. And what are our
minds like? *Eesh.* We're often caught up in our own problems, worries,
and pain—our troubles, real or imagined.

But as we spend time with God, He reshapes our minds. He
leads us to think about what is *true*—not the worst-case scenarios
we imagine. He says to think about what's *honorable*—how people
respect, serve, and build up others. Not what the world focuses on.

He says to think about what's *right* and *pure*. Think about what's
lovely. Think about what's *admirable, excellent,* and *worthy of praise.*

Throw your energy in these directions—because you're with God!

God is saying, *Follow My thoughts. Love what I love. Meet Me in*
My joy and peace.

Reshape my mind, God! Help me focus on what is true,
celebrate Your goodness, and share in Your joy.

Absorb the Good

When it comes to life, the critical thing is whether you take things for granted or take them with gratitude.
G. K. Chesterton

Sometimes there's good all around us and it flies past our radar. We're too preoccupied, anxious, or tired to notice. Or we're so used to things that we take them for granted. God has surrounded us with gifts for us to delight in, and we're not truly conscious of them.

Experts say we need to not only notice the good but also spend some moments *absorbing* it—giving it our full attention, observing how it affects us, and lingering over it enough to let some of that goodness soak into us. It's pretty simple, but it can really change how we feel, in the moment and long-term. [3]

So when you sip a drink from your favorite mug, see tree branches gently sway in the wind, think of a funny moment with your friend, or receive encouragement from a coworker, don't just mindlessly move on to the next thing. Sit with the positive experience for five to twenty seconds. Savor it. Soak in its pleasantness.[4] You'll likely feel some level of genuine joy and gratitude. Can you imagine how doing this more and more could change your daily experiences and mindset?

You have access to so much goodness. God "deals out joy in the present, the now" (Ecclesiastes 5:20 MSG). Actively absorb it! Receive it fully and thank Him deeply.

Help me be a sponge to Your goodness and love, God.

Say Thanks

Jesus asked, "Were not all ten cleansed? Where
are the other nine? Has no one returned to give
praise to God except this foreigner?"
Luke 17:17–18

There was a time when Jesus healed ten men with leprosy. What would you have done if you were them? Take time to thank your healer? That's what only *one* of them did. When that one man realized he was healed, he came back to Jesus, shouting about how grateful he was. He fell to the ground, kneeling at Jesus' feet, thanking Him and giving Him glory for His abundant grace and power.

Jesus asked, "Where are the others?"

Jesus notices gratitude. It's not the reason He gives blessing; generosity is simply His nature. But when He sees us celebrating the Gift Giver, it matters to Him. We're giving the praise and honor that's due to Him and nurturing our relationship with Him. For all we know, those other nine men may never have interacted with Jesus again.

How many times have I been like those nine men, getting gifts from Jesus and going on my way? I want to be someone who is always coming to Jesus, saying "Thank You!" with a full heart, who's ready to shout and kneel and let the whole world know how wonderful He is.

You give me so much, God! I want to take time
to celebrate, thank, and worship You.

Don't Give In to Complaining

All the Israelites grumbled against Moses and Aaron,
and the whole assembly said to them, "If only we
had died in Egypt! Or in this wilderness!"
Numbers 14:2

When God rescued the Israelites from Egyptian slavery, He displayed His power and extravagant love. You'd think that after witnessing God's character in such a profound way, the Israelites would have been full of awe, trust, and praise for a good long time.

Nope. Pretty soon afterward, their main refrain was whining about discomforts. They talked up the good ol' days in Egypt when they had more food choices. When God provided manna, they complained it didn't have meat. They grumbled about Moses' leadership.

God heard it all, and what He wanted for them was far better: to focus on all the good He'd poured out to them and to be grateful, trusting, and loving. In the wilderness, they were no longer slaves. They were free and in the presence of God, who would provide and stay with them. They'd received enough amazing things from His hand to fill their entire lifetimes with praise. But they forgot.

We have the same instincts as the Israelites. Don't give in to grumbling and complaining today. Don't forget God. Remember Him. Thank Him. Praise Him.

Because of who You are and what You've done,
God, I delight and trust in You.

Recall His Works

*One generation commends your works to another; they tell
of your mighty acts. They speak of the glorious splendor of
your majesty—and I will meditate on your wonderful works.*
Psalm 145:4-5

Scripture gives a simple cure for a complaining or discontented
spirit: remembering and being grateful. Doing those things
prompts our hearts to fill up with praise, joy, and trust.

Over and over we see people in the Bible rehearsing the works
of God—and God told them to do this. He knows how our human
minds forget! Our emotions can take over, our present troubles can
take up our whole view, and we can get tossed around in the big waves
of life. But if we're intentional about remembering God's presence and
goodness, our hearts and minds will change.

"Stop and consider God's wonders" (Job 37:14). Take time to
recall how God has revealed Himself throughout history and throughout the world today. Remember how He has protected you, preserved
you, and provided for you throughout your life. Remember how He
has helped and taken care of the people you know.

Do this so your heart can experience awe and wonder and be filled
with adoration and praise.

*Lord, help me to remember and be grateful every
day, so I can adore You and praise You more.*

Rejoice in the Lord Always

On your feet now—applaud GOD! Bring a gift of
laughter, sing yourselves into his presence.
Psalm 100:1–2 MSG

S cripture directs us to have a *mindset* of rejoicing: "Rejoice in the Lord always" (Philippians 4:4). Celebrate who He is. Have a heart that regularly revels in His greatness, generosity, beauty, and love.

This may seem impossible, but it's really about mental habits—daily reminding ourselves of the character of God. Use scriptures like these to guide your thoughts:

- "Yours, O LORD, is the greatness, the power, the glory, the victory, and the majesty. Everything in the heavens and on earth is yours. . . . We adore you as the one who is over all things. . . . Our God, we thank you and praise your glorious name!" (1 Chronicles 29:11, 13 NLT)
- "When I look at the night sky and see the work of your fingers . . . what are mere mortals that you should think about them? . . . Yet you made them only a little lower than God and crowned them with glory and honor." (Psalm 8:3–5 NLT)

Keep coming back to the deep goodness of God that changes you. Keep delighting in Him and praising Him.

My Great King, You are worth rejoicing in—all the time!

Gratitude Magnifies Him

I will magnify him with thanksgiving.
Psalm 69:30 ESV

When we're in pain, gratitude often feels far away. But even as God sits with us in our pain, understanding it perfectly and hurting with us, His abundant goodness hasn't changed. It is still a wellspring of life-giving peace and joy. When we choose to dwell on His beauty, generosity, and goodness, we can be changed even in that place of pain. We can even have gratitude and praise Him.

Psalm 69 gives us an example of this. David was in trouble—truly heart-wrenching stuff—yet here's what he said at the end of the psalm: "I am afflicted and in pain; let your salvation, O God, set me on high! I will praise the name of God with a song; I will magnify him with thanksgiving" (Psalm 69:29–30 ESV).

Even in crisis and distress, David turned to praise and thanks. Whenever we do that, we magnify God—we make Him greater than anything else in our minds and make His character hold the most power in our hearts. We open ourselves up to our source of life and healing and hope.

So make a point to thank Him even when it's hard. Give attention to His goodness; it will build your trust, invite His peace, and open your heart to your all in all.

God, give me the strength to look for things—in Your
character—to be grateful for when I am hurting.

Hannah Chose Gratitude and Joy

My heart rejoices in the LORD! The LORD has made
me strong.... There is no Rock like our God.
1 Samuel 2:1–2 NLT

For years, Hannah longed for a child. She hoped and waited and wept and prayed, and at last, she had her baby boy Samuel.

But before she ever held that sweet bundle in her arms, she'd said to God, "If you will look upon my sorrow and answer my prayer and give me a son, then I will give him back to you. He will be yours for his entire lifetime" (1 Samuel 1:11 NLT).

And Hannah kept her word. Once Samuel was weaned, when he was about three years old, Hannah brought him to the house of God so that he could live and serve there. She would still get to visit him, but she wouldn't be the one nurturing him and seeing him grow up every day.

Even so, when she brought him to the tabernacle she was full of worship. You can find her entire prayer of praise in 1 Samuel 2:1–10. She marveled at God's generosity and power and put her trust in Him for the future. The pain of her loss could have enveloped her, but instead, as she focused on the character of God and what He does for His people, she chose gratitude, hope, and joy.

How can your heart follow Hannah's lead today?

Even when I'm in the midst of loss or difficulty, Lord,
help me find and delight in the goodness You give.

The Benefits of Gratitude

In ordinary life, we hardly realize that we receive
a great deal more than we give, and that it is
only with gratitude that life becomes rich.
Dietrich Bonhoeffer

Gratitude improves our quality of life and opens the door to so many soul-enriching blessings. It brings peace, strength, and joy—and *more*. It has been shown to calm us and bring down our stress hormone levels. It can decrease blood pressure, improve sleep, build immunity, and even possibly "reduce the effects of aging to the brain."[5]

Gratitude lessens negative emotions like frustration, resentment, and jealousy and boosts "positive emotions such as joy, enthusiasm, love, happiness, and optimism."[6] It's been shown to steer us away from comparing ourselves with others, which can make us feel more content, and it can build resilience.[7] Expressing gratitude also helps us feel less isolated, bringing us closer to people and to God.

All in all, it lowers our anxiety and stress.[8]

That's a lot of good stuff—and stuff that sometimes feels elusive, right? What if it's not as elusive as we thought? What if a mindset shift is the game-changer? You take some time to dwell on what's good, train yourself to look for it again and again, and choose positive words when the negative ones come to mind. Try it out. Welcome new richness and goodness in your mind, heart, and body.

God, thank You for directing us toward gratitude and all its gifts.

A Habit of Gratitude

Always give thanks to God the Father for everything.
Ephesians 5:20 NCV

Have you ever kept a gratitude journal? Writing about the good things in our lives trains our thoughts to move away from negativity and deepens our gratitude and joy.[9] Think of it as a super simple way to get some super important results.

Take a little time to write out a few things you're grateful for. What you pick could fall anywhere on the spectrum of significance: a sunny sky, a soft sweater, a delicious meal, an encouraging word, a hug, a project going well, God's forgiveness.[10]

Research shows that being specific in gratitude journaling can produce better results than being general. So instead of listing several things you're grateful for, you could list several specific ways you're grateful for one thing or person.[11] Maybe you'd write about your coworker who joined you for lunch, made you laugh, listened to you intently, pointed out one of your strengths, and helped you see something in a project you didn't notice before.

Whenever you sit down to write, think of it as a treat. Instead of spending those minutes dwelling on your worries, you're getting to just sit with the good stuff in your life and take joy in it.

God, I want to establish habits of gratitude that
generate more positive thought patterns.

A Mega List of Happy Things

*Be grateful for the tiny details of your life and make
room for unexpected and beautiful blessings.*
Henry van Dyke

D on't you get excited and happy when you talk to friends about your favorite things? You can have a similar kind of experience on your own by creating a list of things that bring you joy—pretty much anything you can think of. Try making it your daily gratitude practice. *Enjoy* thinking about all those happy things. After you've created your list, be intentional about noticing and seeking out those joys more often.

For example, if you wrote down that you love pink peonies, maybe you'll stop to look at them and smell them every time you pass them in the grocery store, or decide you'll buy a handful once a month. If you wrote about loving a particular hand lotion, maybe you'll take a few extra seconds to delight in it the next time you use it.

You might even come up with a statement that you tell yourself when you do these things. When you see and smell the peonies, you might think, *God's beauty delights my heart.* When you feel the hand lotion, *Thank You for little joys.*

When we do things like this, we'll open our hearts to whatever "unexpected and beautiful blessings" God has for us next.

*Help me, God, to intentionally receive joy from both my
past and my present, from both big and little things.*

Revisit Your Best Memories

Let them praise the LORD for his great love and for
the wonderful things he has done for them.
Psalm 107:8 NLT

D o you ever feel as though the best times of your life are far away in your past? Well, researchers have some great news: you can benefit from your happiest memories *today.*

One study showed that recalling specific, positive memories correlates with lower stress hormone levels and more activity in the part of our brain that handles "emotion regulation." Another study connected depression with *less* happy memory recollection and linked resilience with *more* happy memory recollection.[12] An expert said revisiting our happiest experiences is "a form of mental time travel" that generates positive feelings in the present. He recommends recalling them "daily or weekly."[13]

Put some time into recalling your favorite experiences. Make a list and write about them, recalling details. Then regularly spend time looking at this list. Let all their goodness settle into your heart and mind.

Use the gifts of your memory and focus to build your faith and joy and change your thought patterns and perspective. Let the best moments of your past pull you closer to His heart of love for you today.

Heavenly Father, fill me with joy and pour Your love into my
heart as I revisit the goodness You've brought into my life.

Share Your Gratitude with Others

*Cultivate the habit of being grateful for every good thing
that comes to you, and to give thanks continuously.*
Ralph Waldo Emerson

Another way to develop and deepen our gratitude is by expressing it to others.

You and a friend could text each other what you're grateful for every day. With your family or roommates, you might go around the table at dinner and talk about something you're glad about.

Whenever anyone does something kind or helpful, make a point of expressing sincere gratitude. Don't wait until later; do it right away. Look the person in the eyes. Show them you mean it. Honor their effort. "Thank you for the care you put into this. Your expertise is amazing." Or, "I'm so grateful for your help today. I really appreciate how you explained things so clearly."

One study showed that people felt happier after expressing gratitude—especially the people who initiated the conversation.[14]

Expressing what you're grateful for kind of cements those good memories in your mind and reinforces their positive impact on you. So take the time to do these basic things to steer your mind toward more peace and joy. And don't forget that when you share your joy with others, your joy multiplies!

*God, I want to affirm, deepen, and share the
goodness I experience by expressing gratitude.*

A Gratitude and Joy Collage

You are my Lord. Every good thing I have comes from you.
Psalm 16:2 NCV

I'm a fan of collages. Even if you're not a "collage person," why not try it out? Make a collage of images and words that represent what you're grateful for and what has brought you joy in life.

Maybe some of these ideas will spark some new ones for you:

- photos of loved ones and people who have influenced, inspired, or encouraged you
- photos of places where you had positive formative experiences
- beautiful photos of nature that inspire awe or peace
- pictures that remind you of times you've laughed a lot or felt happy
- images that represent your favorite activities or things to see, hear, touch, smell, or taste
- favorite book or album covers
- cute pictures of animals that make you smile
- words like *together, love, alive, peace, happy, good, joy, grateful*

Put it up somewhere you can see it regularly and let it make you happy.

I want to create visual reminders of Your love and goodness, Lord. I want to keep remembering Your presence in my life.

Be Intentional with Your Words

A man who is kind benefits himself, but a cruel man hurts himself.
Proverbs 11:17 ESV

E very word that comes out of our mouths makes an impact—they're meaningful for us and for anyone who hears them. And sometimes our word choices are generating more negativity than we realize.

Research has found that people with anxiety tend to use more "absolutist words" like *never, always,* and *complete.*[15] So if you notice yourself making sweeping judgments, consider how you can steer your thoughts in a more objective, positive direction.

Instead of saying, "She never listens to me," you could say, "This isn't the first time she's ignored me. I can find a way to address this."

Instead of saying, "I always make a mess of things," go with, "I've made mistakes, but I'm going to keep trying."

Avoid saying things that aren't 100 percent true, and don't agonize over your disappointments and frustrations. Realize they come and go and you're able to deal with them. Once you've processed them with God, grab on to some truth that can anchor you, and turn your focus to improving the situation. If there's nothing you can do, then still focus on whatever is yours to do. And keep sticking with the words that call out the good and build up others and yourself.

God, help me speak what is true and focus on the good I can see and the good that is possible.

Tips for Finding the Good

The pessimist sees difficulty in every opportunity. The
optimist sees the opportunity in every difficulty.
Winston Churchill

L et's think more about how we can be intentional about finding
and focusing on the good in our lives. Sometimes it really is just
about getting practical—focusing on doing certain actions so that new
joyful feelings will follow.

Here are some ideas:

- Give out compliments frequently and generously.
- Write an encouraging note to someone.
- Think about how you are now strong in ways you used to
  be weak.
- Consider what you gain from your struggles and pain.
- When you make a mistake, write out what you learned. When
  you face a difficulty, write out how you think you could grow
  and develop through it.
- Tell people how you're thankful and how you're celebrating
  God's goodness.
- Praise and thank God in regular rhythms throughout the day.

Lord, enable me to take actions that can help me
nurture a mindset of dwelling on goodness.

Spot the Robber

In the kingdom of God . . . the important things are living
right with God, peace, and joy in the Holy Spirit.
Romans 14:17 NCV

W hen my daughter was in kindergarten, she was working on
mastering the monkey bars at recess. Her teacher reported that
one day my daughter strode out on the playground with a smile and a
gleam in her eye, and said, "Not today, monkey bars."

She did go on to master them eventually, but along the way there
were days when she decided they weren't going to mess with her. She
knew they'd rob her of joy. She looked at them and said, "Not today."

What robs you of joy? What changes your perspective and mood
from optimistic to discontented or worried? Is it regret, perfectionism,
comparison, fear of criticism, or something you're dreading?

Your joy robber may be something you can't simply walk away
from—a health issue, a recurring problem at work, a judgmental person in your community. If that's the case, you can decide to engage
with the issue or person differently. Hold on to something true and
good that will guard you from the negativity. Decide you won't let the
issue or person get the better of you.

Remember that your ultimate source for joy doesn't come from
circumstances. It comes from the One who *is* joy.

God, let Your Spirit of peace and joy reign in
me and guard me from joy robbers.

Notice the Brave Overcomers

Although the world is full of suffering, it is
also full of the overcoming of it.
Helen Keller

I f a child grew up with someone telling her a bedtime story of doom and gloom every night, how would that shape her view of the world? If she instead heard stories of brave overcomers who persevered in patience, problem-solved, and helped others, what would her mindset become then?

The cause and effect here would be pretty clear-cut.

When we've got a steady stream of negative headlines and stories of suffering running along our mental ticker tape, our view of life is going to get dark fast. We must acknowledge and respect the suffering in the world, but we also must not forget to do the same with the overcoming, the persevering, and the bravery.

Look for stories of people who are living in the power of the Holy Spirit. Celebrate how the Spirit alive in them is greater than this world, overpowering the darkness, enabling His people to live in His strength and wisdom, and empowering them to shine His light.

Seeing people respond to hard things in good ways calms us. God is at work in others, and we can count on Him to be at work in us too.

God, help me see how You are alive and
active in people all over this world.

Seek Out the Good

I would maintain that thanks are the highest form of thought;
and that gratitude is happiness doubled by wonder.
G. K. Chesterton, *A Short History of England*

There is so much good in the world that you're bound to run into it. But don't just wait for it to show up; be intentional about seeking it out. Build it into your life.

Get outside and let the beauty of nature lift your spirit. Hang out with people who encourage you, who are quick to laugh with you. Turn on a funny show or audiobook. Exercise and generate some happy hormones. Do something creative and calming. Be adventurous and try a new food or activity. Ask friends to join you for coffee or a walk.

Do something that helps you feel God's nearness and joy. Runner Eric Liddell was said to have "felt God's pleasure" when he ran.[16] If there's something you can do that makes you feel anything like that, make sure you're doing it regularly.

Bring more good things into your life, be present and grateful as you experience them, and ask God to use them to move your heart and mind in the direction He has for you. Give Him thanks as much as you can, and you just might discover "happiness doubled by wonder."

Lead me, Lord, as I seek out good things that will
bring more of Your joy into my life.

Don't Miss It

We also have joy with our troubles, because we know
that these troubles produce patience. And patience
produces character, and character produces hope.
Romans 5:3–4 NCV

S ome time ago I was in the midst of a trial that really knocked me down. I was often in a rough place emotionally, but there were moments when the Holy Spirit shifted my perspective and brought in some light.

One of those moments came after I had processed some heavy feelings and then was able to ask and pray, *What do You want me to learn in this place, where I'm confused and hurting and weary? You're here and active. You bring good things. Don't let me miss what You've got for me. What do You want to show me and teach me?*

Whatever you're in the middle of, see if you can open the door to new possibilities. Ask God to open your mind to the goodness He wants to bring you through the hard stuff. Ask Him to protect you from getting caught in emotions that distract you from the good He's working and from perceiving the darkness to be more powerful than the light.

God, I believe Your goodness is more powerful than
the hard stuff in my life. I open myself to You and the
good work You want to do in and through me.

See Any Fulfilled Hopes?

Do not spoil what you have by desiring what you
have not; but remember that what you now have
was once among the things you only hoped for.
Epicurus

W e can spend so much of our lives anticipating a future season or longing for something we don't have. *I can't wait until . . .* and *If only I could . . .* thoughts can keep us from seeing and enjoying the great things right in front of us.

Another practical way to get us in a mindset of gratitude is to identify the things we currently have that used to be things we wished and hoped for. What did you pray for years ago? How did things play out? Maybe you prayed for a new home, a new job, a new relationship, or a change in a current one. Maybe you prayed about a health issue, a child, or a community. Maybe you asked for peace, freedom from a stronghold, or courage to do hard things.

Make a list of them and thank God for each one. As you walk into the door of your new home or job, or as you step into your day with more peace or courage than you did years ago, take special notice of it. Thank God in your heart again and stay awake to the good gifts that used to be only wishes.

God, don't let me overlook or forget all the amazing ways
You've provided for me and answered my prayers.

Look for the Good in God Himself

As for me, it is good to be near God.
Psalm 73:28

One summer when I was working as a camp counselor, I broke my ankle while I was playing a field game. And it happened right at the beginning of my summer-long counseling gig. So instead of hanging out with a camp full of fun people in the sunshine, leading worship, and helping kids come closer to God's love, I ended up alone on a couch with my leg elevated—for six weeks.

But you know what? It actually ended up being a pretty fulfilling time of study, prayer, and contemplation—a sweet time in my relationship with God. Sure, I still felt rotten and bummed sometimes, but those feelings didn't color the whole thing. God met with me, and He was good.

As I reported on my summer to a friend later that fall, I found myself saying, "Breaking my ankle was hard. But God was better." His goodness prevailed. Because of who He is, He could make a sour time sweet.

When you struggle to find a good thing around you or to experience joy in the good things you're seeing, look to God Himself. Deepen your relationship with Him. Praise. Listen. Respond. See how He'll flood your heart with His goodness, peace, and joy.

God, I believe You are infinitely good. Come and bring more of Your goodness into my heart and life.

Cultivate Gratitude

Pray diligently. Stay alert, with your eyes wide open in gratitude.
Colossians 4:2 MSG

Scripture repeatedly reminds us to be alert. Stay aware. Keep awake. In Colossians 4:2 Paul connects the idea of alertness with prayer and gratitude—pointing out that it's in conversation with God that we cultivate a mindset of being thankful. We give Him our focused attention. We ask for clarity and the ability to see what He wants us to. We give thanks. This practice helps shape our perspective and attitude throughout our days.

If you look at the Greek words translated as "pray diligently," there's a sense of courage and persistence, of devotion and steadfast attention.[17]

All this helps us see how we can move into a mindset that's more grateful and joyful: It's a prayer thing. It's an attention and clarity of mind thing. And it requires courage and persistence. We refuse to let the dark stuff sink us.

Now, does being joyful mean you're flighty or insensitive, overlooking pain or the hard parts of life? No. It means you have the courage to believe that God's goodness is bigger than all the bad. You're living into your purpose as a God-worshiper—celebrating Him and the ways His beauty is showing up in the world.

God, make me persistent in prayer and gratitude
and brave enough to cultivate a life of joy.

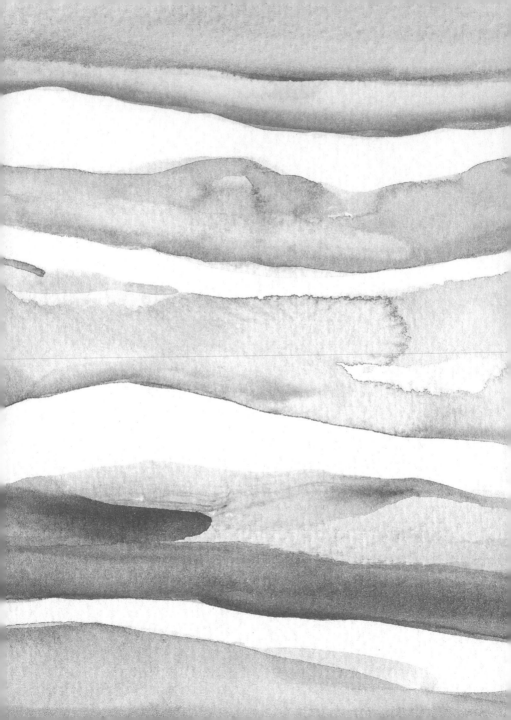

~

Live Out Your Purpose

This month let's cut through the noise and worry to what matters most.

Where do you get your worth? What is your life's purpose? What is essential? Zero in on these things and hold the rest loosely.

No matter what's going on, you can fulfill your purpose: to respond to God with trust and love, to be the unique person He created you to be, to do the best with what's in front of you, to grow in the ways He calls you to, to have a heart of courage and joy.

Every day, you can make your life meaningful to heaven.

Your Heart Is Beating for a Reason

You are God's children whom he loves. . . . Live a life of love.
Ephesians 5:1–2 NCV

B e still and quiet. Put your hand to your heart. Close your eyes. What do you feel?

Life. God is putting life in you right this moment.

Even though there is uncertainty. Even though there is brokenness and pain. Even though there is struggling and fear. God is keeping your heart beating for a reason.

You're alive to know His love and to love.

We've compared the image of a mother with her crying newborn in her arms to our experience with the Father. Return to that image for a moment: she gazes at her precious, unsettled baby with adoration, with both tenderness and strength. His loving gaze is still on you, dear one. It's always on you.

It's okay you don't understand everything. I'm here, He says. I will give you what you need. I'll show you the way. I'll bring beauty and strength and peace. We can be close forever. My heart is wrapped up with yours.

He wants to pull you closer to His love. You're here to be changed by that love, to choose to be identified by it, to grow in it.

Just as His life generates more life in you, His love will generate more love in you. So turn to it. Receive it. Live into it.

I'm alive to receive and give and be changed by Your love, Lord.

Created for His Glory

God is the One who made all things, and
all things are for his glory.
Hebrews 2:10 NCV

L ook around you and what will you see? What God has made and
what is meant for His glory.

"The heavens declare the glory of God," Psalm 19:1 tells us. His
creation shows His goodness, power, and beauty. All of life is designed
for His praise.

You, beloved child of God, are part of that. Do you know what
He's said about His own children? "I have made them for my glory"
(Isaiah 43:7 NLT).

He didn't make you to be defined by fear or pain. He didn't make
you to look within yourself for answers or purpose. He created you to
be all wrapped up in who He is and what He's doing.

Your existence is all about knowing and enjoying God forever. It's
about pointing to His beauty and perfection and worth. Your life is
meant to put His power and loveliness on display. Isn't that amazing?

Thinking on these things calms and settles my heart. My purpose
is about magnifying my God. My life is about loving Him, relying
on Him, bringing others into marveling at Him, and becoming like
Him. As I keep aiming to live in His Spirit, He's going to bring glory
to Himself through me.

Thank You for using my existence for Your great glory, God!

Made for Worship

"The people I formed for Myself will declare My praise."
Isaiah 43:21 HCSB

Today let's think about a fundamental reality that's worth repeated contemplation: God made you for Him. You were designed specifically for Him. You were made for relationship with others too, but it's all in the context of experiencing love in and with and through God, the source of all life and love.

When He formed you, He shaped you to be someone who would need Him and have the capacity to see His beauty. When He recreated you in Christ, He designed you to be, first and foremost, a worshiper—characterized by adoration, relationship, and transformation. He has set you apart, has put you on a different path in life, and is guiding you in a new way to *be*.

So worship is your main thing now, both your focal point and framework: establishing rhythms of communing with Him; finding ways to love and enjoy Him in ordinary moments; experiencing all of life in relationship with Him—listening to Him, responding to Him in love and trust, being changed by Him.

This is purpose: resting in the fact that He is God, being dazzled by Him, saying yes to Him.

I open my heart up to the One I was made for. I
love You, God, with all I am and have!

A Life Directed Toward Heaven

Praise the LORD, my soul; all my inmost
being, praise his holy name.
Psalm 103:1

God uses our worship for His epic, all-important purposes. *Worship transforms you.* Stepping into a life of worship now is training for your life of glory in heaven, one of love, joy, connection, and wholeness. When you "practice" for that, it changes you.

Worship changes the world. Jesus brought the kingdom of heaven to earth and builds it through the hearts of His people. When you love Him and live like Him, you get to bring heaven to earth.

Worship on earth connects you to heaven. You get a glimpse and taste of the joy you'll have there. You do a version of what you'll get to do there forever. You connect with that meaningful life of worship that will continue for eternity.

Worship prepares you for sweet togetherness with God. One day, when you come into heaven and see Him face-to-face, you'll be able to say, "There You are, the One I've been longing for."

Know that every bit of worship matters. Every time you meditate on Scripture and believe God, choose selflessness and generosity and grace, treasure and follow what He says is good and right, you're participating in God's work of transformation and in eternal life itself.

God, I want to live toward heaven in every way I can.

His Kingdom Is Better

Your kingdom is an everlasting kingdom.
Psalm 145:13

Sometimes we're so busy trying to keep up with our tasks and goals that we can't see straight. Maybe we're overcommitted. But is it possible that we're stressed because we're doing stuff we're not even called to do?

Our culture points us toward a self-oriented path, one that leads us to building our own little kingdoms. They look great for a while, but they're fleeting.

God's kingdom, however, is massive. He is eternal, His reign will be eternal, and He gives us the honor of joining Him in it. It is *so much better* than anything we could build on our own.

We're meant to build and steward things—but to do so unto God and for His glory. It helps me to come back to this when I find myself fussing over little stuff in life or feeling small compared to impressive people. Whatever I spend myself on, I want it to be what He values.

So if your head is feeling crowded with concerns, ask God to help you filter out what you don't need to worry about. Remember you're all about His kingdom now, which involves "what God does with your life as he sets it right, puts it together, and completes it with joy. Your task is to single-mindedly serve Christ" (Romans 14:17–18 MSG).

Lord, guide me every day in living a life that's wrapped up with Yours.

What Do You Value Most?

Living a just and holy life requires one to . . . love things . . .
in the right order, so that you do not love what is not to be
loved . . . or have a greater love for what should be loved less.
Augustine, *On Christian Doctrine*

O ne of the church's greatest theologians, Augustine, talked about how God shapes our values and prompts our hearts to love the right things in the right ways. He talked in terms of *disordered loves* and *rightly ordered loves.*

Sin is disordered love—loving something in a way that makes it an idol. Worship is rightly ordered love—loving God most and loving other things based on how they're instruments of God's glory.

When we do this, we don't turn our back on the world; we reach out to it in love. As C. S. Lewis said, "If you read history you will find that the Christians who did most for the present world were precisely those who thought most of the next."[1]

We don't view all earthly stuff as bad; we recognize what God creates and can redeem. We're free to enjoy, engage with, and pursue many things as we see them in the right light.

So stop and ask yourself, *What do I value most? How does what I value relate to God's glory and kingdom?*

When we get our loves and values rightly ordered, anxious thoughts often resolve into the clarity of the big picture.

Help me love the right things in the right ways and love You most of all.

Prioritize the Best Thing

"You are worried and upset about many
things. Only one thing is important."
Luke 10:41–42 NCV

M artha was up to her ears in tasks as a hostess. Jesus and His disciples were visiting, and she was working hard to make things nice for everyone. These were worthwhile tasks—but her labor of love became her top priority. The Beautiful One, the One she was meant to be close with, was *right there* in her home, and she was completely caught up in meal prep.

Her sister Mary didn't miss the chance to get close to Jesus. She sat at His feet and drank Him in, listening to His every word with an open heart. When it became clear that Martha was unhappy about Mary not helping her in the kitchen, Jesus gave her a new perspective.

"Martha, you are worried and upset about many things. Only one thing is important. Mary has chosen the better thing, and it will never be taken away from her" (Luke 10:41–42 NCV).

What is essential? Knowing the heart of our God. Worshiping the One who is lovely and amazing and worthy.

Busyness and anxiety blur our vision and throw our priorities out of whack. Choose what's best. Don't let anything keep you from the most important thing in your life—Jesus Himself.

Help me, Lord, to see how I can make spending
time with You my top priority.

You Want to Join In?

Don't hold back. Throw yourselves into the work of the Master,
confident that nothing you do for him is a waste of time or effort.
1 Corinthians 15:58 MSG

I magine you're on a soccer team, sitting on the bench like usual. The coach comes over and says, "Listen up. We're going to win this game. It'll get intense and crazy hard, but we'll have the victory. It'll be a thrill and honor to be part of it. You want to jump in?"

When you say yes to Jesus, you're on His winning side forever. You're in the kingdom of light, and you get to build it with the way you live. This involves all forms of living in the Spirit—every thought, word, and action of faith and worship; every way you serve and love and help; every time you reach out and reach up; every time you spread truth, peace, and courage.

He's calling you into His very *life*—to be partakers in His divine nature, to be used to accomplish His will, to spend yourself on what counts and will last forever.

You can be part of this winning team either on the bench or in the action. But it's pretty dull and empty just sitting on the bench, isn't it? You want more. You know you're made for more. You're here for the purpose of being in the action.

It's your choice. Will you join in?

God, I want to give myself to You and Your purposes
and spend every day living in Your Spirit.

Freedom from Self-Preoccupation

Do not let selfishness or pride be your guide. Instead, be
humble and give more honor to others than to yourselves.
Philippians 2:3 NCV

S elf-awareness and self-care play critical roles in wellness. But self-
preoccupation will do us in.

Jesus exemplified selflessness and humility. He chose to leave heaven, become human, and take on the role of a servant. He came to give His life and spend Himself for the sake of others.

Jesus taught the exact same themes. In the Sermon on the Mount, He said don't trust in money, don't be selfish, and don't worry—all because you belong to God.

"What I'm trying to do here is get you to relax, not be so preoccu-pied with *getting* so you can respond to God's *giving*. People who don't know God and the way he works fuss over these things, but you know both God and how he works. Steep yourself in God-reality, God-initiative, God-provisions" (Luke 12:29–31 MSG).

We are loved and cared for. He knows how many hairs are on our heads, for goodness' sake. His love frees us to turn away from self-preoccupation and take on the same focus and purpose as Jesus.

He frees us up to live purposefully. *I've got more for you. Want to see how you can give yourself to what matters? Want to pour yourself out in love?*

God, I want to spend my life on love, like Jesus.

He's Got Good Works for You

We are His workmanship, created in Christ Jesus for good works,
which God prepared beforehand that we should walk in them.
Ephesians 2:10 NKJV

God created you in love and joy and wisdom. He knew what He was doing when He designed you. He made you just the way you are for good reason.

And when you say yes to Jesus, He re-creates you and guides you into something else He's prepared for you: good works.

This is important, worthwhile stuff. This is honorable, servant-of-the-Highest territory. Nothing we'd come up with could compare to the immense value of the good works He brings us into.

Isn't it a relief that we don't have to come up with them ourselves? He doesn't put us on the spot and say, "Generate something meaningful and eternal. Figure out something you can do that matters."

No. He says, "Come join Me in My work. Follow Me and partner with Me. I've got just the thing for you."

Can you spot any ways you can join Him today?

Thank You, Lord, for preparing good works for me. Lead me into them!

Alive for Love

"My command is this: Love each other as I have loved you."
John 15:12

G od said the most important things in the world are loving Him and loving others. You're alive for love. Today let's listen to how God guides us into loving the people around us.

"Let us love one another, for love comes from God. Everyone who loves has been born of God and knows God" (1 John 4:7).

"Be completely humble and gentle; be patient, bearing with one another in love" (Ephesians 4:2).

"Love is patient, love is kind. It does not envy, it does not boast, it is not proud. It does not dishonor others, it is not self-seeking, it is not easily angered, it keeps no record of wrongs. Love does not delight in evil but rejoices with the truth. It always protects, always trusts, always hopes, always perseveres" (1 Corinthians 13:4–7).

"Above all, love each other deeply, because love covers over a multitude of sins" (1 Peter 4:8).

"Let love and faithfulness never leave you; bind them around your neck, write them on the tablet of your heart" (Proverbs 3:3).

We love because of Him and through Him. Love changes us. It changes others. It puts His beauty on display and brings the glorious life of heaven to earth. So whatever you do today, do it with love!

Thank You, Lord, for enabling me to love. Make me
a vessel for Your patience, grace, and love.

Do Something for Someone

A single act of love makes the soul return to life.
St. Maximilian Kolbe

Feeling heavy today? Are your concerns or a mix of emotions weighing on you? Try putting your focus elsewhere: do something for someone.

Even the smallest things we do can make a huge difference to others. Give a store clerk a big smile and warm hello. Hold the door open for someone. Go out of your way to help a coworker with something. Make your family's favorite meal for them. Give something from your pantry to a friend. Call an extended family member. Pay for the order of the person in line behind you at the cafe. Check in with your neighbor and see if there's anything you can do for her. Write an encouraging note. Listen intently to someone.

Be the reason people feel seen, cared for, and supported. Let the love of God flow through you to them. And know that as the Spirit works through you, you'll be changed too.

I'm looking for ways to spread Your love today, God.
Work in and through me as I reach out.

Love and Trust, Not Control

In you, LORD my God, I put my trust.
Psalm 25:1

How often do we have anxiety because we care about something or someone immensely? We really want our family members to be safe and healthy. Or to nail our work project. Or to help our struggling friend. This is good and right and beautiful.

But as we focus on doing those things and strive to get results, we feel the responsibility so intensely that it stresses us out. The immediate concerns and tasks are so top of mind that we forget something even bigger than these important good works.

We forget that, first and foremost, we are to respond to God with love and trust. We're alive to worship, not to try to run the show on our own.

It's freeing to come back to this. Your purpose in this world is not riding on everything you touch going just right. Your job is not to fix every problem you see. You do what you can and do your best. You serve and help and love people. But remember: God is in control. He is here, and you are working *with* Him.

So take a beat. Take a deep breath. Turn to Him with a trusting heart. Turn to Him with a loving heart. *What now, Father? I'm ready to follow Your lead.*

Lord, help me remember that doing my best is
meant to be wrapped up in love and trust.

You're Part of an Epic Story

God decided in advance to adopt us into his own family
by bringing us to himself through Jesus Christ. This is
what he wanted to do, and it gave him great pleasure.
Ephesians 1:5 NLT

The story of your life is a beautiful one God is writing. The ups and downs and twists and turns all come together to reveal His goodness and power to the world. You can see only parts of it now, but the Author sees it all and has great plans for what's ahead.

God is not only writing your story; He's also weaving it into His epic story, the one where He proves He is the one true God. He's telling His story of a great rescue, of loyal love and joy, of justice and power. One day no one will be able to deny that He is the God of life, righteousness, and beauty. Every knee will bend to the good and great King.

Each day you live, you're contributing to this all-important story. You play a role. Isn't that *amazing*? You're an instrument in the band. A thread in the tapestry. A line in the poem. It's an unbelievable privilege, and He's had it in mind for you all along. "Even before he made the world, God loved us and chose us in Christ" (Ephesians 1:4 NLT).

He's made you part of His story and part of His purpose. With every act of love and with your very being, you are helping underscore the main theme: *He is our King and He is Love.*

Thank You, Lord, for telling Your beautiful story through me.

Right Now Is Our Chance

Teach us to number our days, that we
may gain a heart of wisdom.
Psalm 90:12

L ife is a timed, mega-marathon race with a surprise finish line—it could show up at any moment. When I watched my mom move through her illness and draw closer to her finish line, I had moments of feeling stunned that *my* body wasn't shutting down. How on earth was it just trucking along, functioning fine? My very life felt like a miracle. Watching her change made me realize that someday I'd change and reach my finish line too. Who knew when it would come? What did I want to make sure I did with my life?

Our culture is resistant to facing mortality. When we bury our heads in the sand, we lose out on a sense of urgency and are quicker to forget the amazing gift of being alive.

We have a chance to throw ourselves into God's purposes *right now*. Tomorrow's not guaranteed. What will we do with today?

When it comes to making the most of your one life on this planet, don't wander aimlessly. Set your eyes on your purpose and actively move in that direction. Use the precious time He's given you to grow into love and make the world more beautiful through the Spirit.

I want to make today count. Give me wisdom
and lead my choices, God.

See Your Uniqueness

I praise you because you made me in an amazing and
wonderful way. What you have done is wonderful.
Psalm 139:14 NCV

Our ultimate purpose is wrapped up with God's purposes, but we each have our own unique gifts and calling. We need to know ourselves well to be able to make the most of those gifts and do what we're uniquely made to do.

Thinking through responses to these questions can help:

- What experiences have brought you the most joy or filled you with wonder?
- Fill in the blank: "I feel my best when _____."
- What do you care most about in the world?
- What needs do you notice and feel drawn to meet?
- What strengths do you see in yourself?
- What have you done that you're proud of?
- The world is wide. What experiences would you like to have? What are your dreams for the future?

God has made you extraordinary and has prepared you to do wonderful things with your life!

God, keep me self-aware so I can sense Your leading
and live out the purposes You have for me.

Gain Insights from Others

Get wisdom and understanding.
Proverbs 4:5 NCV

S ince others can see things we don't, we need to pay attention to what they tell us. They may not always point us in the right direction, but the Spirit can give us discernment. Consider these questions:

- What strengths have others identified in you?
- What have you done that others are proud of?
- What encouraging words from others have stayed with you?

It's also important to notice who we connect with and why. There may be a commonality that helps highlight our unique gifting or calling.

- Who inspires you? Why?
- Who has had the most positive influence on you? How so?
- You're unique, so you shouldn't try to be exactly like anyone else, but is there someone you see and think, *I want to do my own version of that*?

Open my eyes and ears, Lord, to what You're showing me about my unique purposes through others.

Clarity and Vision

There is nothing like a dream to create the future.
Victor Hugo, *Les Misérables*

See if you can get a little more clarity and vision for what might become your focus. Or, if you know what your focus is, rehearse and confirm it. Remind yourself what you're about.

Think about how your strengths and interests overlap with the purposes of God. How does what you care about connect with what God cares about? How can your abilities be used to do things that matter eternally?

Next, write out a purpose statement for your life, and pursuits that support that. What is your life about? How do you want to live in your strengths and build the kingdom?

Last, take a few steps to express your vision and follow your focus. Post a few verses or key statements to guide your thoughts. Create a vision board for all the purposeful, fulfilling experiences you want your future to include. Talk with someone who can help you develop your ideas. Write out some goals for the coming weeks and months.

Come back to all of these things when you feel lost or anxious. If you're holding on to them in your heart and making moves in their direction, you can know you're cultivating a life of purpose.

Give me a vision for the bright and beautiful
future You have for me, God!

Use All You've Endured

Don't waste your pain; use it to help others.
Rick Warren, *The Purpose Driven Life*

A girl who struggled with a learning disorder grew up to do work that mattered to her deeply—running a program for kids with the same problem she'd had. A boy who watched his brother be strengthened through multiple surgeries on his legs became an orthopedic surgeon. A woman with childhood traumas became a counselor to help other people heal from their own.

Our pain and struggles can become instrumental in our development and prepare us for our unique life purposes. God makes our broken places a fertile ground for growth. He doesn't let the hard parts of our lives go to waste; He uses them to prepare us for extraordinary works.

You have your own unique story, unlike anyone else's. You've endured much. What have your struggles and pain made you care about? What insights and abilities have you gained? How could they be related to your unique life purpose?

Ask God to reveal how He's been working in you and where you can go with it. Use all you've gained through your suffering to live in wisdom and bless others.

Help me, God, to use what I've endured to live out my purpose on earth.

Use Money for Good

Honor the LORD with your wealth.
Proverbs 3:9

How do you feel about the size of your bank account? Pretty much everyone thinks, *I wish I had more.* But is gaining as much wealth as possible our purpose in life?

No. Even if we have great wealth, God says, "Don't let . . . the rich boast in their riches. But those who wish to boast should boast in this alone: that they truly know me and understand that I am the LORD who demonstrates unfailing love and who brings justice and righteousness to the earth" (Jeremiah 9:23–24 NLT).

Our purpose in life isn't to have a bunch of money, get a ton of stuff, and fill our days with expensive activities. It's to love God with all we are and all we have. We're to honor Him with our money and submit to Him in all our ways (Proverbs 3:6).

The main issue isn't how much money you have; it's what you *do* with what you have. How can you use your money for good—to meet people's needs, build the kingdom, and join God in spreading love, justice, and righteousness in the earth? Ask Him to show you how to use it as a tool for carrying out whatever He wants, for showing His character to the world, for serving His glory and pleasure. Instead of looking at your bank account and thinking, *I wish I had more,* try thinking, *What might God do with this through me?*

Lead me in using my money for Your good purposes, God.

Use All Your Resources with Purpose

Each of you should use whatever gift you have received to serve others, as faithful stewards of God's grace in its various forms.
1 Peter 4:10

S tewardship is what humanity was originally made for. God told Adam and Eve, "Be fruitful and increase in number; fill the earth and subdue it. Rule over the fish in the sea and the birds in the sky and over every living creature that moves on the ground" (Genesis 1:28).

God has entrusted us with all kinds of resources and it's our job to manage them well. Jesus' parable of the talents shows us that this is an issue of faithfulness: to the man who made the most of what he'd been given, the master said, "Well done, good and faithful servant!" (Matthew 25:23). We want Jesus to be able to say those same words to us one day because of how we used what He gave us.

Think of all that God's given you: time, abilities, materials, relational connections, a body that can move, a mind that can work. How can you use all of these resources for good? How can they go toward helping and loving people and giving God glory? Think what a difference you can make in this world through them.

Remember that faithful stewardship is part of your calling and purpose. Take joy in it! You get to use gifts from God in a temporary world to help build a kingdom that will last forever.

I want to use all I have for Your glory, God. Help me make the most of what You've given me.

Bravery, Not Perfection, Required

The important work of moving the world forward
does not wait to be done by perfect men.
George Eliot, *Janet's Repentance*

I have big dreams. I can't go after them now, though. Someday I will . . . whenever I'm in a better situation.

Have you ever had a thought like this?

There are some dreams God's put in our hearts that we're truly not ready for yet, and we have to wait for the right time to act. But often, something else is going on. We have decided we can't do new things because of a major roadblock we've created for ourselves: *perfectionism.*

If we wait around fixating on our shortcomings or less-than-ideal circumstances, we're going to miss out on parts of life—probably some of the most important stuff. God uses the willing, not the perfect. He's well aware of our human limitations, yet He's set on including us.

There are needs to be met, people to be helped and held, important things to build. What is He drawing your heart toward? Don't wait until you become flawless before you make a move. Say yes to Him and be brave. Jump in and try, just as you are right now. Trust that He'll equip, lead, and empower you. He'll change you as you go.

God has big stuff for you to do with Him.

I surrender my anxiety about perfectionism to You,
God. I believe You can work through me as I am.

Change Ushers in New Purpose

*It was by faith that Abraham obeyed when God called him to
leave home and go to another land that God would give him as
his inheritance. He went without knowing where he was going.*
Hebrews 11:8 NLT

L ife is always changing. One season wraps up, another begins—a
new home and city, a new job or class, a new relationship. The
possibilities are exciting . . . but all those unknowns? They can stir up
the anxiety.

Abram knew that feeling. He was all settled in his homeland when
God said, "I want you to leave what is familiar. Go to a new land. I'm
going to bless you and make you a blessing. Go, because I'm doing
something new for you and through you."

God was going to use this man's obedience to change the world.
And to think Abram could've said, "No, I'm staying where I feel
secure." He would've missed out on what he was meant for.

But Abram said yes. He trusted God and did exactly what He
said. He didn't focus on the unknowns; he focused on what he knew
for sure from God.

Trust God as Abraham did. Walk into new territory with Him.
Remember that He uses the changes in your life to usher you into His
new purposes for you.

*I say yes to Your purposes for me, so I say yes to any
change You lead me into. I trust You, God.*

Meet Him in Your Pain

In my deepest wound I saw your glory and it dazzled me.
St. Augustine

Nobody likes open wounds. It's unsettling to see parts of ourselves that are normally hidden away. But some wounds have a purpose, like when a surgeon cuts through skin to bring healing to a deeper area.

God brings purpose to our pain. He redeems it. He can take senseless suffering and turn it into a place for us to meet Him. Our wounds open up a deep part of us and create an opportunity to experience Him in a new way, see new truths, and be transformed.

Augustine spoke of knowing God in a profound way through pain. As he hurt, he saw God's magnificence like never before. It amazed him and changed him.

Paul spoke of this too. He gave up everything he'd spent his life working to earn just to gain Christ—to know Him and share in His sufferings (Philippians 3). *Knowing Him* didn't mean knowing about Him; it meant knowing Him intimately, experiencing Him in deep and personal ways.

So when the deep parts of you are opened up by pain, meet with Jesus in them. See what new capacity you might have to know Him and soak Him in. Be dazzled by His glory, brilliance, and power. Let Him change you through it. Let Him comfort and strengthen you.

Help me know and love You more deeply through my pain, Jesus.

What's in Front of You

Continue to be strong because of your
hope in our Lord Jesus Christ.
1 Thessalonians 1:3 NCV

Living a life of purpose will look different from season to season. The common thread throughout them all, though, is doing the best with what's in front of you and living from a heart of love, courage, and hope.

Not long ago I had a prolonged recovery time after a surgery. I was limited in what I could do physically—I couldn't run errands, make meals, or take care of people like I usually did.

For a while all I could see was what I couldn't do. But eventually I focused on the value of what I could do: reading with my daughter, encouraging my sister, making my husband laugh, creating books that help people. My life was still full of purpose.

As I wondered how long I'd continue in that state, I needed God's strength and wisdom. He graciously led me to the point where I could say, *As long as my heart is beating I can be brave. Have hope. He makes me alive for a reason, and that reason is to worship and love.*

Whatever season you're in today, however hard some days get, remember that you are alive for love and worship.

Lord, give me a heart of love, courage, and hope,
and help me do my best with today.

Lavish Offerings of Love

"This woman, from the time I entered, has not stopped kissing my feet. . . . She has poured perfume on my feet. . . . Her many sins have been forgiven—as her great love has shown."
Luke 7:45–47

The woman had a bad reputation; everyone knew she was a prostitute. She had no business walking into Simon the Pharisee's house, but *Jesus* was there—Jesus, who changes lives and gives fresh starts, who forgives and redeems. Gathering all her courage, she stepped into Simon's dinner party and knelt down beside Jesus.

She began weeping. Her tears dropped onto His feet, so she wiped them with her hair. Then she kissed them. Next, she poured expensive perfume on them.

Gratitude and adoration were flooding out of this woman. So what if people scrutinized or stared at her? Jesus was worthy, and she was set on pouring out her love and lavish offerings to Him. Her many sins had been forgiven.

My sins have been forgiven too. But how often am I more concerned about what might go wrong in my life than what lavish offerings I can give Jesus? I'm thinking about what *might* happen instead of what He's already done.

Let His extravagant grace result in your extravagant love.

Jesus, You are worthy of all praise and every expression of love I can give You.

Be a Living Sacrifice

I urge you, brothers and sisters, in view of God's mercy, to
offer your bodies as a living sacrifice, holy and pleasing
to God—this is your true and proper worship.
Romans 12:1

You could start this day worried and stressed. Instead, start with a reminder of who you are and what the day is really about.

You are a child of God—someone God pursued, freed, and adopted. You are forgiven, all because God decided to pour out mercy and love to you.

Today, respond to this amazing God by worshiping Him with all you are. Make your life, all your choices, an offering of praise to Him.

Whatever you do, think of it as a way to love God back, and prioritize what He says: "Be joyful in hope, patient in affliction, faithful in prayer" (Romans 12:12). "Act justly and . . . love mercy and . . . walk humbly with your God" (Micah 6:8). Surrender to Him in trust, saying, "Not as I will, but as you will" (Matthew 26:39).

Things may go wrong today, outside of your control. You can control your perspective and your priorities. Whatever happens, your choices are your worship. So embrace what He's done. Respond to His mercy and His presence. Offer your whole self back to Him in love. This would be a day well lived.

Help me, Jesus, to focus more on worshiping
You than on worrying about my life.

Thought Life Worship

Let the words of my mouth and the meditation of my heart be
acceptable in Your sight, O LORD, my strength and my Redeemer.
Psalm 19:14 NKJV

Our life purpose is to love and honor God, and we do that in so many ways—in words, in actions, in attitude, and in the mind. Let's consider a few ways we can honor Him in our minds.

First, we spend time thinking about the One who made and reigns over all creation. We give attention to our King, and join the angels, who say, "Holy, holy, holy is the LORD Almighty; the whole earth is full of his glory" (Isaiah 6:3). We ponder His character, greatness, and wonders, and when we do, it changes our lens on the rest of life.

Second, we sit in the mysteries of God and life with faith. We believe what He reveals and surround any unanswered questions with trust and reverence. We say that God's ways are not our ways, and His ways are perfect (Isaiah 55:8; 2 Samuel 22:31).

Third, we let Him inform how we view everything—discerning what is good and right, turning from selfishness to love, moving from fear to faith. We don't just operate in our reasoning; we ask God for wisdom.

The common theme throughout it all? Exalting Him above anything else in our thoughts. Live out your purpose by worshiping Him with your mind today.

I want to love You with all my mind, Lord.

Worship with Your Body

Do it all for the glory of God.
1 Corinthians 10:31

Have you heard it said that your body is a shell for your soul? Opinions on this differ, but I resonate with theologians like Aquinas, who talked about both embodied souls and ensouled bodies—meaning we're always both, body and soul together.

This helps me think of my actions as prayers, such as marveling at God's stunning world, taking mindful walks, honoring the creation of my body by taking good care of it, reflecting God by creating something of my own—cooking, drawing, painting, gardening, being a steward of the earth and its resources. In all these ways, we're using our human capacity for good in our sphere of the world.

I'd say your body is not just a shell for your soul. Your whole person is God's lovely design. What you do with it matters, so use it for worship. Make all the things you do—even little ones that seem unimportant—part of your relationship with Him. Use all of your life for reaching up to Him, like a plant reaching up for light. Use as many of your minutes as you can for responding to His love. Use the full extent of your existence for interaction with your Maker.

As you make this perspective shift, your everyday moments will hold new meaning. Simple things will become sweet. A new happiness will come into your heart as you feel closer to the One who loves you.

Lord, I want to live with the joy of loving You through my actions.

Live into Who You're Becoming

We are to be remade. . . . We shall find [ourselves to be
what] we have never yet imagined: . . . a son of God,
strong, radiant, wise, beautiful, and drenched in joy.
C. S. Lewis, *God in the Dock*

You're holding uncertainties today. You're carrying questions and concerns. But even as you do, you're on your way to becoming someone new. If you look up, open up, and say yes to God in faith, He'll be the One forming you. And when He forms you, He makes you beautiful.

Just think: God promises to remake you to be like His Son—there's no question about that. It's a certainty you can celebrate.

Your transformation is an ongoing process that happens here and now, and you have a role in it. So live as though you're getting remade. Make choices in the direction of your destiny of being made like Christ. Grow in the ways He's called you to grow.

What are your sights on? Love, joy, peace, patience, kindness, goodness, faithfulness, gentleness, and self-control. Humility and self-lessness. Graciousness and wisdom. Holiness and purity. Fierce trust, resolute obedience, and absolute confidence in the Father. Sweet communion with Him that empowers your life. Beauty. Strength.

Here is meaning and purpose.

Help me, Father, to do my part in becoming a
version of myself that is like Jesus.

Seek Him, Seek Him, Seek Him

God looks down from heaven on all mankind to see if
there are any who understand, any who seek God.
Psalm 53:2

W hat do we do when we feel lost or empty, without a sense of purpose? Unite ourselves with the One who is our source.

What do we do when we're anxious and fearful? Focus on the all-powerful, all-beautiful One.

Scripture points us to a life of seeking God:

- "My heart says of you, 'Seek his face!' Your face, LORD, I will seek." (Psalm 27:8)
- "You, God, are my God, earnestly I seek you; I thirst for you, my whole being longs for you, in a dry and parched land where there is no water." (63:1)
- "I ask only one thing from the LORD. This is what I want: Let me live in the LORD's house all my life. Let me see the LORD's beauty." (27:4 NCV)

We need Him. We're made for Him. So we run to Him. We make our life all about Him.

This is worship and relationship and love—all that you're meant for. Seek Him today!

God, I want my life to be about running to You and loving You back.

~

Now Go with Power

God gives us a spirit of power, not fear. He equips us for life. He enables us to face challenges and manage difficulties.

He also gives us agency and freedom. We can pursue meaningful goals and establish new habits. Even in hard seasons and tough situations, you have the ability to go and do and be so much.

Are you saying yes to what He's offering you? Will you look to Him to empower you? Are you willing to step out of your comfort zone and use what He's given you?

Doing Life with an Empowering God

I . . . pray that you will understand the incredible greatness
of God's power for us who believe him. This is the same
mighty power that raised Christ from the dead.
Ephesians 1:19–20 NLT

When stress and anxiety are issues you're dealing with regularly, you need Someone to calm the storm in you.

But when I'm anxious I want more than relief; I want a sense of steadiness that makes me feel as though I can face whatever's next. I want to be freed and empowered to do what I'm meant to do. I want to feel strong and alive in God.

And that's what God wants too.

He has given us His Spirit to deal with every issue in life. He offers us the same incredible power that raised Jesus from the dead and wants us to use it for living out His will. He lifts us up, pours His resources into us, and sets us in a new direction. He builds us up and calls us into *more*.

Listen. You're not looking at anything He can't help you with. His power is greater than death. The Spirit who lives in His people "is far stronger than anything in the world" (1 John 4:4 MSG). Do this day with your empowering God.

Thank You, Lord, for not only calming my storms but also calling
me into more. Your love and power open up so many possibilities.

He Is Your Portion

My flesh and my heart may fail, but God is the
strength of my heart and my portion forever.
Psalm 73:26

You know those days when you are, shall we say, "in touch with your weakness"? The hard stuff feels especially heavy and worries about the future are especially persistent.

Those are the times you need to remind yourself that it's not the end of the world to feel weak, because you're not on your own. Your powerful God is here with you. You can say with the psalmist and with Jeremiah, "The LORD is my portion" (Lamentations 3:24). Other translations say "inheritance" (NLT) or "all I have" (GNT). God is our all in all. He's our source of true goodness now and forever. He meets our needs and then some.[1]

The verses before Psalm 73:26 read, "I am always with you; you hold me by my right hand. You guide me with your counsel, and afterward you will take me into glory" (vv. 23–24). The God who will resurrect you later will help you do life now. His power, not your weakness, defines you.

So keep turning to the Mighty One and depend on Him. He's got all the resources you need. He will carry you through and make your heart strong.

Thank You, God, for giving Your incredible power to Your people.

Your Problems Plus His Power

All these difficulties are only platforms for the
manifestation of His grace, power and love.
Hudson Taylor, *The Growth of a Work of God*

The centurion had a problem—his servant was paralyzed and suffering. So he went to Jesus.

When Jesus offered to come heal the servant, the centurion said, "Lord, I do not deserve to have you come under my roof. But just say the word, and my servant will be healed."

Jesus answered him, "Let it be done just as you believed it would" (Matthew 8:8, 13).

The centurion, a man who wasn't Jewish, knew where to go with his problem. The same should be said of us.

Not only do we need to be in the habit of going to God with our problems, but we need to reframe our problems as opportunities for Him to do something awesome.

Paul said that our lives are supposed to put God's power on display; we're like jars of clay showing "that this all-surpassing power is from God and not from us" (2 Corinthians 4:7).

Go to Him with all that's hard. Look at your problems *plus* His power and resources. See your difficulties as platforms for His awesomeness—"His grace, power and love."

Use my hardships to reveal Yourself, God!

If He Can Do That, He Can Do This

"The LORD who rescued me from the paw of the lion and the
paw of the bear will rescue me from the hand of this Philistine."
1 Samuel 17:37

When young David saw Goliath, you know where his mind went? To the times he'd experienced God's power in his past. Everyone was cowering to the nasty giant, but David said, "This brute isn't allowed to bully people who belong to the living God! I'll fight him." Can't you just see him lifting his chin and squaring his shoulders?

When he came at Goliath, he didn't have mixed feelings or uncertainties. He was all caught up in the *ableness* of God. "You've got your sword and spear, but I come in the name of the God who fights for Israel. He'll defeat you through me. The world will see that He saves through His unparalleled power, not through swords and spears. This is His battle, and He's going to win" (1 Samuel 17:45–47).

Whoa. Coming. Out. Swinging. What if we approached our battles that way? Think about when you've experienced God's power in your life. When have you stepped out in confidence in Him and seen Him work in and through you? Bring all that into your mindset today. Choose words and actions of faith in the God who is bigger than your giants.

You've empowered me before, Lord, and You can
do it again. I have confidence in You.

He Equips You

His divine power has given us everything required
for life and godliness through the knowledge of Him
who called us by His own glory and goodness.
2 Peter 1:3 HCSB

L et's say you really wanted to make your favorite meal but then realized you didn't have all the ingredients. Or you wanted to carve a pumpkin, but the only tool you had was a plastic spoon. Or you started a new desk job, but no one gave you a computer.

You need to have the right materials and tools in order to do a task.

God knows this well—and that's why He equips us to do life His way. He doesn't say, "See if you can live in My goodness. Come up with some resources. Figure it out on your own." No. He says, "Come closer. Know Me better. Rely on Me more."

He sustains us and gives us wisdom. He fills our hearts with peace and strength. He helps us endure unbelievable stuff and keep choosing what He says is right and beautiful. He gives us all we need for life and godliness—to respond to Him in worship and make our lives about loving Him.

So if you're feeling drained or weak or worried, lift your eyes to your Equipper. Show Him you want to know Him more and rely on the power and resources He provides.

Through Your power and Spirit alive in me, God,
equip me with all I need to do this day.

Armor Up

Be strong in the Lord and in his mighty
power. Put on the full armor of God.
Ephesians 6:10–11

D o you have a bear of a day ahead of you? Maybe you're feeling worried or short on resources. Maybe you're already anticipating how tough it'll be not to give in to temptations that come when you're stressed or frustrated.

Totally typical human stuff. We're all in this place. That's why Paul told his friends to be strong in *God's* mighty power—not to try to muster up their own, which would dwindle away super fast.

So how do we do that? We rely on what He's given us: truth, righteousness, the gospel of peace, faith, salvation, and His Word (Ephesians 6:14–17). We "stand firm . . . and pray in the Spirit on all occasions with all kinds of prayers and requests" (vv. 14, 18).

When you're worried, put your faith in Him. When you're feeling like a failure, remember He's made you righteous through His grace. When you're afraid, remember He was mighty to save your soul and will be mighty in your future too. When you're stressed, return to truth: He is always with you, and He's able to empower you and work things out for good in your life.

Put on God's armor today. Get yourself covered head to toe with His resources. You can be strong and resilient because of Him.

God, help me bring Your armor into every hard moment today.

He Makes You a Conqueror

We are more than conquerors through him who loved us.
Romans 8:37

H ave you been through some tough stuff? Paul did too. He pretty much lived and breathed tough stuff.

He was persecuted and imprisoned. He was whipped, beaten, and stoned. He survived three shipwrecks, including a stretch of time where he was stranded at sea, and lots of travels to all sorts of dangerous places (2 Corinthians 11:23–28).

Outrageous afflictions. Unthinkable suffering. How in the world did he make it through? Well, in the same letter where he mentioned all these hardships, he praised "the Father of compassion and the God of all comfort, who comforts us in all our troubles" (1:3–4). And in another letter he said, "If God is for us, who can be against us? . . . We are more than conquerors through him who loved us" (Romans 8:31, 37).

Paul wasn't just naturally awesome. God made him a conqueror throughout all those unbelievably hard things. God can make us conquerors throughout our hard things too.

The victory He accomplishes through us is no close call. He's so much bigger than what we face! He loves us, empowers us, and makes us resilient. Rely on your God of compassion, comfort, and power today.

Apart from You, God, there's no way I could
survive. But with You, I'm a conqueror.

A Farmer Became a Warrior

"The LORD is with you, mighty warrior."
Judges 6:12

The Israelites were suffering because of the villainous Midianites who had been invading the Israelites' land, stealing their livestock, and destroying their crops.

So God told Gideon, a humble farmer, that He'd use him to solve this problem. His angel said, "God is with you, mighty warrior!" Gideon figured there was some kind of mistake. But the angel continued, "I'm sending you to save Israel from the Midianites. Go in strength."

Gideon pushed back. "How can *I* do this? I'm from the weakest clan in our tribe. I'm the youngest in my family."

But God's message was "I'll be with you and enable you to defeat them."

When it came time for battle, God led them to surprise the Midianites at night, surrounding their camp with torches, and to terrorize them with sounds of trumpets and shouts. In their panicked confusion, the Midianites ended up running for their lives.

God led the Israelites to victory through someone who didn't see himself as capable. Are you looking at something and thinking, *If only I were capable*? Maybe God's given you strength you're overlooking. See how He wants to make you mighty for what's next.

God, I believe that You empower me to do what You want me to do.

His Forever Love Is Fuel

We know and rely on the love God has for us.
1 John 4:16

M aybe you feel like you're running out of steam to keep tackling the next thing. Maybe you're concerned something bad is coming up around the corner. Or maybe you're hung up on your weaknesses and afraid about making mistakes.

Dare I say you could be all of the above? I've definitely been there.

Whether you're weary or worried or caught up in perfectionism, you need to come to God and receive something: His abundant, unconditional, forever love. That is the gas you need in your tank. And it comes from time spent with your Father.

He will keep you going when you're worn out. His power is incomparable and miraculous.

He will assure you that whatever comes, He'll always stick with you. You have a Helper who never runs off.

And He will remind you that your failures don't stop His enduring love. He's not turning His back on you when you drop the ball. He's supporting you and cheering you on, like a bighearted dad who's proud of his kid for getting in the game. So you lock eyes with Him, take a deep breath, and soak in His smile, then get back up again.

This love is loyal and enduring. It's energizing, freeing, and life-changing. Let it fill up your heart and be the fuel for your life.

Father, Your forever love is the reason why I can do today.

New Position, New Perspective

*He gives strength to the weary and increases the power
of the weak. . . . Those who hope in the LORD will renew
their strength. They will soar on wings like eagles.*
Isaiah 40:29, 31

Holly started following Jesus when she was forty, so for decades she'd lived out patterns of worry. Between her high-stress job, health problems, and family drama, she had a lot to manage, and she'd obsess over her problems and worst-case scenarios.

But once Holly got to know Jesus and stayed close with Him, she was able to focus on new realities: *He can handle what you can't. He can enable you to do what you think you can't.*

She wasn't overwhelmed by her lack of power; she was standing with the One who had all the power. It was no longer, *How am I going to handle this on my own?* It was, *How might He empower me?*

She'd pray, *You are my good Father who gives good gifts. Come bring wisdom and guidance. Come bring energy and strength to my body. Come bring more joy and courage to my heart. Be my mighty provider and help me move forward in the power You give.*

You're standing in the same position as Holly is—with the One who has all the power. You can have the same perspective she has, trusting in Him and ready to do new things you can't do on your own. Be someone who keeps depending on your God.

Provide me, Father, with what I need and what only You can give.

His Joy Gives You Strength

Do not grieve, for the joy of the LORD is your strength.
Nehemiah 8:10

There are days I look at myself and can see only the ways I'm weak and failing. We can be pretty cruel to ourselves. It's good to be self-aware and recognize what we need to work on; we just can't let ourselves drown in discouragement. We're works in progress!

When the people of Israel returned from exile to rebuild their lives in the promised land, they gathered in Jerusalem to hear the law of Moses read aloud—and the result wasn't exactly uplifting. In that moment the people were confronted with just how far they were from the kind of goodness and holiness God wanted for them, and they began to weep.

But God's leaders gave the most beautiful response to the people's tears: "Do not grieve," they said, "for the joy of the Lord is your strength." They didn't offer platitudes or downplay the people's failures. They went right to that fundamental truth: *God takes joy in you, just as you are.*

When you and I look honestly at our imperfections, we need more than vague optimism. We need strength to step forward in hope. And that strength comes from the heart of God. He's bursting with enduring love for His people. *I'm right here with you, beloved.*

Your strengthening joy and love just keep going,
Lord, no matter how much I fall short.

Here's an Escape Route

When you are tempted, [God] will also give you a way
to escape so that you will be able to stand it.
1 Corinthians 10:13 NCV

M alia walked in her house after an awful day at work. During dinner, one child was whining about not liking the food, another threw a handful of meatballs at a sibling, and the other knocked over his milk and full plate to the floor.

Malia was about to blow.

At this point, she had a choice: either turn to God for help or see where her big emotions would take her. If she chose the latter, she might find herself throwing something across the room in anger and frightening her kids. If she chose the former, she might ask her oldest child to clean up the mess while she took a minute in another room to cool down. She could take some deep breaths and pray, *God, fill me up with the power and peace I need to do the rest of this day.*

When we're stressed, we're more likely to be tempted to make wrong choices. But God never lets us stray into territory where we have no choice.

In the desert, Jesus relied on Scripture to fight temptations (Matthew 4:1–10). Do the same and ask the Spirit to make you strong and help you choose the escape route God is sure to provide for you.

Thank You, God, for always making a way for me
to choose the goodness You have for me.

God Empowers the Imperfect

The Spirit of the LORD came powerfully upon him.
Judges 14:6

S amson was chosen by God to help the Israelites start to break free from the Philistines. God blessed him with extraordinary strength. But even though Samson was set aside for great things, he repeatedly didn't live into that. He used his gift of physical strength for his own personal interests, which often got him into trouble.

His lowest moment was when he was imprisoned, blinded, and getting mocked by his enemies. He called out, "Sovereign LORD, remember me. Please, God, strengthen me just once more" (Judges 16:28). And God did. Samson pushed the two main pillars of the Philistines' temple and it collapsed, killing everyone in it, including himself. In spite of Samson's mistakes, God ultimately still used him for the purpose He said He would: beginning to free His people from the Philistines.

Samson's story is a cautionary one—it's always foolish to not obey God. But his story illustrates something beautiful: God doesn't require us to have our act together before He empowers us and accomplishes great things through us.

If you feel too far gone, remind yourself: It's not too late; take courage and ask Him to strengthen you.

*My faith is in Your goodness and power, not
my own. Use me as I am, God.*

Commit Yourself to Him

The eyes of the LORD search the whole earth in order to
strengthen those whose hearts are fully committed to him.
2 Chronicles 16:9 NLT

E very day you get to make an important choice: Will you say yes to God throughout the day? We'll never do this perfectly, but we keep aiming for it.

Here's why: He is our Creator, Sustainer, and Savior; He is worthy of our worship. He is our source for life; we need Him. He defines who we are; we have to stay close to Him to remember that.

Maybe today you can set yourself on course to staying committed to Him by picking up your Bible and a journal, choosing a few verses, and writing them out. Then turn them into prayers or mantras.

You might say something like, *I will trust in You with all my heart and lean not on my own understanding. I'll acknowledge You in all my ways (Proverbs 3:5–6). Help me do everything in love (1 Corinthians 16:14). I love You, O Lord, my strength (Psalm 18:1).*

God is looking for people to strengthen. Prepare your heart to receive His help by finding little ways day in and day out to commit yourself to Him, and you'll find His strength will be there when you need it.

I belong to You, God. I want to honor You,
listen to You, and give You my best.

Do Your Part

"Come, follow me."
Matthew 4:19

G od empowers us to do all kinds of things. But He also calls us to action.

When Peter and Andrew were working as fishermen, Jesus said to them, "Come, follow me."

When Lazarus was dead in his tomb, Jesus called, "Lazarus, come out!" (John 11:43).

When a paralyzed man lay on a mat, Jesus told him, "Get up, take your mat and go home" (Matthew 9:6).

That paralyzed man went for it, even though his previous attempts to get up had failed over and over. People who heard Jesus call Lazarus to get moving likely thought He was crazy. When Peter and Andrew followed Jesus, they were doing something completely new, shifting their lives in a whole different direction.

As we answer Jesus' calls to action throughout our lives, we'll probably be able to identify with these people. Sometimes we'll have to move in a direction we haven't been able to before. Sometimes people around us won't get it. Other times we'll be embarking on something totally new because Jesus said, "Come."

Come, follow Me. Come, step into the life I'm giving you.

> *Jesus, You call me to do my part, and I will. Help me see what You want me to do and have the courage to do it.*

Take a Risk and Trust

"Someone did touch me, because I felt power go out from me."
Luke 8:46 NCV

The woman who'd been bleeding for years sought out Jesus in a crowd, even if only to touch His clothes. It'd be a risk—would He get angry? She couldn't be sure, but she had hope. She took a risk and, with faith in Him, reached out and touched the fringe of His robe. As soon as she did, she was healed.

Jesus asked, "Who touched me?" When no one fessed up, He said, "Someone did touch me, because I felt power go out from me."

The woman fell to His feet trembling and explained herself.

Jesus replied, "Daughter, you took a risk trusting me, and now you're healed and whole. Live well, live blessed!" (Luke 8:48 MSG).

Trusting Jesus often means taking risks. It also often means connecting with His power.

The same thing happened for Joshua as he walked around the walls of Jericho, following God's surprising plan for victory. The same thing happened for Peter when he stepped out of the boat and onto the water's surface. This is part of doing life with an empowering God. We reach out to Him in faith and put ourselves in His hands, then move forward in the strength He gives.

How will you show that you're putting your trust in Him today?

God, You are all-powerful and worthy of my trust!

Agency and Hope

When will we ever learn that there are no hopeless situations,
only people who have grown hopeless about them?
Charles Swindoll, *Wisdom for the Way*

W hen the Israelites were slaves in Egypt, the monstrous Pharaoh ordered the Israelite baby boys to be killed. He wanted to shrink their population and keep them under his control.

When an Israelite woman named Jochebed gave birth to a son, she could have felt powerless. She could have resigned herself to the horrible circumstances, thinking, *My boy is doomed. He'll never live.* But Jochebed didn't. She knew she had agency, so she got industrious. She took a basket and put tar on it, so it'd glide like a boat on water. And she got brave. She put her three-month-old boy, little Moses, in that basket and set it in the reeds of a riverbank. And she got strategic. She had her daughter keep watch on the basket from afar.

Later, after Pharaoh's daughter found the baby and took pity on him, Moses' mother had the chance to serve as his nurse (Exodus 1:8–2:9)!

Jochebed couldn't have known how things would play out, but she still did her part, and God used her bravery to preserve her son's life. Next time your circumstances seem insurmountable, follow Jochebed's lead. Do what you can do and trust God to do what you can't.

Help me, God, to not feel paralyzed by difficulties.
Show me the next step that I can take.

The Ripple Effects of Faith

I alone cannot change the world, but I can cast a
stone across the waters to create many ripples.
Mother Teresa

Do you ever feel helpless in a society with big, overarching problems, surrounded by forces out of your reach? It might tempt you to throw your hands up and feel stuck. But we always have the option of taking acts of faith and knowing that God might use them in surprising ways.

Let's look again at Jochebed. When she gave birth to Moses, she couldn't exactly go negotiate with Pharaoh and talk him out of his decree to kill infants. But she didn't just throw her hands up. Instead, she took an act of faith and made an effort to keep her baby alive. She couldn't have known that her choice would lead to an Israelite living in Pharaoh's own home—the Israelite who would one day rescue God's people from Pharaoh! God used one small event to set off a whole series of events that freed Israel.[2]

We can't know how little acts of faith might have ripple effects. It's easy to think that if we don't hold powerful positions maybe our actions won't matter much. But God works through His faithful people! Our small acts of obedience just might be part of His big plan.

Lord, I'm choosing acts of faith because I love You
and want to be available for You to use.

Your Faith Matters to Jesus

When Jesus heard [the centurion], he marveled and
said to those who followed him, "Truly, I tell you,
with no one in Israel have I found such faith."
Matthew 8:10 ESV

C helsea had been getting up early to read her Bible and pray for months. During that time she was also regularly inviting people into her home, donating food and clothes, and reaching out to her estranged brother, hoping for reconciliation. For some reason at the two-month mark, Chelsea wondered, *Does all of this matter? Does God care about what I'm doing?*

The answer to her question was: Yes. Absolutely. Big-time.

Jesus notices faith. He told the bleeding woman and a blind man, "Your faith has healed you" (Mark 5:34; 10:52). He "saw" the faith of the men who lowered their paralyzed friend down through a roof to reach Him (Luke 5:20). He told a persistent Canaanite woman, after she repeatedly asked Him to heal her daughter, "You have great faith!" (Matthew 15:22–28). He *marveled* at the faith of the centurion and said, "Truly, I tell you, with no one in Israel have I found such faith."

Jesus notices and responds when we express faith in Him. Don't underestimate how important your faith is to Him. Express it every way you can. Act according to it all the time. Know that Jesus delights in people who honor Him with a heart full of love and faith.

Jesus, I put my faith in You and I will keep choosing to express it.

Fishermen Became Bold Messengers

"Don't be afraid; from now on you will fish for people."
Luke 5:10

Peter, James, John, Andrew, and Philip were all fishermen. They weren't students of the law or religious leaders. They weren't known for their influence or eloquence. Fishing was their thing. But knowing Jesus changed them. His mission became their thing, and He equipped them to do it.

Early in Peter's relationship with Jesus, He provided a miraculous catch of fish. When Peter saw this he was overcome with awe and his own unworthiness. He said, "Go away from me, Lord; I am a sinful man!" (Luke 5:8).

But Jesus assured Peter, "Don't be afraid; from now on you will fish for people."

Peter became a disciple not because he was especially good or able, but because he responded to Jesus with humility and belief in who He is.

The five fishermen all went on to heal people in Jesus' name and confidently speak His truth to all who'd listen. They, along with several other ill-qualified men, became Jesus' bold messengers. It was a complete transformation from where they'd been—all because of God's power at work in them.

If God could do that in them, what might He do in you and me?

I'm willing to be used for Your glory, God.
Transform me any way You choose.

Deborah's Courage and Confidence

It is God who arms me with strength and keeps my way secure.
Psalm 18:32

I s there something in your life you know you need to grab hold of? Need an inspiration for doing it? Think about Deborah.

She was a prophet, judge, and leader in Israel. God revealed to her that He'd save Israel from the Canaanites, who'd been oppressing them for twenty years, and He'd use an Israelite named Barak to do it. Through him, God would lead the Israelites to defeat the Canaanites in battle.

Deborah called for Barak to come to her so she could tell him about this. When he heard about it, he wasn't so sure. "If you go with me, I will go," he said. "But if you don't go with me, I won't go."

"Certainly I will go with you," was Deborah's reply (Judges 4:8–9). She had no hesitation.

When it came time to charge into battle, Deborah said to Barak, "Go! This is the day the LORD has given [the Canaanites] into your hands. Has not the LORD gone ahead of you?" (v. 14). And she and Barak led the army to their victory in battle.

Deborah was totally aligned with God's will and completely confident in His power. Bravery and wisdom were emanating from this woman! She saw what God wanted to happen, and she went after it.

If God wants you to do something, don't hesitate. Do a Deborah.

Lord, I'm ready to step forward with confidence in Your power.

You Get to Decide a Lot

Live as free people, but do not use your freedom as
an excuse to do evil. Live as servants of God.
1 Peter 2:16 NCV

S ometimes we get so familiar with our situation in life that we lose
sight of how many options we have. We actually get to decide a lot
about our lives. Think about some of the biggest issues on your mind
right now. What are all the things you could do about them?

Maybe you are more capable than you think.

Maybe you're feeling anxious about things you need to go and do
something about. And the issue now is whether you are going to do it.

Will you take that class and learn what you need to know? Will
you see the doctor about that health issue? Have that difficult conversation with a loved one? Reach out for help to manage your overload
of responsibilities? Say no when you need to? Cultivate a community
by building relationships?

There's a lot within your grasp. You get to make choices. Maybe
you need to come at some of the hard stuff from a different angle or
with more determination. Your choices can open up all kinds of new
possibilities.

You have freedom. What are you going to do with it?

Help me, God, to think openly about possibilities
and have the courage to do new things.

Live Like You're Free and Empowered

Suddenly an angel of the Lord appeared and
a light shone in the cell. . . . "Quick, get up!" he
said, and the chains fell off Peter's wrists.
Acts 12:7

W hen Peter was in prison, God sent an angel to break him out. God made the chains on his wrists fall off and told him to rise up and move. He even provided a personal escort to help him get out of there! Peter responded with faith, following every word from God.

Imagine for a minute if Peter had responded differently. What if he'd been so devastated by his imprisonment that he just ignored the angel? What if he was caught up in his own despair or fear and went on living as if God hadn't freed him—even though his chains were on the floor?

Sometimes we do something like this. We live defeated or with fear or hesitancy, thinking we're stuck with no other option. But God pursued us and made us His, and now His love shapes our identity. He frees us and empowers us to do more than we ever thought possible. And our job is to live like it.

Are there issues or thoughts that seem to keep you chained up? Bring them to God. Ask Him to speak to you about them. Let Him remind you that He calls you free and empowered. Rely on His Spirit to escort you out of that stuck place.

Help me, Father, to step into the reality You've created for me.

The Power of Micro Habits

The strength of a man's virtue should not be measured
by his special exertions, but by his ordinary life.
Blaise Pascal, *The Thoughts of Blaise Pascal*

H ow can someone go from not being able to run a city block to running twenty miles? Gradual progress. They work up to it little by little.

Is there a goal or lifestyle change you want to pursue, but it just feels out of reach? Instead of making a grand resolution that basically involves reinventing yourself overnight, try developing a micro habit to build a bridge between where you are and where you want to be.

Want to exercise more? Start doing just a few sit-ups every day. Stick with it and you'll gradually be ready to do a smidge more daily.[3]

It'll help if you connect the new habit to an activity you already do, so it becomes a prompt, and if you have some kind of reward or celebration moment afterward.[4] So maybe you'll drink some water during your commute, then look at the empty space in the water bottle and notice you feel refreshed, not parched. Or you'll go over that Bible verse you're memorizing when you wash your hands, then think, *I did it!*

So the next time you think of something you want to start doing, don't despair about how hard it feels. Try a super-easy version of it, be consistent, and know that little by little, you *will* change.

Lord, help me take consistent small steps toward growth.

Create and Use Momentum

Life is like riding a bicycle. To keep your
balance, you must keep moving.
Albert Einstein

A lexa was stressed and drained. She could see what she needed to change in her life, and she was inspired to make it happen, but it was *a lot*. She'd need to drop some commitments and start exercising, eating right, sleeping more, building connections with people, and spending more time outside. *Uh . . .* where to begin?

Sometimes it helps to focus on one area of life and gain some momentum. Alexa first made it her mission to improve her sleep habits, which helped her not only feel better physically but also gain a sense of confidence that she could accomplish change. Next, she dropped some commitments. Afterward she again thought, *Okay, I can do this*. Then she started exercising, and pretty soon she felt a lot more energized and focused. The momentum she gained from one area of growth strengthened her and propelled her into another.

If there's more than one area of life you want to change, try focusing on just one. Once you start feeling like a rock star for making progress, bring that energy and confidence into another sphere. Once you get yourself trucking along toward improvement in one area, you'll feel more optimistic about making changes in others.

Help me, Lord, to pursue change in a way that
multiplies my energy and confidence.

Persistence

Our greatest weakness lies in giving up. The most certain
way to succeed is always to try just one more time.
Thomas A. Edison

Have you seen Michelangelo's massive and outrageously detailed paintings in the Sistine Chapel? Can you even imagine accomplishing that? When he was assigned the work, he didn't think of himself as a painter, only a sculptor. He accepted the task with uneasiness but ended up expanding the original assignment, ultimately painting the whole ceiling and parts of the walls. It took him four years to do it.[5] Persistence got him to the finish line.

Thomas Edison famously made countless attempts at his inventions before finding success, but it paid off: he eventually held more than one thousand patents.[6] When his factory burned down in 1914, he said, "Although I am over sixty-seven years old, I'll start all over again tomorrow."[7] It was the response of a man who'd had a lot of practice at continuing to make effort after failure.

Do you want to shoot for that kind of persistence and resilience with me? We'll need it to reach our worthwhile goals.

Whether you're aiming to take better care of yourself or build more meaning into your life, be persistent. Even when it seems too hard or things don't go well, keep at it. Someday someone might say of you, "She just never gave up, and look where that took her!"

Jesus, help me be persistent in moving toward worthwhile goals.

Rise Up After Setbacks

Nothing can be done without hope or confidence.
Helen Keller

What puts a damper on our persistence? Setbacks. Obstacles. Mistakes. But we get to choose how we see those things.

We can use guiding thoughts like these: *This is a bump in the road, not a wall. This does not diminish my capabilities and potential. I get to decide whether this stops me. This will lead me to a better strategy. I'll use this to improve.*

The words we choose make all the difference for our mindset. Stick to words of hope and confidence rooted in the God you belong to. Remember verses like these: "With God's power working in us, God can do much, much more than anything we can ask or imagine" (Ephesians 3:20 NCV). "God is able to bless you abundantly, so that in all things at all times, having all that you need, you will abound in every good work" (2 Corinthians 9:8). We can do anything God wants us to do in His strength (Philippians 4:13). Nothing is too hard for Him (Jeremiah 32:17).

If you choose this kind of perspective, you'll be able to jump back up with hope and get moving again with confidence.

Spirit of God, steer my mind toward the
positive possibilities You can create.

Ask, Seek, Knock

"Ask and it will be given to you; seek and you will find;
knock and the door will be opened to you."
Matthew 7:7

Olive had some complicated work dynamics. Problems were affecting her that she had no way of changing. Was there an appropriate way she could address them? She needed wisdom and discernment.

Sophie was constantly finding herself snapping at her kids. They were in difficult stages, and her stress levels were high because of other life issues, but did it have to be this way? She needed patience, gentleness, and self-control.

Rochelle was feeling deeply discouraged and sad after her husband left her. Could she ever recover? She needed peace, hope, and joy.

What could these women do? Turn to their good Father. He wants to "give good gifts to those who ask him" (Matthew 7:11).

How often do we forget that He said to *ask* Him? Whether it's fruits of the Spirit we need or someone to step in and help us, we can seek God and ask Him to provide.

What have you been assuming you need to deal with on your own?

God, I'm going to keep seeking You and
what You want to provide for me.

Resolve Not to Procrastinate

The lazy will not get what they want,
but those who work hard will.
Proverbs 13:4 NCV

D o you tend to put things off? Whenever I do this, it amps up my stress level. Something that's not really that hard *becomes* hard because I keep thinking about it and putting it off.

And if I do this with several things at once? I'm basically creating a load of unnecessary drama for myself.

I'm much happier when I have a mindset of attacking hard things. At some point I heard the phrase "better now than later," and it stuck in my brain. Now it's often what I tell myself when I'm considering procrastinating, and as I start doing the task, I pretend I'm doing some clever life hack that is going to make my life *so* much easier later.

Sometimes we procrastinate because of fear, and if that's the case, we need to address the fear. Other times it's just a lack of self-discipline. We just don't feel like it, and other things are more interesting.

Catch yourself when you're about to do this. Remember that you'll need to say no to some things in order to have a "better now than later" approach. Tell yourself the reason it's good to do the hard task. Think how you'll be freeing up your mind and lowering your stress level by just knocking it out *now*.

Help me, God, to have the discipline and courage
to tackle my tasks now rather than later.

He Says, "Go"

"So now, go. I am sending you to Pharaoh to bring
my people the Israelites out of Egypt."
Exodus 3:10

How often is our anxiety high because of something we're *not* doing?

Sometimes we know we should be doing something, like exercising, but we've convinced ourselves we're too busy so we're not even thinking about it anymore. Other times we refuse to look at something we ought to be addressing, like paying a bill or resolving an issue with a family member. One way or another we're turning away from the healthy and right choice, and somewhere deep inside us, we feel unsettled about it.

What do you think God says about this? To sit where you are because it's just too hard? Nope. He says to go after the healthy and right thing. To rely on Him to face your challenges.

You'll have to be brave to move forward, but you won't be going alone. You can see it as a chore or as an adventure.

God says, "Go." But remember He also says, "Do not fear, for I am with you; do not be dismayed, for I am your God. I will strengthen you and help you; I will uphold you with my righteous right hand" (Isaiah 41:10).

Show me what healthy and right things You
want me to do in Your strength, God.

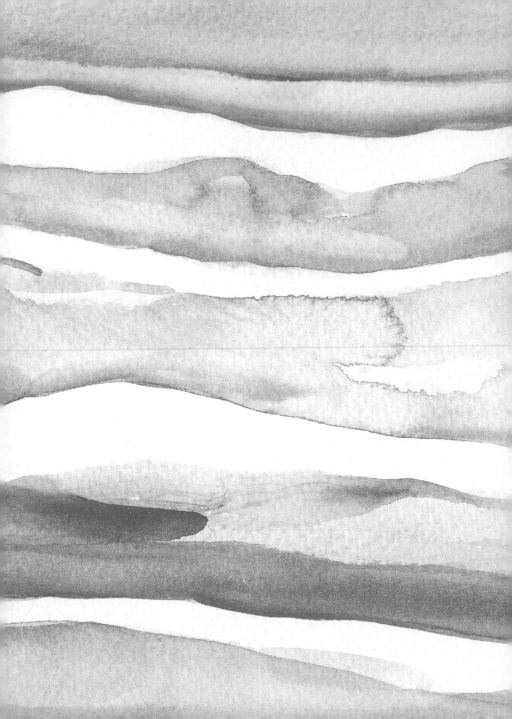

~

Be Sunshine

What is it like to live in the light and keep working through your difficulties with God? You daily open yourself up to Him; absorb His bright beauty, strength, and peace; and shine that out to everyone in your orbit.

Advent is the season of anticipating and welcoming the arrival of Jesus, the Light of the World. What better time to think about living in His light and bringing it to others?

We Receive His Light

With you is the fountain of life: in your light we see light.
Psalm 36:9

When was the last time you walked around a super-dark room? Remember how it felt? You don't really know what you're doing and you can easily get confused about where you are. At any moment you could trip over a step or ram into a wall or break something.

And how different is it when you flip that light switch? Completely different. Like night-and-day different.

When we try to do life without God's help, we're stuck in the dark. But when we turn to Him, the Light of the World, we have His presence to calm us, His power to strengthen us, and His wisdom to guide us. He surrounds us with His love and fills us with His life.

He makes all the difference.

The next time your worries are darkening your world, remember you don't have to get stuck alone there. Your God is light and power and goodness, and He wants to fill your world with His presence.

Come bring more of Your life and light to me, God!

Living Daily in the Light

"I am the light of the world. Whoever follows me will
never walk in darkness, but will have the light of life."
John 8:12

Have you ever opened a window shade just a little, to have only a bit of light come in? Then maybe later you opened it more so it made the room brighter, or all the way so the room was full of light?

That's a picture of what it's like when we repeatedly invite more of God's light into our lives. Whenever we turn to Him, we're opening our minds and hearts to Him more. We're saying, *Come with Your truth and power. Come with Your calm and strength.* The more we do it, the more His light floods in.

It's good for us to do it in the morning as we're establishing our mindset for the day and in the evening when we're processing our experiences. It's good to do throughout the day in the midst of difficult moments of conflict or anxiety, or in brief moments of quiet.

Come to Him and be honest about your mistakes and needs. Embrace His truth and grace. Soak in His beauty and praise Him for His wonders and holiness. Let Him lead you away from any lies or hopelessness. When you do these things, His light will change how you see things and brighten your perspective.

I open myself to You right now, God. Come
brighten Your light in my life.

He Makes Us Radiant

I sought the LORD, and he answered me; he delivered me
from all my fears. Those who look to him are radiant.
Psalm 34:4–5

Moses spoke with God on Mount Sinai, and when Moses came down, "his face was radiant because he had spoken with the LORD" (Exodus 34:29). The presence of God had changed him.

Jesus made it possible for you and me to come intimately close to God through His grace. When we do, we can be like Moses, "our faces shining with the brightness of his face. And so we are transfigured much like the Messiah, our lives gradually becoming brighter and more beautiful as God enters our lives and we become like him" (2 Corinthians 3:18 MSG).

Know that when you encounter God, you will be changed. When you let Him live in you, you'll be transformed. When you continually go to Him with your troubles and needs and fears, when you keep trusting Him and saying yes to Him, you won't be the same. You'll be radiant. His peace, strength, and joy will become part of you.

Seek Him today. Ask Him to make your heart and your life brighter and more beautiful through His presence.

Come change me through Your presence, God.
I want to shine out Your beauty.

You Are a Light

"You are the salt of the earth. . . . You are the light of the world."
Matthew 5:13–14

W hen you light a match and transfer that flame to a candlewick, the flame duplicates. The light that was once in only one place spreads to another.

Jesus says, "I am the Light of the World, and I want to make you the light of the world too. I want to live in you and use you to bring My presence into your part of the world."

When you put your faith in Him, you receive His light—His Spirit of peace and joy, His Word of truth and power. You'll think and act differently than people who don't know Him. Your life will become a vessel for His glory.

You're going to have problems and pain in the world just like everyone else, but you can still declare His praises with your life. You can still let the Spirit lead you. You can "let your light shine before others, that they may see your good deeds and glorify your Father in heaven" (v. 16). Today, look for ways to put the love, courage, and hope you receive from God on display so the world can see who He is.

God, brighten the light in this world through me.

Spread Love and Happiness

Spread love everywhere you go. Let no one ever
come to you without leaving happier.
Mother Teresa

When I'm stressed out, I bring my stress into every room I walk into. When I keep focusing on what's causing it and how my anxiety feels, I'm basically feeding it—and spreading it to others in some way.

But when I manage my stress by taking care of myself, turning my anxious thoughts into prayers, and letting go of what I can't control, I can bring a different presence into a room. I'll be able to spread something much more positive to people.

Easier said than done, right? But it's good to remind ourselves of the power we have—that our mindset and behavior impact the people around us and help create the environment we share with them. It's as though we're a domino touching other dominos, and we get to choose how we contact them. We can choose to focus on bringing goodness and cheer to others. When we do, our own anxiety often lifts.

Even though things aren't perfect in your life, you can still decide that you're going to make an effort to bless the people around you. So take care of them, connect with them, and work hard for their benefit. Make them feel loved, seen, respected, and enjoyed. Be sunshine— warm and strong and bright with God's light and joy.

God, make me sunshine for others today.

How Love Looks

Anyone who loves their brother and sister lives in the light.
1 John 2:10

Chloe is cooking a meal for her neighbor who just had surgery. Yesterday she spent a couple of hours listening to her brother share about his life struggles and encouraging him. Tomorrow she'll take her elderly dad to a doctor's appointment and write a note of encouragement to her coworker—the one she often disagrees with.

Chloe is stressed about plenty of her own stuff, but she's still receiving and giving God's love. It's part of living in the light.

Augustine once asked and answered a big question: "What does love look like? It has the hands to help others. It has the feet to hasten to the poor and needy. It has eyes to see misery and want. It has the ears to hear the sighs and sorrows of men."[1]

Reach out to bless people you don't know well and loyally care for people closest to you. Proverbs 17:17 says, "A friend loves you all the time, and a brother helps in time of trouble" (NCV). See others through the hard times and share the joy of the good times. As you do, you'll live in God's love, help others strengthen and grow, show His character to the world, and get a taste of the sweet unity we'll know in heaven. Live in the light.

God, help me use my hands, feet, eyes, and ears for love.

Really Listen

Always be willing to listen and slow to speak.
James 1:19 NCV

W hen Kyra and Wren got together for coffee or lunch, Wren usually did most of the talking. Kyra asked questions and listened as Wren opened up about her work struggles and relationship issues and spiritual questions. Kyra didn't really mind; she could tell Wren really needed a safe place to share and process all this stuff. And if she could be the one to provide that, great.

She didn't know that after every conversation, Wren felt validated and encouraged, and her prayers had more faith and hope. Wren felt God's love through Kyra.

Sometimes our role is simply to listen. Not to fix or to counsel, but just to hear and know about someone's experience with them. We may not even resonate with what we hear, but we can still show respect and offer acceptance of the person.

Do you seek to understand more than you seek to be understood? Are you curious about others' thoughts and compassionate toward them? You might be surprised how much good it does for both of you—for you to put your mind on something other than your own concerns, and for the other person to feel known and heard. Be willing to really listen and to let God show His love through you.

Show me who You want me to give a listening ear to today, Lord.

Speak Life

The tongue has the power of life and death.
Proverbs 18:21

We often go about our days expressing our thoughts as they come without realizing the immense power they hold—both for others and for ourselves. Our words can either build up or tear down, multiply hope or reinforce pessimism, point to truth or amplify fear.

"Careless words stab like a sword, but wise words bring healing" (Proverbs 12:18 NCV).

Those are some pretty serious consequences, mirroring the life-and-death talk from Proverbs 18:21. We've experienced this ourselves, right? You can probably remember when someone said a hurtful word that soured a relationship or blurted out an opinion that diminished your view of your capabilities. That's why Paul told believers, "Let everything you say be good and helpful, so that your words will be an encouragement to those who hear them" (Ephesians 4:29 NLT).

So start with guiding your own thoughts toward truth, hope, and love. Discipline yourself not to say every thought that comes to mind, and carefully choose what you do say. Use words that point out people's good qualities, prompt them to believe what God says, and help them step into His good will for them. Affirm, accept, and love them. And live into those powerful, good words yourself.

Lord, may my words be all about truth, hope, and love, spreading strength, life, and goodness.

Greet and Acknowledge Others

Greet one another.
Romans 16:16

One of my favorite college professors would always walk down the classroom hallways with a big smile on his face and excitedly greet every student he passed—by name. I would see him coming toward me from the other end of the hall and look forward to when it'd be my turn. "Hi, Carrie!" he'd say as he passed me, and I'd happily return his greeting. It seemed like the whole hallway of people started smiling and walking a little peppier as a result. That man was a beaming bright light.

What genuine greetings have you received from people that left you feeling good? The people probably looked you in the eye, smiled, shook your hand or waved, and said your name. Maybe they said something else positive or kind. And they did all these things in a sincere manner. Their effort made a difference for you.

You come across people every day; how do you treat them?

Make a point to greet them with warmth. Be a welcoming presence that's willing to engage. Give a sign—even a small one—that they're seen and valuable. Acknowledge that they are God's creation and He knows and cares for them. Extend a bit of strength and love to them, and you'll feel more strength and love in you too.

Use me, Lord, to lift up others in simple ways today.

Stay Connected

"I am the vine; you are the branches. If you remain in me and I in
you, you will bear much fruit; apart from me you can do nothing."
John 15:5

Have you put up Christmas decorations yet? Twinkle lights are my favorite part. It makes me so happy to see all those bulbs give a beautiful soft glow at night.

Think for a minute how those strands of lights are like our relationship with Jesus. If you have one of those little bulbs all by itself—disconnected from a strand—it won't do anything. But if it's secured into a socket on a strand that's plugged in, it'll light right up. Jesus is the strand, and we are the light bulbs. Jesus is the vine, and we are the branches. We need to live connected to Him in order to bring His light and fruit into the world.

Anne Graham Lotz said, "The first secret to loving others is to immerse yourself in a love relationship with God the Father, God the Son, and God the Holy Spirit—and abide there."[2]

Remember that you're not supposed to be a light in your own strength. Remain in Him. Live with Him as your power source. Let your love flow from His love.

I'm going to keep turning my heart and mind toward
You, God, welcoming Your light and power.

Everyday Generosity

A generous person will prosper; whoever
refreshes others will be refreshed.
Proverbs 11:25

Zacchaeus was a tax collector who'd been stealing money from people. Was he afraid he wouldn't have enough? Was he just really greedy? Maybe both. In any case, he wasn't trusting in God to help him and take care of him.

But when Zacchaeus met Jesus, he changed. Zacchaeus said, "Look, Lord! Here and now I give half of my possessions to the poor, and if I have cheated anybody out of anything, I will pay back four times the amount" (Luke 19:8).

Focusing on God made him *want* to do what was right and to bless people. Receiving God's generosity prompted him to offer generosity to others. He also sounded *super* excited about it.

Don't you feel the same way when you give something to someone? Initiate some of that joy for yourself and others today. You don't have to go to the extreme Zacchaeus did, but maybe you can do something small in the same direction. Buy your coworker's lunch, hand a granola bar to someone who's hungry, or give a book to a friend to encourage her. Make an effort to be generous and see how it refreshes others and you.

God, show Your heart to others through my generosity today.

Be a Peacemaker

"Blessed are the peacemakers, for they will be
called children of God. . . . Love your enemies
and pray for those who persecute you."
Matthew 5:9, 44

Megan had a family member named Susie who was extremely antagonistic toward her. Susie regularly criticized Megan and complained about her to others.

Megan felt hurt, but she kept a soft heart toward Susie. She thought of Jesus' words about loving people who don't love you and being a peacemaker. She actually began going out of her way to serve and encourage Susie. Not only did it often defuse the tension between them, it also made Megan feel stronger. She felt closer to God.

God loved us when we were His enemies—that's how lovely and strong He is. And He says to us, "Come join Me in My life. Love and bring peace like I do. Be My children."

That's why He tells us to make every effort to do what leads to peace and edifies others (Romans 14:19). To bear with people and forgive them instead of being quick to grumble or fight.

When we feel pretty far from all that, we can start here: "Let the peace of Christ rule in your hearts" (Colossians 3:15 ESV). When we've gone to Him to receive peace, we'll be able to offer it.

Heavenly Father, I want to live like Your child. Bring
peace to my part of the world through me.

Hospitality

Open your homes to each other.
1 Peter 4:9 NCV

W hen I was in college and missing the home I grew up in and my mom who'd recently passed away, there was a woman who lived near campus and had been a friend of our family for years. She'd invite me into her home for a meal or a movie or an overnight stay. Whenever I was there with her, I felt so cared for, as though I had a place to belong, to be known, to rest. She was generous to me not only by giving me food and a spot on her comfy couch but also by having good conversations with me. She treated me like I was special and made me feel loved.

Sometimes we can think that hospitality isn't really a big deal, but it can make a huge difference in people's lives—even if they're not as obviously needy as I was in college. You never know how much someone could benefit from a nurturing environment and a visit that builds them up. Actually, couldn't we all use that, anytime?

Look for people to invite into your home. Make an effort to make them feel celebrated and cared for. Your home doesn't have to be perfect. Focus on meeting their needs and making them comfortable. Stay engaged with them, listening and sharing. Be genuine and generous. Allow God's love to move among you.

Strengthen me to be hospitable and generous, Lord.

Write a Brightening Letter

There is more hunger for love and appreciation
in this world than for bread.
Mother Teresa

W ho in your life do you appreciate? Maybe there's someone at work who is always making people's lives easier, is super thorough in her work, or never complains. Have you ever let her know you notice what she's doing and think it's wonderful?

Maybe a person in your community is an amazing leader or helper, or there's someone from your past who often comes to mind as an inspiration for you now. Don't you think they'd love to hear your thoughts?

Everybody's busy, but imagine if you carved out a few minutes to write out a note to someone, telling them what you appreciate about them. It would absolutely brighten their day. And it would brighten your day too! Part of what makes it so special is that it's not required. So consider offering a special gift to someone, a letter of genuine appreciation, and see if it doesn't give you a boost of joy.

Jesus, I want to go out of my way to lift up others.

Shake Off Offenses

*A person's wisdom yields patience; it is to
one's glory to overlook an offense.*
Proverbs 19:11

Have people been doing things recently that you've found conde-scending or insulting? Have you been finding yourself thinking about it? We've all gone through phases of focusing on how we've been treated. But when we do it a lot—and we're basically caught up in our need to receive honor and respect—we reap negativity.

It's exhausting for us to always be on the lookout for offenses. It's hard for other people to be around us. It closes us off from others. It keeps us from focusing on receiving and giving God's love and grace.

And it all starts with us not living from our true identity: a loved, forgiven, empowered child of God.

The next time someone rubs you the wrong way, why not just let it go? Decide that you won't let it invade your focus on God's goodness. Decide that you don't need them to treat you in a particular way in order for you to be strong, secure, and loving.

And don't look for trouble. Believe the best about others' inten-tions and keep a soft heart. Let Scripture guide you: "Be kind to one another, tenderhearted, forgiving one another, as God in Christ for-gave you" (Ephesians 4:32 ESV).

Lord, You make me strong enough to forgive and choose love.

Do It Anyway

*People are often unreasonable, irrational, and
self-centered. Forgive them anyway.*
Mother Teresa

How often have you started an interaction with someone, intending to be loving or kind, but then the person does something irritating—and you change your mind?

If everyone always simply reacted to the flaws in the people around them, there'd be a lot less love and kindness in the world.

Love and kindness are not meant to be conditional based on people's worthiness. They're gifts you just decide to give.

Mother Teresa posted some sayings in her home for children, which included, "If you are kind, people may accuse you of selfish, ulterior motives. Be kind anyway. . . . If you are honest and sincere, people may deceive you. Be honest and sincere anyway. . . . The good you do today will often be forgotten. Do good anyway. . . . In the final analysis, it is between you and God. It was never between you and them anyway."[3]

Other people are going to make their own choices; don't spend a lot of time worrying about that. Spend more time answering the question, *How do I want to live?*

*God, I'm living unto You. I'm going to honor
and love You through my choices.*

Winter Wisdom

The earth is full of his unfailing love. By the word of the LORD the
heavens were made, their starry host by the breath of his mouth.
Psalm 33:5–6

Have you been spending a lot of time inside these days? Where I live, temperatures and daylight hours drop in the winter, so we spend more time indoors and get a lot less sunshine and fresh air. If you're in a similar climate, you may hardly ever see daylight these days because it's dark when you walk into your workplace in the morning and dark when you leave in the evening.

And how is it for our mood and mental state to live so cooped up and see less light? Not great. Less exposure to sunlight means less vitamin D, which activates happy hormones like dopamine and serotonin.[4] It also affects the body's circadian rhythm, which can cause anxiety, worsen mood, and impact sleep.[5]

So take all the steps you can to connect with nature even in cold and dark seasons. Open your curtains and blinds so natural light floods in. Even if it's gray and cloudy, step outside and lift your face up to the sky. Take a few minutes on your lunch break to inhale fresh air. Bundle up on weekends for a walk outside. Receive the energy from the elements in God's beautiful world. It'll make you stronger and brighter.

God, make me intentional about enjoying the natural
resources You're providing in this season.

Today Can Be Awesome

Give every day the chance to become the
most beautiful day of your life.
Mark Twain

D o you wake up hopeful? Maybe you start out pretty chipper but
after a few setbacks your attitude crashes. Maybe it depends on
whether it's a weekend, or just what season of life you're in.

Whatever your mindset or mood is today, give today a chance.
Don't assume it's going to be bad or rule out good things. Who knows?
This day could bring you a remarkable experience or a memory you'll
treasure forever.

If things go sideways by midmorning, don't write off the whole
day as a bummer. Give it a chance to get better. If it's been one frustration after another all day long, remember the day's not over yet! The
evening could turn out to be sweet and happy.

Whatever you do next after you put this book down, bring some
joyful hope to it. Think how awesome things could be right around
the corner. Think about what could go right, and how you can keep
choosing joy even if it doesn't. Resolve that you'll give every hour of
your day the chance to have good in it and that you'll do what you
can to *bring* good to it too.

God, I take joy in the day You've made and look
forward to experiencing its goodness.

A Sweet Scent

*God uses us to spread his knowledge everywhere like
a sweet-smelling perfume. Our offering to God is this:
We are the sweet smell of Christ among those who are
being saved and among those who are being lost.*
2 Corinthians 2:14–15 NCV

Have you ever walked into a house that had a bad odor? Maybe it
smelled like a stinky barn or rotten eggs or burnt broccoli. Not
exactly inviting.

But how about when you walk into a house that has gingerbread
cookies baking in the oven, a real Christmas tree with the perfect pine
scent, a fire in the fireplace, and some vanilla candles burning? *Ahhh.*
It makes you want to be there—and never leave.

Our presence can be like a sweet smell to others. When we allow
Jesus to live in us, we bring His truth and love wherever we go. It's part
of our thoughts, words, and actions. It permeates the environment of
every interaction we have with people.

When you give someone grace because you've received grace,
you help others know Jesus. When you reach out to someone who's
hurting, faithfully take care of your family, or show integrity in your
workplace, you're letting people see God's heart.

There's a lot in your life today that you can't control. But you get
to decide whether you'll bring the sweet smell of Christ to others.

Jesus, lead me in becoming like a sweet scent both to You and to others.

Inhale, Exhale

He himself gives everyone life and breath and everything else.
Acts 17:25

Make a point to take some deep breaths today. When you do, try making the exhale nice and long—maybe twice as long as the inhale. Some research shows that a longer exhale can make us calmer.[6] And remember to breathe from your lower abdomen, not your chest, since breathing from your chest can actually make you more anxious.[7]

Try thinking some simple, short prayers as you do these breaths.
Inhale. *You are love.* Exhale. *You're right here.*
Inhale. *You are strength.* Exhale. *You are peace.*
Inhale. *Fill me.* Exhale. *Surround me.*
Inhale. *You are for me.* Exhale. *You secure me.*
Inhale. *I trust You.* Exhale. *I love You.*
Inhale. *Shine Your light to me.* Exhale. *Shine Your light through me.*
Use whatever words mean the most to you.

Let the breath that comes in and out of you remind you of the living God who is able to reach into your heart with power and love and do more good in and through you than you can imagine.

Lord, bring Your power and calm to me with each breath I take.

The Greatness of Servants

*"Whoever wants to become great among you must be your
servant. . . . For even the Son of Man did not come to be served,
but to serve, and to give his life as a ransom for many."*
Mark 10:43, 45

A baby was born in Bethlehem so that He could grow up and give
His life away. Jesus came to us to pour Himself out in love and
service.

So it's no wonder that when He found His disciples striving for a
position of honor in God's kingdom He told them, "Whoever wants
to become great will serve others."

The way Jesus talked about God's kingdom kept surprising the
disciples—and it's still pretty shocking even today. How often do we
give our highest respects to people in humble, service-oriented positions? Jesus turns the world upside down: those who are considered
lowest in the ranks are actually on top.

When you choose to serve others, know that Jesus honors your
choice. He'd say you're pursuing true greatness.

John Bunyan wrote, "You have not lived today until you have done
something for someone who can never repay you." Can you see a need
to meet? Go make a difference. Can you find a way to lift someone
up? Go do it. Be generous with your time and effort. Live like Jesus
did, giving yourself to love and service.

I praise You, Jesus, for being the greatest servant of all.

Be Actively Available to God

"I am the Lord's servant," Mary answered.
"May your word to me be fulfilled."
Luke 1:38

An angel appeared to Mary and told her astonishing news: Mary would have a baby who'd be the Son of God. In that moment, Mary had a choice. She could have pushed back, saying, "No, that doesn't seem likely. I don't believe you."

But instead, she said, "I am the Lord's servant. May your word to me be fulfilled." She said yes to God.

No matter how many times I think about this, I'm always stunned that God chose to send the Savior in a way that involved the cooperation of a human.

Today He wants us, even with our weaknesses, to be participants in His work too. And in order for that to happen, we have to make ourselves available to Him. Mary did this in a profound way—she gave her body, heart, time, and future to her new role as a mother.

How can you follow Mary's lead and be more available to God? Maybe you need to be open to making a change. Maybe it's simply a matter of pausing and praying more often before reacting, or showing more of God's patience to your family.

Instead of focusing on what's stressing you today, think about how you can be used by God in every situation you're in.

I am Your servant, God. Use me any way You choose.

A Bright Star of Hope

May those who fear you rejoice when they see
me, for I have put my hope in your word.
Psalm 119:74

The wise men saw a bright star, and they had hope and joy: the King was coming. They started traveling in the direction of that star so they could go worship the King.

That bright light in the sky changed their lives.

When you and I choose to live with faith and put our hope in God, we are like a bright star for others to see. They can look at us and have hope and joy. It might even change how they live their lives and prompt them to worship Him too.

Maybe you don't feel too bright and shiny today—the holiday season can be difficult. But you can keep putting your hope in God in all kinds of ways. Whenever you feel stressed or anxious today, pause and tell God you trust Him. Whenever you don't know how to handle something, pray for His help. Moment after moment let faith lead your thoughts. Then let your faith come out in your words and actions as much as you can.

Do it because He is worthy, but know that you just might inspire hope and joy in others too.

As I put my hope in You, Lord, make me like a bright
star that will bring others closer to You.

Spread Joy

To shed joy around, to radiate happiness, to cast light upon
dark days, to be the golden thread of our destiny, and the very
spirit of grace and harmony, is not this to render a service?
Victor Hugo, *Toilers of the Sea*

When the angels appeared to the shepherds to tell them about the birth of Jesus, they said they brought "good news of great joy" (Luke 2:10 ESV). Jesus' presence brings us joy today too. Whenever we share that joy with others, we are "rendering a service" and making the world brighter.

Do you know people who are always sharing something they're happy about? Don't you just love that?

How about you—do you typically let other people know when you have a joyful moment and give them some of your joy? Be active about finding ways to let people know how you're experiencing that God is good, His grace is enough, and His provision is real.

Sometimes what's blocking us from living this way is that we just get stuck on our frustrations. But we can reframe our perspective. We might originally think, *I need my situation to be a certain way and other people to do particular things in order to be happy and loving.* But instead, we can think, *I've already got reasons to be happy and loving. God fills me with love and joy. I'm grateful for what He's poured out. I'd love to shower it over you too!*

God, I want to spread the joy, light, and grace You give me to others.

Emmanuel Arrived

You have made us for Yourself, and our hearts
are restless until they rest in You.
Augustine, *The Confessions*

Years ago in a simple, ordinary place, a baby was born. God stepped into His creation, breathing air like we do, crying and feeling the cold like we do, sharing love and closeness like we do.

Emmanuel arrived. The God who made us for Himself drew so close to us that He became one of us.

He's the only One your heart can truly rest in. And He is here.

The Prince of Peace. The Bread of Life. The Good Shepherd. The Friend of Sinners. The Light of the World. The King ushering in His kingdom. The One who is perfect love and joy.

Lift up a happy heart, sing a beautiful song, shout out a praise—He is here!

I praise and adore You with all I am, King Jesus.

Get Caught Up in What He's Doing

*Set your minds on things above, not on earthly things. For
you died, and your life is now hidden with Christ in God.*
Colossians 3:2–3

J esus came to earth to do His Father's will. He's still at work this
very minute, and He says to His followers, "Come, join Me."

It's only natural that we should answer that call, since we've
invited His Spirit to live in us. We've said yes to receiving His eternal
life and to connecting ourselves to Him forever. Because He lives, we
live. And because He does the Father's will, we do too.

Eugene Peterson summarized Paul's message to the Colossian
believers like this: "If you're serious about living this new resurrection life with Christ, *act* like it. Pursue the things over which Christ
presides. Don't shuffle along, eyes to the ground, absorbed with the
things right in front of you. Look up, and be alert to what is going on
around Christ—that's where the action is" (3:1–2 MSG).

I'll probably be tempted to get absorbed with the earthly stuff
in front of me today. Probably repeatedly. But I'm going to try to
notice the Spirit's leading away from that, shifting away from self-
preoccupied thoughts and toward the questions, *What is Jesus doing?
How can I join Him?*

Want to join me?

*You are my life, Jesus, so lead me in the focus and
purpose You want me to have in this world.*

Benefits of Service

I showed you that by this kind of hard work we must help
the weak, remembering the words the Lord Jesus himself
said: "It is more blessed to give than to receive."
Acts 20:35

Whenever you feel too stressed to volunteer to help someone, give it a second thought. It may actually be exactly what you need to do.

In a large group study, researchers found that volunteering once a month increased the odds of happiness by 7 percent, and volunteering twice a month bumped it up to 12 percent. Serving others makes people happier. It draws our attention away from our difficulties and can pull us out of negative thought patterns.[8] It can lower our stress levels, steer us away from anxiety, and bring more meaning into our lives.[9] It also can decrease chronic pain and blood pressure and even increase longevity.[10] That's a lot of benefits!

Think back to the last few times you've gone out of your way to help someone. How did it make you feel? Glad about your ability to help? Happy about the difference you made? Satisfied knowing that what you did meant something?

Jesus said you'll be more blessed when you give than when you receive. Do you believe Him? If you're feeling stressed or short on joy, make room in your life to help others.

Lord, show me ways I can serve and give to others today.

Content in Any Situation

I have learned the secret of being content
in any and every situation.
Philippians 4:12

I s it possible to have joy in a hard situation?
Paul said yes, it is.

Like most of us, he experienced a variety of seasons in life. Sometimes he had plenty of what he wanted; sometimes he didn't have enough. But even when his circumstances were rough and he had to live with unmet needs, he knew how to be content.

He talked about all this in his letter to the Philippians, right before he said, "I can do all things through Christ, because he gives me strength" (v. 13 NCV). He wrote the letter *while in prison* and mentioned the ideas of joy, gladness, and rejoicing sixteen times, including when he said, "Rejoice in the Lord always. I will say it again: Rejoice!" (v. 4).

Paul's joy came from His relationship with God, the One whose Spirit produces peace, hope, joy, and love. Yours can too.

Today, whatever happens, remember contentment is possible. You're doing life with the One who's full of joy! Shift your thoughts toward Him. Experience Him through whatever you're going through. Ask for His perspective and help. He will strengthen you and bring you joy.

Make my heart content, Lord, as I focus on You.

Decide to Worship No Matter What

I will always thank the LORD; I will never stop praising him.
Psalm 34:1 GNT

When everything fell apart and went to ruin in Job's world, he expressed his grief and sadness—he "tore his robe and shaved his head" (Job 1:20). But after that, he did something surprising.

"He fell to the ground in worship and said: 'Naked I came from my mother's womb, and naked I will depart. The LORD gave and the LORD has taken away; may the name of the LORD be praised'" (vv. 20–21).

In the days that followed, he struggled to understand his crisis, reeling with emotions. But he also worshiped. We see it clearly in his initial response to suffering and later on, after God revealed His majesty and wonder to Job. "I know that you can do all things," Job said to God. "No purpose of yours can be thwarted" (42:2).

What if you and I decided we were going to worship God no matter what? When things are awesome, when things are blah, when things are the worst, we'll praise the One on the throne. We can choose to think, *My God is the one true God. He is wonderful and worthy. So I'll honor Him. I'll set my mind on His goodness and set my heart on worshiping Him.*

When we make that choice, we make His kingdom of light a little brighter wherever we are.

You are God and I am not. I will keep worshiping You, my King.

A Confident Heart

Every tomorrow has two handles. We can take hold of
it with the handle of anxiety or the handle of faith.
Henry Ward Beecher

What's coming tomorrow remains unknown today. It'll probably be a mix of good and hard. Be brave to meet it.

Why? Because you are not alone, and because your extravagantly good God is designing your life to fit into the big, beautiful story of His glory and love.

You could give in to fear—but don't. Join the chorus of believers from throughout the ages who say, "His love makes us brave. His power gives us hope. His presence gives us peace. His grace makes us loving. His joy makes us strong. He's the source for all that our hearts need, and He always will be. He is wonderful!"

You'll have problems and pain, and you'll lament the sorrows in our world—just like Jesus did. But keep trusting and worshiping. Keep holding on to His Word and loving Him. Rely on Him for strength and confidence.

Grab the handle of faith for all your tomorrows. Hang on to the precious promises of your Father, remembering how He's blown you away with goodness before. Look to Him to provide for you moment after moment.

I'm choosing faith and confidence in You, Lord.

A Prayer for the Future

"Give your entire attention to what God is doing right
now, and don't get worked up about what may or may
not happen tomorrow. God will help you deal with
whatever hard things come up when the time comes."
Matthew 6:34 MSG

M y loving Father, you are always right here with me. Help me listen to Your voice of love and remember who You say I am. Remind me that I'm doing each day with You, my empowering God. You make me an overcomer and conqueror.

I believe You are greater than anything I fear and anything I'll face. May I navigate my thoughts away from anxiety and dwell on truth. Help me find the good and live in Your joy. Shine Your light and love all around me.

My confidence is in You, almighty God. "When I am afraid, I will put my trust in you" (Psalm 56:3 NLT). Whatever else I feel, "I will hope in your name, for your name is good" (52:9). Your love for me is loyal and unfailing.

Bring Your calm, steady strength to my mind. Use my every struggle to bring more of Your power and beauty into my life.

I open myself up entirely to Your Spirit and offer You my heart, full of praise and adoration!

I trust You and love You, my Father and King.

Notes

JANUARY 1–31

1. Christopher Bergland, "Diaphragmatic Breathing Exercises and Your Vagus Nerve," *Psychology Today*, May 16, 2017, https://www.psychologytoday.com/us/blog/the -athletes-way/201705/diaphragmatic-breathing-exercises-and-your-vagus-nerve.
2. Edith Zimmerman, "I Now Suspect the Vagus Nerve Is the Key to Well-Being," *The Cut*, May 9, 2019, https://www.thecut.com/2019/05/i-now-suspect-the-vagus-nerve-is -the-key-to-well-being.html.
3. "Supporting Vagus Nerve Function; Is This the Missing Link to Improving Mental Health?," Food for the Brain Foundation, https://foodforthebrain.org/supporting -vagus-nerve-function-is-this-the-missing-link-to-improving-mental-health/.
4. Jenna Fletcher, "How to Use 4–7–8 Breathing for Anxiety," *Medical News Today*, February 12, 2019, https://www.medicalnewstoday.com/articles/324417.
5. Bergland, "Diaphragmatic Breathing Exercises and Your Vagus Nerve."
6. Ilene Ruhoy, "11 Ways to Stimulate Vagus Nerve Function for Better Gut and Mental Health," MBG Health, July 17, 2019, https://www.mindbodygreen.com/articles/how -to-support-vagus-nerve-for-better-gut-and-mental-health.
7. Courtney E. Ackerman, "83 Benefits of Journaling for Depression, Anxiety, and Stress," *Positive Psychology*, April 15, 2021, https://positivepsychology.com/benefits -of-journaling/.
8. Philip Yancey, *Disappointment with God: Three Questions No One Asks Aloud* (Grand Rapids, MI: Zondervan, 2009).
9. "Psychic Services Industry in the US—Market Research Report," IBIS World, April 9, 2021, https://www.ibisworld.com/united-states/market-research-reports/psychic -services-industry/.

FEBRUARY 1–29

1. "The Meaning of Shalom in the Bible," New International Version Bible, https://www .thenivbible.com/blog/meaning-shalom-bible/.

MARCH 1–31

1. John Locke, *An Essay Concerning Human Understanding*, Vol. 1
2. Daphne M. Davis and Jeffrey A. Haynes, "What Are the Benefits of Mindfulness?" *Monitor on Psychology* 43, no. 7 (July/August 2012), https://www.apa.org/monitor /2012/07–08/ce-corner.
3. *Swindoll Study Bible* NLT (Carol Stream, IL: Tyndale House, 2018), 911.

APRIL 1–30

1. Will Kynes, "God's Grace in the Old Testament: Considering the Hesed of the Lord," *Knowing and Doing* (Summer 2010), https://www.cslewisinstitute.org /webfm_send/430; and John J. Parsons, "Putting the Chesed of Adonai Before Your Eyes," Hebrew for Christians, https://www.hebrew4christians.com/Meditations /Chesed/chesed.html.
2. Scholar R. C. Sproul points out how the idea of chesed is seen in Paul's words in Romans 8:31: "If God is for us, who can be against us?" Sproul says the teaching that God is for us "captures this whole concept of loyal love." See "The Lovingkindness of God," lecture by R. C. Sproul in the Loved by God series, Ligonier Ministries, video, 20:50, https://www.ligonier.org/learn/series/loved_by_god/the-lovingkindness -of-god/.
3. William Shakespeare, *Othello* (Cambridge: Cambridge University Press, 2018, e-book), 136.
4. "What Is Meant by Saying 'God Is My Portion'?," Compelling Truth, https://www .compellingtruth.org/God-is-my-portion.html.
5. Elisabeth Elliot, *Passion and Purity: Learning to Bring Your Love Life Under Christ's Control* (Grand Rapids, MI: Baker, 2002), 62.
6. Andrea Bonior, "The Health Benefits of Hope," *Psychology Today*, March 31, 2020, https://www.psychologytoday.com/us/blog/friendship-20/202003/the-health-benefits -hope.
7. Kirsten Weir, "Mission Impossible," *Monitor on Psychology* 44 no. 9 (October 2013), https://www.apa.org/monitor/2013/10/mission-impossible.
8. See Gretchen Rubin, *The Happiness Project* (NY: Harper, 2018), 35–36 for a discussion on the concept of acting the way you want to feel.
9. Allie Volpe, "Science Says You Need to Plan Some Things to Look Forward To," *Vice*, December 29, 2020, https://www.vice.com/en/article/7k9wvb/science-says-you-need -future-plans-to-look-forward-to-during-pandemic.
10. Henri Nouwen, *Finding My Way Home: Pathways to Life and the Spirit* (New York: Crossroad Publishing, 2004), 101.
11. Isaac Asimov, *How Did We Find Out About Sunshine?*, http://www.arvindguptatoys .com/arvindgupta/sunshinepix.pdf; and Tom Metcalfe, "Afraid of the Dark? Why Eclipses Frightened Ancient Civilizations," Live Science, https://www.livescience .com/60139-why-eclipses-frightened-ancient-civilizations.html.
12. Quoted in Henri Nouwen, *Reaching Out: The Three Movements of the Spiritual Life* (New York: Image Books, 1986), 36. This quote is often attributed to Henri Nouwen, but he stated in this book that a friend once wrote it to him.

1. Shaoni Bhattacharya, "Brain Study Links Negative Emotions and Lowered Immunity," *New Scientist*, September 2, 2003, https://www.newscientist.com/article /dn4116-brain-study-links-negative-emotions-and-lowered-immunity/.

2. Discussed in Gretchen Rubin, *The Happiness Project* (p. 36), supported by the quote, "Action and feeling go together, and by regulating the action, which is under the more direct control of the will, we can indirectly regulate the feeling, which is not." This quote is from William James, *Talks to Teachers on Psychology and to Students on Some of Life's Ideals* (New York: H. Holt, 1914), 98.

3. Andrea L. Bell, "The Biology of Calm: How Downregulation Promotes Well-Being," *Good Therapy*, October 27, 2016, https://www.goodtherapy.org/blog/biology-of-calm -how-downregulation-promotes-well-being-1027164.

4. Harvard Medical School, "Understanding the Stress Response," July 6, 2020, https:// www.health.harvard.edu/staying-healthy/understanding-the-stress-response.

5. Bell, "The Biology of Calm."

6. "Calming a Wigged Out Autonomic Nervous System Using the Vagus Nerve," Innis Integrative BodyMind Therapy, November 21, 2017, https://www.innisintegrativetherapy .com/blog/2017/11/21/calming-a-wigged-out-autonomic-nervous-system-using-the -vagus-nerve; Terry Hurley, "Activating the Parasympathetic Nervous System to Decrease Stress and Anxiety," Canyon Vista Recovery Center, October 26, 2018, https://canyonvista.com/activating-parasympathetic-nervous-system/; and Harvard Medical School, "Understanding the Stress Response."

7. "7 Ways to Keep Your Nervous System Relaxed in Times of Stress," *The Optimist Daily*, May 6, 2020, https://www.optimistdaily.com/2020/05/7-ways-to-keep-your -nervous-system-relaxed-in-times-of-stress/.

8. Amy Blankson, *The Future of Happiness: 5 Modern Strategies for Balancing Productivity and Well-Being in the Digital Era* (Dallas: BenBella Books, 2017).

9. Lindsey Hyslop, "4 Big Benefits of Getting Less Screen Time," Fitbit, November 29, 2018, https://blog.fitbit.com/screen-time/; and "Benefits of Reducing Your Screen Time," Barnsley College Alumni and Friends, https://www.barnsley.ac.uk/benefits -of-reducing-your-screen-time/.

10. Julia Dellitt and Katie Horwitch, "5 Ways Screen Time Impacts Your Health," *Aaptiv*, https://aaptiv.com/magazine/ways-screen-time-impacts-health.

11. Matthew Thorpe and Rachael Link, "12 Science-Based Benefits of Meditation," *Healthline*, October 27, 2020, https://www.healthline.com/nutrition/12-benefits-of -meditation#9.-Improves-sleep.

12. Ruth Graham, "This Is Your Brain on Faith," *U.S. Catholic*, June 10, 2014, https:// uscatholic.org/articles/201406/this-is-your-brain-on-faith/.

13. Barbara Bradley Hagerty, "Prayer May Reshape Your Brain . . . and Your Reality," NPR, May 20, 2009, https://www.npr.org/templates/story/story.php?storyId =104310443.

14. Hagerty, "Prayer May Reshape Your Brain."

15. Jill Seladi-Schulman, "What to Know About Your Brain's Frontal Lobe," *Healthline*, April 20, 2020, https://www.healthline.com/health/frontal-lobe#fast-facts.

16. Graham, "This Is Your Brain on Faith."
17. Jenna Fletcher, "Why Sleep Is Essential for Health," *Medical News Today*, May 31, 2019, https://www.medicalnewstoday.com/articles/325353.
18. Fletcher, "Why Sleep Is Essential for Health."
19. Eric Suni, "Mental Health and Sleep," Sleep Foundation, September 18, 2020, https://www.sleepfoundation.org/mental-health.
20. Michael J. Breus, "12 Tips for Better Sleep in Bad Times," WebMD, October 4, 2001, https://www.webmd.com/sleep-disorders/news/20011004/12-tips-better-sleep-troubled-times.
21. Eric Suni, "Healthy Sleep Tips," Sleep Foundation, July 30, 2020, https://www.sleepfoundation.org/sleep-hygiene/healthy-sleep-tips.
22. Stacy Simon, "10 Tips to Get More Sleep," American Cancer Society, May 5, 2020, https://www.cancer.org/latest-news/how-to-get-more-sleep.html.
23. "Is Your Bedroom Preventing a Good Night's Rest?," *Today*, March 2, 2006, https://www.today.com/news/your-bedroom-preventing-good-nights-rest-wbna11641852.
24. Eric Suni, "How Smell Affects Your Sleep," Sleep Foundation, October 23, 2020, https://www.sleepfoundation.org/bedroom-environment/how-smell-affects-your-sleep.
25. Suni, "Healthy Sleep Tips."
26. "Is Your Bedroom Preventing a Good Night's Rest?"
27. Arlene Semeco, "The Top 10 Benefits of Regular Exercise," *Healthline*, February 10, 2017, https://www.healthline.com/nutrition/10-benefits-of-exercise.
28. Crystal Raypole, "How to Hack Your Hormones for a Better Mood," *Healthline*, September 30, 2019, https://www.healthline.com/health/happy-hormone#exercise.
29. Academy of Nutrition and Dietetics, "How Much Water Do You Need?" Eat Right, November 6, 2019, https://www.eatright.org/food/nutrition/healthy-eating/how-much-water-do-you-need.
30. Markham Held, "Your Brain On: Dehydration," *Shape*, August 6, 2014, https://www.shape.com/lifestyle/mind-and-body/your-brain-dehydration.
31. "Water, Depression, and Anxiety," Solara Mental Health, https://solaramentalhealth.com/can-drinking-enough-water-help-my-depression-and-anxiety/.
32. "Dehydration Literally Makes Your Brain Shrink," IOL Health, April 25, 2018, https://www.iol.co.za/lifestyle/health/diet/dehydration-literally-makes-your-brain-shrink-14641122.
33. Ashley Marcin, "How Much Water You Need to Drink," *Medical News Today*, July 26, 2017, https://www.medicalnewstoday.com/articles/318623#recommendations.
34. Lindsay Sparks, "How Eating Is a Form of Self-Care," Feed Your Spark, https://www.feedyourspark.net/blog/how-eating-is-a-form-of-self-care.
35. Jamie Forward, "Sugar Is Wreaking Havoc on Your Hormonal Health," *Observer*, February 13, 2018, https://observer.com/2018/02/sugar-is-wreaking-havoc-on-your-hormonal-health/.
36. "Top 10 Nutrient-Dense Foods," Sunbasket, https://sunbasket.com/stories/top-10-nutrient-dense-foods.
37. Susan McQuillan, "Organize Your Space, Declutter Your Mind and Tidy Up," *Psycom*, August 10, 2020, https://www.psycom.net/organize-clutter-mind-tidy-up.

38. Daniel K. Brown, Jo L. Barton, and Valerie F. Gladwell, "Viewing Nature Scenes Positively Affects Recovery of Autonomic Function Following Acute-Mental Stress," *Environmental Science & Technology* 47, no. 11 (June 4, 2013): 5562–69, https://www.ncbi.nlm.nih.gov/pmc/articles/PMC3699874/.

39. Allison Michelle Dienstman, "10 Unexpected Benefits of Spending Time in Nature," Goodnet, March 24, 2019, https://www.goodnet.org/articles/10-unexpected-benefits-spending-time-in-nature.

40. Marelisa Fabrega, "8 Reasons Why You Need to Spend More Time in Nature," Daring to Live Fully, https://daringtolivefully.com/spend-more-time-in-nature.

41. J. Thompson Coon et al., "Does Participating in Physical Activity in Outdoor Natural Environments Have a Greater Effect on Physical and Mental Wellbeing Than Physical Activity Indoors? A Systematic Review," *Environmental Science & Technology* 45, no. 5 (March 1, 2011): 1761–72, https://pubmed.ncbi.nlm.nih.gov/21291246/.

42. Fabrega, "8 Reasons Why You Need to Spend More Time in Nature."

43. Lawrence Robinson, Melinda Smith, and Jeanne Segal, "Laughter Is the Best Medicine," HelpGuide, https://www.helpguide.org/articles/mental-health/laughter-is-the-best-medicine.htm.

44. "ANXIETY: Find the Humor, Find the Cure," Anxiety and Depression Association of America, February 27, 2018, https://adaa.org/learn-from-us/from-the-experts/blog-posts/consumer/anxiety-find-humor-find-cure.

45. Robinson, Smith, and Segal, "Laughter Is the Best Medicine."

46. "Levity," Dictionary.com, https://www.dictionary.com/browse/levity.

47. Kai Lundgren, Lawrence Robinson, and Robert Segal, "The Health and Mood-Boosting Benefits of Pets," HelpGuide, https://www.helpguide.org/articles/mental-health/mood-boosting-power-of-dogs.htm.

48. Andrea Beetz, Kerstin Uvnäs-Moberg, Henri Julius, and Kurt Kotrschal, "Psychosocial and Psychophysiological Effects of Human-Animal Interactions: The Possible Role of Oxytocin," *Frontiers in Psychology* 3 (2012): 234, https://www.ncbi.nlm.nih.gov/pmc/articles/PMC3408111/.

49. Lundgren, Robinson, and Segal, "Health and Mood-Boosting Benefits of Pets."

50. Joe Bagliere, "Science Shows Watching Cute Animals Is Good for Your Health," CNN, September 27, 2020, https://www.cnn.com/2020/09/27/us/watching-cute-animals-study-scn-trnd/index.html.

51. Matthew J. Zawadzki, Joshua M. Smyth, and Heather J. Costigan, "Real-Time Associations Between Engaging in Leisure and Daily Health and Well-Being," *Annals of Behavioral Medicine* 49 (2015): 605–15, https://link.springer.com/article/10.1007/s12160-015-9694-3?sa_campaign=email/event/articleAuthor/onlineFirst.

52. W. Eriksen and D. Bruusgaard, "Do Physical Leisure Time Activities Prevent Fatigue? A 15 Month Prospective Study of Nurses' Aides," *British Journal of Sports Medicine* 38, no. 3 (June 2004): 331–36, https://www.ncbi.nlm.nih.gov/pmc/articles/PMC1724835/.

53. Jaime L. Kurtz, "Six Reasons to Get a Hobby," *Psychology Today*, September 15, 2015, https://www.psychologytoday.com/us/blog/happy-trails/201509/six-reasons-get-hobby.

54. Ashley Stahl, "Here's How Creativity Actually Improves Your Health," *Forbes*, July 25, 2018, https://www.forbes.com/sites/ashleystahl/2018/07/25/heres-how

-creativity-actually-improves-your-health/?sh=63536d9f13a6; and Elizabeth Bennett, "Could Creativity Be the Cure for Anxiety?," *Balance*, January 5, 2018, https:// balance.media/benefits-of-creativity/.

55. Colette DeDonato, "How Being More Creative Improves Your Mental and Physical Health," Lifehack, https://www.lifehack.org/articles/lifestyle/how-being-more-creative-improves-your-mental-and-physical-health.html.

56. Stahl, "Here's How Creativity Actually Improves Your Health."

57. Allison S. Gremillion, "Colors and Emotions: How Colors Make You Feel," 99 Designs, https://99designs.com/blog/tips/how-color-impacts-emotions-and-behaviors/.

58. Melanie Curtin, "Neuroscience Says Listening to This Song Reduces Anxiety by Up to 65 Percent," *Inc.*, May 30, 2017, https://www.inc.com/melanie-curtin/neuroscience -says-listening-to-this-one-song-reduces-anxiety-by-up-to-65-percent.html.

59. "Definition and Quotes About Music Therapy," American Music Therapy Association, https://www.musictherapy.org/about/quotes/.

60. "A Study Investigating the Relaxation Effects of the Music Track Weightless by Marconi Union in Consultation with Lyz Cooper," Mindlab, https://www .britishacademyofsoundtherapy.com/wp-content/uploads/2019/10/Mindlab-Report -Weightless-Radox-Spa.pdf.

61. "How Smell Affects Your Body and Mind," *SAGA*, July 16, 2020, https://www.saga .co.uk/magazine/health-wellbeing/mind/how-smell-affects-your-body-and-mind.

62. "14 Calming Scents to Help You Unwind," *Homesick*, July 30, 2020, https://homesick .com/blogs/news/14-calming-scents-to-help-you-unwind; and Annette McDermott, "The 18 Essential Oils for Anxiety," *Healthline*, March 7, 2019, https://www .healthline.com/health/anxiety/essential-oils-for-anxiety.

63. "Psychology and Smell," Fifth Sense, https://www.fifthsense.org.uk/psychology-and -smell/.

64. Michelle Trudeau, "Human Connections Start with a Friendly Touch," NPR, September 20, 2010, https://www.npr.org/templates/story/story.php?storyId=128795325.

65. Matthew Tull, "Use Your 5 Senses to Manage Stress Levels."

66. Christina Kozlowski, "The Best Fidget Toys to Relieve Stress and Anxiety," *Autism Parenting Magazine*, March 23, 2021, https://www.autismparentingmagazine.com /fidget-toys-to-relieve-stress-anxiety/; and Alyssa Mertes, "Do Stress Balls Work?," Quality Logo Products, July 23, 2020, https://www.qualitylogoproducts.com/promo -university/do-stressballs-work.htm.

67. Tull, "Use Your 5 Senses to Manage Stress Levels."

68. Wanda Thibodeaux, "This Might Be the Simplest Scientific Way to Get Rid of Stress You've Ever Heard Of," *Inc.*, September 17, 2018, https://www.inc.com/wanda -thibodeaux/this-might-be-simplest-scientific-way-to-get-rid-of-stress-youve-ever -heard-of.html.

69. Stacy Horn, "Singing Changes Your Brain," *Time*, August 16, 2013, https://ideas.time .com/2013/08/16/singing-changes-your-brain/.

70. "The Health Benefits of Singing a Tune," *Chicago Tribune*, March 15, 2018, https:// www.chicagotribune.com/suburbs/advertising/todayshealthywoman/ct-ss-thw-health -benefits-of-singing-a-tune-20180314dto-story.html.

JUNE 1-30

1. Helen Keller, *The Story of My Life* (n.p.: Doubleday, Page, and Co., 2009), 182, https://www.google.com/books/edition/The_Story_of_My_Life/QNpEAAAAYAAJ ?hl=en&gbpv=1&dq="We+could+never+learn+to+be+brave+and+patient+if+there+w ere+only+joy+in+the+world."&pg=PA182&printsec=frontcover.

2. John Bunyan, *Grace Abounding to the Chief of Sinners: A Brief Account of God's Exceeding Mercy Through Christ to His Poor Servant, John Bunyan,* updated and illustrated ed. (Abbotsford, WI: Aneko Press, 2017, Kindle edition).

3. Jesse Greenspan, "10 Things You May Not Know About Winston Churchill," History, June 17, 2020, https://www.history.com/news/10-things-you-may-not-know-about -winston-churchill.

4. Anne Watt, "Overcoming Obstacles: How Winston Churchill's Struggles Fueled Success," Learning Liftoff, January 13, 2015, https://www.learningliftoff.com /overcoming-obstacles-winston-churchill/.

5. Douglas J. Hall, "Churchill's Elections," International Churchill Society, https:// winstonchurchill.org/resources/reference/churchills-elections/.

6. Eleanor Roosevelt, *You Learn by Living* (Louisville, KY: Westminster John Knox, 1983), 29.

JULY 1-31

1. Kira M. Newman, "Is Social Connection the Best Path to Happiness?," *Greater Good Magazine,* June 27, 2018, https://greatergood.berkeley.edu/article/item/is_social _connection_the_best_path_to_happiness.

2. Emma Seppala, "Connectedness & Health: The Science of Social Connection," Stanford Medicine Center for Compassion and Altruism Research and Education, May 8, 2014, http://ccare.stanford.edu/uncategorized/connectedness-health-the -science-of-social-connection-infographic/.

3. Jill Suttie, "Four Ways Social Support Makes You More Resilient," *Greater Good Magazine,* November 13, 2017, https://greatergood.berkeley.edu/article/item/four_ways _social_support_makes_you_more_resilient.

4. Review of "Health and Behavior: The Interplay of Biological, Behavioral, and Societal Influences," PubMed, 2001, https://pubmed.ncbi.nlm.nih.gov/20669491/.

5. Jamie Ducharme, "Why Spending Time with Friends Is One of the Best Things You Can Do for Your Health," *Time,* June 25, 2019, https://time.com/5609508/social -support-health-benefits/.

SEPTEMBER 1-30

1. "How Do Trees Change in the Fall?," National Park Service, September 25, 2019, https://www.nps.gov/articles/how-do-trees-change-in-the-fall.htm.

2. Jessica Stillman, "Gratitude Physically Changes Your Brain, New Study Says," *Inc.,* January 15, 2016, https://www.inc.com/jessica-stillman/the-amazing-way-gratitude -rewires-your-brain-for-happiness.html.

3. Leslie Becker-Phelps, "Counting Your Blessings Isn't Enough," *Psychology Today,* November 19, 2018, https://www.psychologytoday.com/us/blog/making-change

/201811/counting-your-blessings-isn-t-enough; and Leslie Becker-Phelps, "The Good Life: Pause, Observe, and Absorb Positives," *Psychology Today*, July 24, 2017, https://www.psychologytoday.com/us/blog/making-change/201707/the-good-life-pause-observe-and-absorb-positives.

4. Rick Hanson, "Taking in the Good," *Greater Good Magazine*, November 1, 2009, https://greatergood.berkeley.edu/article/item/taking_in_the_good.

5. Lauren Dunn, "Be Thankful: Science Says Gratitude Is Good for Your Health," *Today*, November 26, 2015, https://www.today.com/health/be-thankful-science-says-gratitude-good-your-health-t58256.

6. Robert Emmons, *Gratitude Works! A 21-Day Program for Creating Emotional Prosperity* (San Francisco: Jossey-Bass, 2013), 9.

7. Amy Morin, "7 Scientifically Proven Benefits of Gratitude," *Psychology Today*, April 3, 2015, https://www.psychologytoday.com/us/blog/what-mentally-strong-people-dont-do/201504/7-scientifically-proven-benefits-gratitude.

8. Madhuleena Roy Chowdhury, "The Neuroscience of Gratitude and How It Affects Anxiety & Grief," *Positive Psychology*, April 27, 2021, https://positivepsychology.com/neuroscience-of-gratitude/.

9. "Gratitude Journal," Greater Good in Action, https://ggia.berkeley.edu/practice/gratitude_journal.

10. "Gratitude Journal."

11. Emmons, *Gratitude Works!*, 33–34.

12. Markham Heid, "The Power of Positive Memories," *Elemental*, December 5, 2019, https://elemental.medium.com/the-power-of-positive-memories-86c2441ffe07.

13. "Why Memories Can Boost Your Mood," *Psychologies*, May 17, 2012, https://www.psychologies.co.uk/self/why-memories-can-boost-our-mood.html.

14. "Science of Happiness," Soul Pancake, https://soulpancake.com/portfolio_page/science-of-happiness/.

15. Mohammed Al-Mosaiwi and Tom Johnstone, "In an Absolute State: Elevated Use of Absolutist Words Is a Marker Specific to Anxiety, Depression, and Suicidal Ideation," *Clinical Psychological Science* 6, no. 4 (2018): 529–42, https://journals.sagepub.com/doi/full/10.1177/2167702617747074. Here's a discussion by one of the researchers that is easier to understand: Mohammed Al-Mosaiwi, "People with Depression Use Language Differently—Here's How to Spot It," *The Conversation*, February 2, 2018, https://theconversation.com/people-with-depression-use-language-differently-heres-how-to-spot-it-90877.

16. Based on a line from the movie *Chariots of Fire*: "I believe that God made me for a purpose. But he also made me fast, and when I run I feel his pleasure." A screenwriter likely wrote it, but others confirm that it does represent Eric Liddell's perspective and experience.

17. "G4342 προσκαρτερέω - Strong's Greek Lexicon Number," https://studybible.info/strongs/G4342.

OCTOBER 1–31

1. C. S. Lewis, *Mere Christianity* (Grand Rapids, MI: Zondervan, 2001).

NOVEMBER 1–30

1. "What Is Meant by Saying 'God Is My Portion'?"
2. *Life Application Study Bible*, notes on Exodus 2:3ff, p. 98.
3. Sabina Nawaz, "To Achieve Big Goals, Start with Small Habits," *Harvard Business Review*, January 20, 2020, https://hbr.org/2020/01/to-achieve-big-goals-start-with -small-habits.
4. Maria Godoy, "'Tiny Habits' Are the Key to Behavioral Change," NPR, February 27, 2020, https://www.npr.org/2020/02/25/809256398/tiny-habits-are-the-key-to -behavioral-change; and "How Habits Work," Charles Duhigg, https://charlesduhigg .com/how-habits-work/.
5. Nick Greene, "15 Lofty Facts About the Sistine Chapel," Mental Floss, August 15, 2016, https://www.mentalfloss.com/article/84176/15-lofty-facts-about-sistine-chapel.
6. "Failing for Success: Thomas Edison," Intellectual Ventures, January 26, 2016, https:// www.intellectualventures.com/buzz/insights/failing-for-success-thomas-edison.
7. Richard Feloni, "Thomas Edison's Reaction to His Factory Burning Down Shows Why He Was So Successful," *Business Insider*, May 9, 2014, https://www.businessinsider.com /thomas-edison-in-the-obstacle-is-the-way-2014-5.

DECEMBER 1–31

1. Augustine of Hippo, *The Confessions*.
2. Anne Graham Lotz, *My Heart's Cry* (Nashville, TN: Thomas Nelson, 2005), 144.
3. "Mother Teresa: 'Do It Anyway,'" The Prayer Foundation, https://www.prayer foundation.org/mother_teresa_do_it_anyway.htm.
4. "Cold Weather and Anxiety (and How to Address It)," Transformation, March 27, 2019, https://www.mytransformations.com/post/cold-weather-and-anxiety-and-how-to -address-it.
5. Erica Silva, "The Pendulum of Seasonal Change," Anxiety Resource Center, October 6, 2018, https://anxietyresourcecenter.org/2018/10/the-pendulum-of-seasonal -change/.
6. Christopher Bergland, "Longer Exhalations Are an Easy Way to Hack Your Vagus Nerve," *Psychology Today*, May 9, 2019, https://www.psychologytoday.com/us/blog/ the-athletes-way/201905/longer-exhalations-are-easy-way-hack-your-vagus-nerve.
7. Sheryl Ankrom, "8 Deep Breathing Exercises to Reduce Anxiety," *Very Well Mind*, March 20, 2021, https://www.verywellmind.com/abdominal-breathing-2584115.
8. Calvin Holbrook, "Why Is Volunteering Important? These 7 Great Reasons Show the Benefits," Happiness, https://www.happiness.com/magazine/personal-growth/ why-volunteering-is-important-benefits/.
9. Jeanne Segal and Lawrence Robinson, "Volunteering and Its Surprising Benefits," HelpGuide, https://www.helpguide.org/articles/healthy-living/volunteering-and-its -surprising-benefits.htm.
10. "7 Scientific Benefits of Helping Others," Mental Floss, https://www.mentalfloss.com /article/71964/7-scientific-benefits-helping-others.